Positive Psychotherapy for Psychosis

Positive Psychotherapy for Psychosis describes a new psychological intervention, which for the first time applies emerging research from the field of positive psychology specifically to psychosis. The book contains guidance on adapting the approach for use in individual treatments, and on providing part of the intervention, either as individual sessions or by integrating Positive Psychotherapy for Psychosis sessions into other treatments.

Divided into two sections – Theory and the Intervention Manual – this book offers methodologically rigorous research, case studies and detailed aims and instructions for clinicians and therapists. The structured, step-by-step manual, for use with clients, includes downloadable handouts, session materials, activities, guides and therapist tips. The manual will be a practical, positive and innovative resource for mental health professionals, providing all the material needed to deliver this evidence-based approach that is designed to improve wellbeing and reduce symptoms experienced by people living with psychosis.

Positive Psychotherapy for Psychosis will be of interest to mental health clinicians working with people with psychosis, as well as clinical and counselling psychologists, psychiatrists, mental health nurses, psychotherapists, social workers, occupational therapists, support workers and peer support specialists.

Mike Slade is Professor of Mental Health Recovery and Social Inclusion, University of Nottingham. His research interests include recovery-focused mental health services and increasing citizenship and social inclusion experiences. Mike has written 250 academic articles and 11 books, including *Personal Recovery and Mental Illness* and *Wellbeing, Recovery and Mental Health*. Information about his research can be found at www.researchintorecovery. com.

Tamsin Brownell is a researcher in mental health services. She helped to develop *Positive Psychotherapy for Psychosis* while working as a Research Assistant at the Institute of Psychiatry, Psychology & Neuroscience, King's College London. Her main research interests are the development and evaluation of therapeutic interventions and user-led services for mental health, particularly in psychosis and eating disorders.

Dr Tayyab Rashid is a licensed clinical psychologist and researcher at the Health & Wellness Centre, University of Toronto Scarborough (UTSC), Canada. He developed and empirically validated an innovative therapeutic approach called Positive Psychotherapy with Dr Martin Seligman at the Positive Psychology Centre, University of Pennsylvania, during his doctoral studies. Tayyab has trained mental health professionals and educators internationally and has also worked with survivors of 9/11 families and Asian Tsunami survivors. Published in peer-reviewed journals, an invited keynote speaker, his work has also been featured in the *Wall Street Journal*, *Maclean's*, Canadian Broadcasting Corporation and at the TEDx (www.tayyabrashid. com).

Dr Beate Schrank is a consultant psychiatrist, therapist and senior researcher at the Department of Psychiatry and Psychotherapy, University Clinic Tulln, Karl Landsteiner University for Health Sciences, Austria. She conducted the work reported in this book as part of her PhD degree at the Institute of Psychiatry, Psychology & Neuroscience, King's College London. Beate's main research interests focus on social psychiatry as well as on the conceptualisation and application of positive psychological variables, such as hope or wellbeing, to people with severe illness, both mental and physical.

Positive Psychotherapy for Psychosis

A Clinician's Guide and Manual

Mike Slade, Tamsin Brownell, Tayyab Rashid and Beate Schrank

 Routledge
Taylor & Francis Group

LONDON AND NEW YORK

First published 2017
by Routledge
2 Park Square, Milton Park, Abingdon, Oxon OX14 4RN

and by Routledge

711 Third Avenue, New York, NY 10017

Routledge is an imprint of the Taylor & Francis Group, an informa business

British Library Cataloguing in Publication Data
A catalogue record for this book is available from the British Library

Library of Congress Cataloging in Publication Data
Names: Slade, Mike, author. | Brownell, Tamsin, author. | Rashid, Tayyab, author. | Schrank, Beate, author.
Title: Positive psychotherapy for psychosis: a clinician's guide and manual for Wellfocus PPT / Mike Slade, Tamsin Brownell, Tayyab Rashid, and Beate Schrank.
Description: London; New York: Routledge, 2017. | Includes bibliographical references.
Identifiers: LCCN 2016022875| ISBN 9781138182868 (hbk) | ISBN 9781138182875 pbk) | ISBN 9781315545776 (ebk)
Subjects: | MESH: Psychotic Disorders—therapy | Psychotherapy—methods
Classification: LCC RC512 | NLM WM 200 | DDC 616.89—dc23
LC record available at https://lccn.loc.gov/2016022875

ISBN: 978-1-138-18286-8 (hbk)
ISBN: 978-1-138-18287-5 (pbk)
ISBN: 978-1-315-54577-6 (ebk)

Typeset in Stone Serif
by Florence Production Ltd, Stoodleigh, Devon, UK

E-resources at: www.routledge.com/9781138182875

Printed and bound by CPI Group (UK) Ltd, Croydon, CR0 4YY

Contents

Illustrations

Figures

Tables

Box

Contributors

Prof. Mike Slade is Professor of Mental Health Recovery and Social Inclusion at University of Nottingham. He led the work reported in this book while working as a Professor of Health Services Research at the Institute of Psychiatry, Psychology & Neuroscience, King's College London, and a Consultant Clinical Psychologist in South London. His main research interests are recovery-focused and outcome-focused mental health services, user involvement in and influence on mental health services, wellbeing in psychosis, staff-patient agreement on need, residential alternatives to inpatient services, and developing measures, for example, INSPIRE, Camberwell Assessment of Need, and Threshold Assessment Grid. His research programme is described at researchintorecovery.com.

Tamsin Brownell is a researcher in mental health services. She helped to develop *Positive Psychotherapy for Psychosis* while working as a Research Assistant at the Institute of Psychiatry, Psychology & Neuroscience, King's College London. Her main research interests are the development and evaluation of therapeutic interventions and user-led services for mental health, particularly in psychosis and eating disorders.

Tayyab Rashid is a licensed clinical psychologist and researcher at the Health & Wellness Centre, University of Toronto Scarborough (UTSC), Canada. Dr Rashid developed and empirically validated an innovative therapeutic approach called Positive Psychotherapy with Dr Martin Seligman at the Positive Psychology Centre, University of Pennsylvania, during his doctoral studies. Dr Rashid has trained mental health professionals and educators internationally and has also worked with survivors of 9/11 families, Asian Tsunami and flood relief workers in Pakistan. Published in peer-reviewed journals, an invited keynote speaker, Dr Rashid's work has also been featured in the *Wall Street Journal, Canadian Broadcasting Cooperation* and at the TEDx. See www.tayyabrashid.com for more information.

Dr Beate Schrank is a consultant psychiatrist, therapist and senior researcher at the Department of Psychiatry and Psychotherapy, University Clinic Tulln, Karl Landsteiner University for Health Sciences, Austria. She conducted the work reported in this book as part of her PhD degree at the Institute of Psychiatry, Psychology & Neuroscience, King's College London. Her main research interests focus on social psychiatry as well as on the conceptualisation and application of positive psychological variables, such as hope or wellbeing, to people with severe illness, both mental and physical.

Her research has most recently involved the development and evaluation of services and therapeutic interventions for these client groups.

This book is based on the WELLFOCUS study, which was funded by Guy's & St Thomas' Charity (Ref G101016). It was undertaken at King's College London and South London and Maudsley NHS Foundation Trust, with support from the National Institute for Health Research (NIHR) Biomedical Research Centre for Mental Health. Martin Seligman supervised and funded the initial validation of Positive Psychotherapy. We thank the trial facilitators (Nicola Gawn, Zara Kanji, Steven Livingstone, Matthew Richardson, Simon Riches and Marieke Wrigley) and participants, and Sherry Clarke, Tony Coggins and Andre Tylee for their contributions to the development and evaluation of the intervention. Data were also collected by Agnes Chevalier, Zivile Jakaite, Charley Larkin, Simon Riches and Judy Tchikaya. Invaluable administrative assistance was provided by Kelly Davies, Becks Leslie, Davina Malcolm and Linda Sulaiman.

Foreword

The promotion of recovery in mental health services is considered standard practice; however, definitions of recovery vary considerably across countries, individuals and professionals. Researchers, clinicians, peers and policymakers have worked tirelessly to develop recovery-oriented interventions. As a result, the concept of recovery-oriented services has become an established practice incorporated into most modern mental health interventions. The operationalization of recovery into services and treatment interventions has not been as clear (Le Boutillier *et al.*, 2011). Identifying the specific recovery-oriented elements of an intervention can be challenging.

Common components of recovery have included person-centered elements such as hope, meaning and purpose as well as the themes of coping, healing and wellness (Onken, Craig, Ridgway, Ralph, and Cook, 2007). Recovery-oriented interventions have operationalized these elements through strategies including the pursuit of a person's goal, developing a new skill, and developing a strategy to reduce symptom distress or to improve a functional limitation such as found in skills training approaches. Many recovery-oriented practices have emphasized shared decision-making where a person collaborates with a provider in the pursuit of recovery (Drake, Deegan, and Rapp, 2010). These approaches have informed recovery in treatment, but they may not fully empower persons to achieve a personally meaningful and gratifying recovery. A review of recovery has consistently revealed that recovery is more than just an absence of symptoms or the remediation of deficits (Davidson, O'Connell, Tondora, Lawless, and Evans, 2005). Recovery also includes the growth and development of a person's abilities, functioning and strengths. Many of the current elements of recovery-oriented interventions continue to focus on the remediation of deficits or removal of symptoms rather than the discovery of a person's strengths.

Encompassed within the definition of recovery is living a full and meaningful life and fostering mental health and wellbeing. Reducing symptoms, improving recovery and supporting positive mental health can be a collaborative process. Recovery-oriented services need to focus on more than only the removal of symptoms as the standard for recovery. The array of recovery-oriented services should embrace elements that enhance wellbeing and help individuals fulfil a more complete vision of recovery.

The development of the Positive Psychotherapy for Psychosis intervention is a novel recovery-oriented approach in the treatment of psychosis.

Slade, Brownell, Rashid and Schrank approached recovery from the viewpoint of positive mental health and closing the gap in recovery support. The strategies in Positive Psychotherapy for Psychosis embrace a well-rounded recovery and focus on enhancing positive emotions, a cornerstone in the promotion of wellbeing.

Positive Psychotherapy for Psychosis is a targeted intervention that offers a diverse approach to building positive mental health through building strengths, strengthening positive social connections and fostering individual meaning and purpose. This programme delivers a nontraditional approach to recovery-oriented services that does not centre on illness-specific deficits but instead emphasizes engagement in a meaningful and purposeful life. Participation in Positive Psychotherapy for Psychosis offers people the opportunity to address the gaps often overlooked in traditional interventions and to take meaningful steps towards recovery.

Slade, Brownell, Rashid and Schrank have created a programme that is both flexible and can be incorporated into existing mental health services to enhance recovery-oriented care. The manual includes specific guidelines to support clinicians implementing this approach and handouts for persons in recovery that guide them to integrate the strategies into their daily lives. The information in the manual is both accessible and appealing to support a consistent and sustainable implementation of a group-based intervention. The research supporting a positive psychology intervention continues to grow and the adaptations for people with psychosis were thoughtful and effective at helping people achieve a more complete recovery.

The field of recovery in mental health continues to grow rapidly and the tools to address recovery in treatment can be difficult to identify. Positive Psychotherapy for Psychosis is a valuable tool in recovery-oriented services for people with psychosis. The diversity and flexibility of the intervention along with the user-friendly materials promote a wider dissemination and implementation. Recovery is about hope and this book contains hope for people with psychosis to be more than their illness and to live a rich, rewarding and full life.

Piper S. Meyer-Kalos, PhD, LP
Minnesota Center for Chemical and Mental Health, St. Paul, MN

References

Davidson, L., O'Connell, M. J., Tondora, J., Lawless, M., and Evans, A. C. (2005). Recovery in serious mental illness: A new wine or just a new bottle? *Professional Psychology: Research and Practice, 36*(5), 480–87.

Drake, R. E., Deegan, P. E., and Rapp, C. (2010). The promise of shared decision making in mental health. *Psychiatric Rehabilitation Journal, 34*(1), 7–13.

Le Boutillier, C., Leamy, M., Bird, V. J., Davidson, L., Williams, J., and Slade, M. (2011). What does recovery mean in practice? A qualitative analysis of international recovery-oriented practice guidance. *Psychiatric Services, 62*(12), 1470–76.

Onken, S. J., Craig, C. M., Ridgway, P., Ralph, R. O., and Cook, J. A. (2007). An analysis of the definitions and elements of recovery: a review of the literature. *Psychiatric Rehabilitation Journal, 31*(1), 9–22.

Abbreviations

ABS	Affect Balance Scale
ACR	active constructive responding
ACT	acceptance and commitment therapy
BPRS	Brief Psychiatric Rating Scale
CBT	Cognitive behavioural therapy
CBTp	Cognitive behavioural therapy psychosis
CHIME	Connectedness, Hope, Identity, Meaning and Empowerment
CI	Confidence Interval
CINAHL	Cumulative Index to Nursing and Allied Health Literature
DSM-IV	Diagnostic and Statistical Manual Version IV
EBE	l'Echelle de Bien-Etre
EMBASE	Excerpta Medica dataBASE
ENJ	Enjoyment
EQ-5D	European Quality of Life-5 Dimensions
ES	Empowerment Scale
GNP	Gross National Product
HoNOS	Health of the Nation Outcome Scale
HRQoL	Health-Related Quality of Life
IHS	Integrative Hope Scale
ICD-10	International Classification of Diseases Version 10
ITT	Intention-to-treat
LQoL	Lehman Quality of Life
LQoLP	Lancashire Quality of Life Profile
LSI	Life Satisfaction Index
LS	general life satisfaction
MANSA	Manchester Short Assessment of Quality of Life
MBCT	mindfulness-based cognitive therapy
MEDLINE	Medical Literature Analysis and Retrieval System Online
MHI-38	Mental Health Inventory – 38 item
MHI-5	Mental Health Inventory – 5 item
MRC	Medical Research Council
ONS	Office of National Statistics
p	probability

PANAS	Positive and Negative Affect Scale
PERMA	Positive emotions, Engagement, Relationships, Meanings and Accomplishments
PGWI	Psychological General Wellbeing Index
PPI	Positive Psychotherapy Inventory
PPT	Positive Psychotherapy
PWI	Personal Wellbeing Index
Q-LES-Q	Quality of Life Enjoyment and Satisfaction Questionnaire
QOLI	Quality of Life Inventory
RCTs	Randomised controlled trials
RES	Rogers' Empowerment Scale
RSES	Rosenberg Self-Esteem Scale
RSPW	Ryff's Scales of Psychological Wellbeing
SAS-II	Social Adjustment Scale II
SAWB	Scale for the Assessment of Wellbeing
SBI	Savoring Beliefs Inventory
SCS	Sense of Coherence Scale
SD	standard deviation
SDHS	Short Depression-Happiness Scale
SEES	Subjective Exercise Experiences Scale
SF	Short Form
SHPS	Snaith-Hamilton Pleasure Scale
SPWB	Scale of Psychological Wellbeing
SSLS	Subjective Satisfaction with Life Scale
SSQ-72	Signature Strengths Questionnaire
SWN	Subjective Wellbeing under Neuroleptics Scale
USA	United States of America
VIA	Values in Action
WEMWBS	Warwick-Edinburgh Mental Wellbeing Scale
WHO	World Health Organization
WHO-5	World Health Organization 5 item Health Index
WHOQOL	World Health Organisation Quality of Life
WHOQOL-BREF	World Health Organisation Quality of Life – BREF
YuQoL	Yu Quality of Life for mental health scale

CHAPTER 1

Introduction

This book is about a new intervention for people living with a diagnosis of psychosis. This group of disorders is high prevalence, high burden and often long-term.[1] The most common psychosis diagnosis is schizophrenia, and it is estimated that 200,000 people live with schizophrenia in England alone.[2] Despite continued progress in the development and evaluation of treatments for schizophrenia and other psychoses, a high proportion of people continue to suffer from symptoms and disability. Hence, innovations in treatments for psychosis have international relevance.

We believe,[3] as do other commentators,[4–6] that research on wellbeing can inform the development of new approaches to supporting the recovery of people living with psychosis. As a result, we undertook a research study, funded by Guy's and St Thomas' Charity between 2009 and 2015. The study developed and evaluated a new manualised intervention called Positive Psychotherapy for Psychosis, which aims to improve wellbeing in people with psychosis. We published some of the study findings in individual academic papers.[7–15] This book brings together the complete body of work, including the revised manual for the new intervention.

In this chapter, we outline how the understanding of wellbeing has evolved over time. We tell this story in some detail, for three reasons. First, the concept of wellbeing is not yet well-defined in relation to people with severe mental illness such as psychosis.[16] Therefore, marshalling and organising the complex history of wellbeing is a sensible starting point. Second, this story illustrates many of the challenges in improving wellbeing in people living with psychosis. This helps to make more explicit some of the choices made in developing Positive Psychotherapy for Psychosis. Third, describing the history of wellbeing introduces many of the constructs used in positive psychology – the study of wellbeing – which were used in developing Positive Psychotherapy for Psychosis.

The remainder of the chapter then makes the links between recovery and wellbeing explicit, and describes the structure of the rest of the book.

What is wellbeing?

Wellbeing has been a topical policy focus in recent years and has attracted research interest across health conditions. An explicit description of the concept of wellbeing is often absent in research.[14] Four academic strands of wellbeing research can be differentiated:

1   Economic Strand: The earliest phase, grounded in economic research. Wellbeing is framed in terms of national wealth, social determinants, development and general quality of life.
2   Medical Strand: Grounded in medical research, wellbeing is framed in relation to disorder and illness.
3   Psychological Strand: Grounded in psychological research, wellbeing is framed in terms of subjective and mental concepts.
4   Integrative Strand: The latest phase, informed by economic, medical and psychological phases, with a distinct focus on positive psychology and recovery research.

We now discuss each phase, with a particular focus on the birth of the psychological conception and its evolution into the contemporary, integrative phase. The primary focus is to show how wellbeing has shifted from being conceived as a collectivist concept with objective measures, to being conceived as an individualistic concept with subjective measures. This transition was instrumental in wellbeing becoming a key concept in mental health.

From the economic phase to the medical phase

In the economic strand, wellbeing was initially conceived of primarily in collectivist terms. Measuring and comparing the wellbeing of populations (rather than individuals) was first undertaken by economists in the early twentieth century. Initially, financial indicators of wellbeing such as Gross National Product (GNP) were used to measure and compare. As these failed to discriminate between countries of similar developmental status, alternative economic indices were proposed to estimate societal functioning.[17] These composite measures further increased the validity of wellbeing estimates. Today, they are known as 'Quality of Life' measures. First, they included purely objective measures, such as mortality, nutrition, literacy, clean water supply or education.[18] Later, 'subjective' indicators such as affect, wellbeing or life satisfaction were added to capture how people actually feel about their lives.[19] Composite measures of population wellbeing are still developed today. For example, the UK Office for National Statistics (ONS) has developed a new assessment of population wellbeing, including subjective domains such as spirituality, personal and cultural activities, political participation or life satisfaction in addition to environmental and sustainability issues and UK economic performance.[20]

Inclusion of population level health indicators, for example, mortality, into composite measures evolving from economic research signifies the emergence of the medical strand to wellbeing research. The addition of subjective measures, for example, life satisfaction, signifies the emergence of the psychological strand to wellbeing research. Medical research also marks a shift in that it emphasises *individual* health status in understanding wellbeing. Health research is another major application of the concept of quality of life, in this context called Health-Related Quality of Life (HRQoL).

HRQoL has attracted substantial research since its introduction, as well as criticism for its lack of uniformity and clarity. The terms 'health related quality of life', 'quality of life' and 'wellbeing' are often used interchangeably, and few articles claiming to measure HRQoL provide a definition or identify constituent domains.[21] Conceptualisations and measures of HRQoL can be described according to a number of defining features, for example, generic versus disease specific, or objective versus subjective. Individual measurement tools often cover widely different dimensions, including access to resources and opportunities, environmental factors, social relationships, employment, leisure activities, sex life, mobility or satisfaction with social domains. The unifying feature of HRQoL concepts is their focus on illness symptoms and functioning based on the assumption that illness and disability inhibits full wellbeing.[22]

While physical health symptoms and functioning are major domains within HRQoL, measurement tools also often use the terms wellbeing and mental health (i.e. the absence of mental illness symptoms) interchangeably.[23] Examples of generic HRQoL measures with a mental health or wellbeing sub-scale include the World Health Organisation Quality of Life (WHOQOL) questionnaires with their domain on 'psychological health',[24] the European Quality of Life-5 Dimensions (EQ-5D) questionnaire with its 'anxiety and depression' domain,[25] or the Short Form (SF) measures, with their 'emotional wellbeing' domain assessing feeling happy, sad, depressed or anxious.[26] Other scales use a more elaborate conceptual foundation grounded in and overlapping with psychological conceptions of wellbeing. For example, the Lancashire Quality of Life Profile[27] (LQoLP) and the Manchester Short Assessment of Quality of Life[28] (MANSA) base their wellbeing domain on concepts of affect balance, life satisfaction and happiness.

One issue in measuring HRQoL in people with mental disorders is the potential distortion of subjective assessments due to 'psychopathological fallacies', most prominently the 'affective fallacy', which indicates that the momentary affective state can influence people's judgement about their overall life.[29] This is most problematic in cases where HRQoL measures contain 'emotional' items relating to feelings of depression and anxiety, as is the case, for example, in the Quality of Life in Depression Scale.[30] Quantitative results support the 'affective fallacy' as depressive symptoms have been shown to have an independent and significantly negative effect on subjective ratings of HRQoL.[31]

A second issue concerns the reliability of subjective assessment in people with psychiatric disorders. This concern led to the inclusion of supposedly objective assessment methods, derived from clinicians or family members.[32] However, subjective assessment has become more accepted as people with severe mental illness were shown to reliably and consistently complete self-rating questionnaires.[33] Moreover, the views of clinicians and family members may be biased, and service users' subjective position is argued to be no less true in case it diverges from an outsider. In fact, 'insider' and 'outsider' perspectives have been shown to differ due to differing values placed on contextual factors and a tendency towards a negative bias from the outsider perspective.[34] This supports the meaningfulness of the subjective assessment of wellbeing. While in HRQoL, subjective and objective measures still co-exist, the psychological approach has completely shifted to subjective assessment.

The emergence of the psychological phase

Psychological research has created specific conceptualisations and measures to capture wellbeing in its own right without embedding it within other constructs such as national development or HRQoL.

As with HRQoL, a review on psychological concepts of wellbeing criticised frequently missing or ambiguous definitions and the interchangeable use of similar terms.[35] Distinctive features of the psychological approach include its focus on subjective experience and personal feelings, and on positive mental health and functioning, for example, positive affect, life satisfaction, autonomy, competence or personal growth.[36-38] Moreover, specific wellbeing concepts allow for peak experiences (e.g. peak positive affect) or for the temporary cessation of affective experience during flow.[39] Such specific states of wellbeing may bring symptomatic relief, which will not be captured in measures of HRQoL.

Differences between measures of HRQoL and psychological wellbeing are empirically confirmed by their only moderate statistical correlations. Factor analysis including twelve scales assessing HRQoL and seven psychological wellbeing scales showed the two concepts to generally load on separate factors. Correlations between these scales ranged between 0.05 and 0.63, but mostly around 0.2–0.4.[40]

Despite broad agreement that wellbeing is a subjective condition in which positive feelings dominate, there is disagreement over more detailed ingredients of wellbeing in the psychological approach. Diverging views are often grouped under two broad perspectives: hedonic and eudaimonic.[36,41] In this context, *hedonism* usually refers to maximising pleasure and happiness while reducing pain. The *eudaimonic* perspective maintains that not all desires yield wellbeing when achieved, even though they might produce pleasure. Instead wellbeing means to live in accordance with one's true self and derives from personal growth and self-actualisation, from actively contributing, holding virtue and doing what is right. Happiness may be a pleasant result of this way of living but not its core.

Another organising principle for psychological wellbeing concepts is the distinction between the absence of mental illness symptoms and the presence of positive mental health, for example, framed as positive emotion. This is reflected in an increasing focus on positively framed items in wellbeing questionnaires.

One rationale for including positively framed variables (e.g. 'I have felt cheerful and in good spirits', 'I woke up feeling fresh and rested') into measurement tools was the observation that a substantial proportion of people in the general population rarely or never report occurrences of psychological distress symptoms.[42] For example, the US national comorbidity survey found a proportion of 14.9 per cent of people from twenty-six samples worldwide to qualify for the diagnosis of a mental disorder.[43] This introduces a ceiling effect,[23] that is, a zero score on a depression scale indicates the absence of depression but not the presence of happiness.[44] Including characteristics of psychological wellbeing (e.g. zest, interest in and enjoyment of life) increases measurement precision and distinguishes among persons who receive perfect scores on measures of psychological distress.[42] An example of a scale covering both ends of a continuum is the Depression-Happiness Scale.[45] The World Health Organization 5 item Health Index (WHO-5) goes one step further. It contains only positive items and assesses emotional wellbeing. However, although framed positively, the WHO-5 still covers core dimensions of depression and has proven to be a sensitive tool for screening for depression and suicide risk.[46] This may indicate that simply rewording negative to positive items may not be sufficient to meaningfully capture wellbeing.

The complex interrelations between the mental health domain in HRQoL and assessment tools designated to specifically measure mental health or wellbeing are exemplified by the RAND health survey. The original survey included the 38-item Mental Health Inventory (MHI-38) to assess mental health.[42] The MHI-38 had assimilated fifteen questions from Dupuy's General Wellbeing Index.[36] Later, the MHI-38 was condensed into the 5-item MHI-5, which was in turn used as the mental health sub-scale in the 'Short Form' HRQoL measures (e.g. SF-36 and SF-20).[47] In addition, from the same item pool, items were adapted into the WHO-5, which aims to assess positive mental wellbeing.[23] These measurement overlaps show the gradual development from purely deficit-focused HRQoL measures to measures of positive wellbeing.

Measuring subjectivity in the psychological strand

Despite their contrasts, the hedonic and eudaimonic views are not independent but overlap conceptually and correlate with each other with varying magnitude. The same issue of contrasting but overlapping dimensions also applies to a view of wellbeing as lack of mental illness versus positive mental wellbeing, or positive versus negative affect.[48] Hence, measurement tools for wellbeing may be better described according to their focus on affective, cognitive and multidimensional components.

Affective measures

Assessment tools that conceptualise wellbeing in terms of affect usually use the term affect to refer to mood states or feelings, without acknowledging the psychological distinctions between affect, emotion and feelings. These scales assume that wellbeing is the degree to which positive feelings outweigh negative feelings. They measure positive and negative feelings either as two distinct dimensions resulting in separate scores or in one overall 'balance score'. Prominent examples are the Positive and Negative Affect Scale (PANAS),[49] Bradburn's Affect Balance Scale (ABS),[41] the Affectometer[50] and the Everyday Feeling Questionnaire.[51] The overlap between affective wellbeing measures and measures of psychiatric symptoms is empirically supported by high correlations especially with depression.[45]

Cognitive measures

Affective and cognitive measurement strategies overlap. An example for the intersection between emotional and cognitive understandings of wellbeing is Diener's concept of 'subjective wellbeing' and the corresponding Satisfaction With Life Scale,[52] which assesses positive affect and subjective life satisfaction. Similarly, the Oxford Happiness Inventory defines happiness as a combination of positive affect or joy, satisfaction and the absence of distress and negative feeling.[53]

Purely cognitive measures of wellbeing include single-item questionnaires asking one question such as 'How satisfied are you with your life overall?' or 'Taking everything into consideration, how would you say you are today?'[36] This requires respondents to reflect on their overall state of life including all individually relevant domains.[54] As with HRQoL, the 'affective fallacy' caveat applies to global cognitive ratings, as they may be influenced by momentary affective states.[55] At the same time, global ratings are thought to better reflect subjective valuation since different areas of life may be valued differently by individuals.[56,57]

Global cognitive measures of wellbeing have been widely applied and inspired the theory of 'subjective wellbeing homeostasis'. This theory is based on the finding that mean population values of overall life satisfaction typically vary only within a narrow range. On a scale from 0 to 100, people in Western countries answer the question for overall life satisfaction roughly around 75; in non-Western countries, the average lies around 70.[58] The theory of subjective wellbeing homeostasis is comparable to the homeostatic regulation of body functions. It proposes that subjective wellbeing is maintained within narrow margins (a 'set point') by a set of psychological devices, for example, cognitive bias, personality factors and adaptation. Hence, people maintaining a normally functioning homeostatic system show little fluctuation in wellbeing as a consequence of normal variations in their living conditions. Only highly unusual events cause the level of global subjective wellbeing to change temporarily, but it will return to its previous level over time, for example, the subjective happiness of both lottery winners and paralysed accident victims soon returns to previous levels.[59] The conclusions that may be drawn for the measurement of wellbeing in general are that the classic 'life as a whole' question is useful as an estimate of the personal set-point of wellbeing, and is unlikely to change as a result of a therapeutic intervention.[60]

Multidimensional measures

Multidimensional wellbeing concepts and their corresponding measures include widely varying psychological dimensions apart from affective and cognitive aspects. Even though multidimensional wellbeing concepts are most comprehensive, none of them covers all potential wellbeing dimensions. No single concept can be regarded generally superior to others as their utility strongly depends on the target group to which they are applied.

Ryff's multidimensional concept of 'psychological wellbeing' and corresponding Scale of Psychological Wellbeing (SPWB)[57] captures positive functioning with a focus on life span development, individuation, maturity and self-actualisation.[61] The scale's unstable factor structure has attracted criticism but the particularly comprehensive concept is still used today and informs other conceptualisations of wellbeing. Likewise, the Warwick-Edinburgh Mental Wellbeing Scale (WEMWBS) covers a comprehensive understanding of wellbeing including affective-emotional aspects, cognitive-evaluative dimensions and psychological functioning.[62,63] Other multidimensional wellbeing scales exist, such as the l'Echelle de Bien-Etre (EBE), which aims to capture variations in wellbeing following changing environmental and personal circumstances.[64]

Integrative phase

The World Health Organisation (WHO) defines health as 'a state of complete physical, mental and social wellbeing and not merely the absence of disease or infirmity' and mental health as 'a state of wellbeing in which the individual realises his or her own abilities, can cope with the normal stresses of life, can work productively and fruitfully, and is able to make a contribution to his or her community'.[65] These highly inclusive definitions of wellbeing and mental health span both poles of the spectrum, that is, illness or the absence thereof as well as optimum or peak states.

Researchers, mainly in psychology, have devised equally comprehensive and overarching definitions of well-being and health, that is, of a good life, by including components of all previously outlined approaches. While the medical and psychological approaches are usually covered, the economic approach is represented to a lesser degree. This varying emphasis is partly supported by empirical research showing that the goodness of life is commonly judged by people according to happiness, meaning and – to a lesser extent – wealth.[66]

In the integrative approach, positive mental health receives explicit attention. This added focus on the positive instead of just on deficits corresponds with the introduction of a recovery orientation in mental health research and practice as well as with the emergence of the academic discipline of positive psychology. Both developments provide an important context for the good life approach in a mental health context.[3]

However, the concept of positive mental health is also far from uniform. One proposed organisation identifies six models of positive mental health from the literature:[67] (i) 'above normal', that is, supremely functioning, empathic, socially competent, resilient, self-actualised, future oriented, autonomous and self-aware; (ii) 'positive psychology', that is, character strength, talents and enablers; (iii) 'maturity', that is, reflecting theories of life time development with greater maturation reflecting better mental health; (iv) 'social-emotional intelligence'; (v) 'wellbeing', that is, happiness depending on genetic, environmental and personality factors and (vi) 'resilience'. This suggested classification again stresses how diverse and entangled the concepts of wellbeing and mental health are and how subjective their classification is.

The Complete State Model of Mental Health is another classification proposed to provide clarity for research and practice.[68] This conceptual framework includes both poles of mental health and wellbeing. Mental illness lies on a spectrum from absent to present. Wellbeing lies on a spectrum from low to high. This notion of a dual continuum may be particularly relevant in a mental health context, because it highlights that people can experience wellbeing at the same time as experiencing mental illness. Wellbeing in this model is conceptualised to include all aspects summarised in the psychological approach (i.e. positive affect, satisfaction and psychological wellbeing according to Ryff's comprehensive definition[69]) and social wellbeing.[70]

There is substantial variation in the definition and measurement of wellbeing. Probably an integrative approach to the concept – which emphasises the many influences on a good life – best reflects its complexity and may hence be most suitable for use in mental health research and practice.

The links between wellbeing and recovery

Recovery has emerged as the international guiding orientation for mental health systems. A recovery orientation is embedded in the national mental health policy in many countries across the Anglophone world[71–75] and elsewhere.[76,77] Box 1.1 shows how recovery is defined and operationalised in different countries.

At least rhetorically, recovery has also been embraced by professional groups. In England, for example, the principles of recovery have been adopted by clinical psychology,[83] mental health nursing,[84] occupational therapy,[85] psychiatry[86] and social work.[87] Perhaps the most influential professional group internationally is psychiatry in the USA, which has also embraced the term.[88]

Wellbeing overlaps with recovery, in several ways

The definition in Box 1.1 from the USA, by Bill Anthony, is routinely cited as the consensus definition of recovery internationally,[89] and uses many of the same constructs discussed earlier in relation to wellbeing. Systematic review evidence identifies key recovery processes such as Connectedness, Hope, Identity, Meaning and Empowerment (the CHIME framework).[90] These mirror the emergent understanding of wellbeing as a multidimensional construct.

BOX 1.1 International definitions of recovery and recovery support

Australia

Elements of this approach include targeted workforce development, establishment of an effective peer support workforce and expansion of opportunities for meaningful involvement of consumers and carers . . . This approach should promote the individual's value and strengths, encourage participation and relevant and equitable service provision. (p. 6)[78]

Austria

Mental health services can be helpful if they succeed in fostering control, choice and hope, but harmful if they undermine self-determination and convey pessimism and hopelessness. (p. 14)[79]

Canada

The concept of recovery is built on the principles of hope, empowerment, self-determination and responsibility . . . the approach to recovery has been broadened to include the concept of wellbeing, so that, with some adaptations to the different stages of life, the principles of recovery can apply to everyone. (p. 16)[72]

England

A greater ability to manage their own lives, stronger social relationships, a greater sense of purpose, the skills they need for living and working, improved chances in education, better employment rates and a suitable and stable place to live. (p. 21)[75]

Hong Kong

The process and outcomes by and in which a person affected by mental illness regains his/her level of functioning ('being'), sense of hope for the future ('becoming') and connection with oneself and others ('belonging'). (p. 43)[80]

Netherlands

We use 'recovery' as a guiding principle in the care and treatment of the client. The term 'recovery', derived from the client movement, indicates the desire to counterbalance the one-sided focus on the disorder itself, which has dominated for a long time . . . Recovery involves an active acceptance of problems and restrictions and a gradual transition in identity from patient to citizenship. (p. 20)[77]

New Zealand

Recovery is commonly defined as living well in the community with natural supports. Recovery does not always mean people will return to full health or retrieve all their losses, but people can and do live well despite this. (p. 11)[81]

USA

A deeply personal, unique process of changing one's attitudes, values, feelings, goals, skills and/or roles. It is a way of living a satisfying, hopeful and contributing life even within the limitations caused by illness. (p. 14)[82]

From a recovery perspective, it has been argued that mainstream solutions should be preferred over specialist solutions to mainstream problems,[91] and that fully supporting recovery involves the promotion of normal entitlements of citizenship.[92] This is consistent with the Transcendent Principle of Personhood, which states that 'people with severe mental illness are people'.[93] The same perspective emerges from the wellbeing research reviewed earlier, and from research into associated concepts such as mental capital.[94] The integrative approach implies that a wide range of factors need to be focussed on in developing interventions to improve wellbeing. Factors such as employment, friendship, exercise, sex or prayer are as important for people with severe mental illness as for any other group in society.

Wellbeing is possible in people experiencing mental illness. Research informed by the Complete State Model of Mental Health indicates that wellbeing can coexist with mental illness. For example, a cross-sectional survey of 3,032 adults in the USA found that only 7 per cent of the population experienced both mental illness and were languishing (low mental health), whereas 15 per cent experienced mental illness and moderate mental health, and 1 per cent experienced mental illness and flourishing (high mental health).[95] This mirrors the emergent possibility that recovery is relevant to all people with mental health problems.[96]

Finally, there is an empirical association between wellbeing and improved functioning, increased resilience and life satisfaction.[97] The evidence suggests that wellbeing confers a protective value against the onset or reoccurrence of mental illness.[98]

This linkage between wellbeing and recovery indicates the need to develop and evaluate new interventions targeting wellbeing and its associated dimensions, such as self-worth, meaning and hope.[99] A promising resource to draw on is evidence from the academic discipline of positive psychology.[100] The promotion of wellbeing is a focus of this discipline, which has shifted away from ameliorating deficits (e.g. symptoms) toward building positive emotions, character strengths and meaning.[101] Positive Psychotherapy (PPT) is a specific intervention developed from positive psychology principles. In this book, we describe how PPT was modified to Positive Psychotherapy for Psychosis, and then further refined following evaluation in a randomised controlled trial.

Structure of the book

This book presents the empirical basis for the intervention, and then provides clinicians with a comprehensive, step-by-step manual of instructions for providing Positive Psychotherapy for Psychosis to people with psychosis. The scientific framework for Positive Psychotherapy for Psychosis is the Medical Research Council (MRC) Framework for Evaluating Complex Health Interventions.[102] The three phases of this framework involved establishing the theory (described in Chapters 2 and 3), developing a model and intervention manual (described in Chapter 4) and refining the intervention through evaluation in a randomised controlled trial (described in Chapter 5).

Chapter 2 gives an overview of positive psychology, focussing on the development of PPT as a specific intervention approach, which has been developed and evaluated in non-clinical populations and in people with common mental disorders such as depression.

Chapter 3 describes the theory base for the new intervention for people with psychosis. Positive Psychotherapy for Psychosis is based on methodologically rigorous research, including data from systematic reviews and qualitative research involving people with psychosis using mental health services (i.e. the target group for the intervention) and mental health service staff.

In Chapter 4, we describe how this theory was used to modify standard PPT into Positive Psychotherapy for Psychosis. We identify the rationale for adding, modifying and removing elements from standard PPT.

Once the intervention was developed, we evaluated Positive Psychotherapy for Psychosis in a randomised controlled trial across out-patient and in-patient settings. The trial design and outcome and process evaluation findings are outlined in Chapter 5, and a description of how the intervention was modified in the light of results from the trial is given.

Chapter 6 summarises our experience of providing Positive Psychotherapy for Psychosis. It uses a question-and-answer structure, to maximise relevance to therapists considering using Positive Psychotherapy for Psychosis in their work. We also provide guidance on adapting the approach for use in individual treatments, and for integrating Positive Psychotherapy for Psychosis sessions into other psychotherapeutic treatments.

The remainder of the book is the intervention manual for the final version of Positive Psychotherapy for Psychosis. Although we recommend familiarity with Chapters 1–6, the manual is written as a standalone document. The theory base is briefly rehearsed, and the intervention described. A synthesis of findings from delivering the intervention is given, as a guide for therapists.

Each of the thirteen structured sessions is then presented, in a consistent and highly accessible format. Each session description includes a brief summary of relevant theory for therapists, session materials, a clear statement about the aims of the session and detailed instructions for each activity and homework assignment. Implementation guidelines are provided, based on our experience of providing the intervention in a number of mental health service settings. We also provide troubleshooting guides for each session, to address common clinical issues. Additionally, each session includes therapist tips for exercises, showing clinicians how to approach some of the more difficult questions that may arise in practice. Case studies are included that illustrate how two anonymous clients progress, based on the findings from providing the therapy during the randomised controlled trial. The manual is followed by all necessary handouts as appendices, which are ready to copy and distribute to clients.

CHAPTER 2

Positive Psychotherapy

Positive psychology

The academic discipline of positive psychology developed from Martin Seligman's 1998 Presidential Address to the American Psychological Association, initiating a shift in psychology's focus towards the positive aspects of human experience, positive individual traits and more generally the positive features that make life worth living.[101] Positive psychology was originally defined as follows:

> The field of positive psychology at the subjective level is about valued subjective experiences: wellbeing, contentment, and satisfaction (in the past); hope and optimism (for the future); and flow and happiness (in the present). At the individual level, it is about positive individual traits: the capacity for love and vocation, courage, interpersonal skill, aesthetic sensibility, perseverance, forgiveness, originality, future mindedness, spirituality, high talent, and wisdom. At the group level, it is about the civic virtues and the institutions that move individuals toward better citizenship: responsibility, nurturance, altruism, civility, moderation, tolerance, and work ethic[101]
>
> (p. 5)

In terms of content, today, positive psychology serves as an umbrella term to accommodate research endeavours that started both before and after the introduction of the movement by Seligman and Csikszentmihalyi. Related research spans a diverse range of disciplines, such as education,[103] sport psychology,[104] family medicine,[105] cancer care[106] or brain injury rehabilitation.[107]

Among the centrally important areas of work in positive psychology research is the development and investigation of strategies that would make people lastingly happier. A range of approaches intended to promote wellbeing have been tested in intervention research, such as mindfulness therapy, forgiveness therapy, gratitude therapy and various forms of wellbeing therapy.[108]

Positive psychology and mental health services

In mental health services and research, the strong focus on illness, symptoms and deficits began to shift towards strengths and resources only in recent decades. The World Psychiatric Association remarks in its official journal that 'psychiatry has failed to improve the average levels of happiness and wellbeing in the general population'[109] (p. 71), suggesting that the promotion of wellbeing is among the duties of the mental health system. Lately, wellbeing has also become a policy focus. For example, in the UK, the Office for National Statistics (ONS) now publishes national[110] statistics on wellbeing, as well as international comparisons.[111] This shift in the mental health field coincides with the consumer-led recovery movement that has evolved since the 1980s, and argues for a focus on wellbeing regardless of the presence of mental illness. Recovery in this context refers not to symptom remission but to people (re-)engaging in their life on the basis of their own goals and strengths, and finding meaning and purpose through constructing and reclaiming a valued identity and valued social roles.[3] These goals of the recovery movement are highly congruent with those of positive psychology.

While positive psychology was originally associated with the scientific study of optimal human functioning and with refocusing psychology away from adversity and illness towards understanding 'how normal people flourish under more benign conditions'[101] (p. 5), positive psychology approaches have since been successfully expanded to various populations including people with disorders and in adverse conditions. The two movements, recovery and positive psychology, are highly complementary.[3,112,113] They share a similar focus, but the former has so far been largely built on personal accounts, theories and opinions with empirical research lagging behind,[114] while the latter offers a quantitative research focus in need of theory and contextual knowledge on which to base its application.

A meta-analysis of fifty-one studies of positive interventions demonstrated significantly improved wellbeing and decreased depressive symptoms for people with depression.[115] A more recent meta-analysis of thirty-nine positive psychology randomised studies involving 6,139 participants concluded that positive psychology interventions can be effective in enhancing subjective and psychological wellbeing and reducing depressive symptoms.[116]

Positive psychotherapy

So far, wellbeing research has focused on a variety of groups, including the general population across the lifespan[117] and on physical health problems such as cancer[118] and HIV/AIDS.[119] There have been calls for a stronger focus on wellbeing in mental health systems,[6] especially in relation to supporting recovery.[113] However, despite the increasing evidence base for its efficacy, and the calls for including more positive approaches in mental health interventions, positive psychology ideas have been slow to be incorporated in mental health services.

TABLE 2.1 Standard 14-session PPT

Session	Content	Homework
1 Orientation to PPT	Group guidelines, importance of homework, presenting problems are discussed	Positive Introduction (a story of when you were 'at your best')
2 Character Strengths	Identify (up to five) character strengths using the Values in Action (VIA) Classification of Character Strengths questionnaire, possibly with family/friends	Blessing Journal (identify three good things each night)
3 Signature Strengths	Identify signature strengths	Signature Strength Action Plan
4 Good vs. Bad Memories	Memories and cognitive reappraisal are discussed	Writing Memories (focusing on bad memories and distress)
5 Forgiveness	Transforming forgiveness into positive emotions	Forgiveness Letter (not necessarily delivered)
6 Gratitude	Enduring thankfulness, good/bad memories are discussed	Gratitude Letter and Visit
7 Mid-Session Feedback	Recap Signature Strengths Action Plan, Forgiveness, Gratitude. Discussion of progress	None
8 Satisficing vs. Maximising	Discuss settling for 'good enough' rather than exploring almost all possible options	Plan areas that could benefit from satisficing
9 Hope, Optimism and Posttraumatic Growth	Consider unexpected/unintended positives. Optimism, hope and new opportunities are discussed. Growth from trauma is explored	One Door Closes One Door Opens
10 Positive Communication	ACR is discussed	Active Constructive Responding
11 Signature Strengths of Others	Character strengths of family are discussed	Family Strengths Tree
12 Savouring	Take time to notice various elements of an experience. Savouring techniques are discussed	Planned Savouring Activity
13 Altruism	Giving the gift of time to help others is discussed	Gift of Time
14 The Full Life	Integration of positive emotions, engagement, positive relationships, meaning and accomplishment. Discuss ways to sustain positive changes	None

The most promising strategies in positive psychology have been combined into one overall intervention named Positive Psychotherapy (PPT).[120] PPT is a psychological therapy that focuses on strengths and positive experiences in order to promote wellbeing. In contrast to some traditional psychotherapies, PPT is strengths-focused rather than problems-focused. PPT attends to problems or symptoms, such as negative memories and forgiveness, but in doing so refocuses to positives. PPT exercises focus on mindfully savouring enjoyable moments or activities; recording blessings or good things, active constructive responding (ACR) in social interaction, identifying character strengths and using them in activities either alone or with others; and focussing on positives through otherwise negative events or memories, or concepts like forgiveness and gratitude.[121,122]

The standard PPT intervention manual describes how to provide PPT to people with depression and to non-clinical samples, with 6-session and 14-session versions.[121] The 14-session version is summarised in Table 2.1.

PPT and strengths

To illustrate PPT, we now describe how strengths are assessed. Rather than a simple approach of identifying and using more of the top five strengths, PPT adapts a comprehensive strength assessment approach, which entails following steps:

1 The client sees twenty-four pictures of strengths, usually through a slide show, with each picture appearing briefly (usually 5 seconds) with a title of strength. Clients are asked to mark five to six strengths, which they 'feel' best represent their personality. This step can also be completed by giving each client a set twenty-four pictures and asking them to select five. Table 2.2 lists the twenty-four strengths.
2 Clients read brief descriptions of the twenty-four strengths, without their titles/names, and identify five, not ranked, that best describe their personality. The descriptions are shown in Table 2.3.
3 Clients are requested to ask two significant others (a family member and/or a friend) to complete a strengths sheet, which includes description of twenty-four strengths, without title, and return the worksheet to clients in a sealed envelope.
4 Finally, clients then complete a self-report measure either online or using a hard copy. This measure, Signature Strengths Questionnaire (SSQ-72), assesses twenty-four strengths through three behaviour items each.[123]

Data from all these sources is aggregated to determine the client's signature strengths. The assessment process described above can be abbreviated according to clinical conditions and logistics. For example, for some clinical conditions, eliciting feedback from a friend and a family member may not be feasible in a specific time frame. In other cases, due to language barriers, the descriptions can be simplified. Nonetheless, clinicians are encouraged to assess strengths from at least two sources, as it could be reassuring for

TABLE 2.2 Character strengths

Strength	Description	Strength	Description
1	Creativity	13	Citizenship and teamwork
2	Curiosity	14	Fairness
3	Open-mindedness	15	Leadership
4	Love of learning	16	Forgiveness
5	Perspective	17	Humility
6	Bravery	18	Prudence
7	Persistence	19	Self-regulation
8	Integrity	20	Appreciation of beauty
9	Vitality	21	Gratitude
10	Love	22	Hope and optimism
11	Kindness	23	Humour and playfulness
12	Social intelligence	24	Spirituality

clients who are likely to focus more on their deficits. After the assessment, clinicians encourage clients to share memories, experiences, real-life stories, anecdotes, accomplishments and skills, which illustrate their signature strengths throughout the course of treatment. At the same time, clinicians also invite clients to conceptualise their presenting issues as lack or access of strengths. In doing so, clients are encouraged to develop a key strength of psychological flexibility. Kashdan and Rottenberg define psychological flexibility as the ability to adapt to fluctuating situational demands, reconfiguring strengths, shifting perspective and balancing competing desires, needs and life domains.[124] In PPT, the psychotherapist helps clients to carefully reconceptualise that certain challenges could be due to competing demands of two strengths, such as should one be honest or kind with a close friend who may be involved in unethical behaviour; self-regulation in one domain of life (e.g. eating or exercises) may be associated with weak interpersonal relationships; fear of failure or giving up may be associated with persisting with goals or pursuits which may be unrealistic; forgiving loved ones for their transgression without a concrete behaviour change may compromise fairness.

The impact of PPT on therapists

The very nature of psychotherapy can require psychotherapists to listen to graphically detailed descriptions of horrific events and bear witness to the psychological (and sometimes physical) aftermath of acts of intense cruelty and/or violence. If psychotherapy largely entails confronting negative memories and adverse experiences – both subtle and severe – then the

TABLE 2.3 Description of character strengths

Strength	Description
1	I am good at thinking of new and better ways of doing things.
2	I love to explore things, ask questions and am open to different experiences and activities.
3	I am flexible and open-minded; I think through and examine all sides before deciding.
4	I love to learn many ideas, concepts and facts in school or on my own.
5	Friends consult with on important matters as they consider me to be wise beyond my age.
6	I do not give up in face of hardship or challenge, even when I am afraid.
7	I finish most things; even if I get distracted, I am able to refocus and complete the task.
8	I consider myself to be a genuine and honest person, known to be trustworthy and act consistent with my values.
9	I am energetic, cheerful and full of life.
10	Showing and receiving genuine love and affection come naturally to me.
11	I love to do kind acts for others, often without being asked.
12	I manage myself well in social situations and am known to have good interpersonal skills.
13	I am an active community or team member, and contribute to the success of my group.
14	I stand up for others when they are treated unfairly, bullied or ridiculed.
15	Others often choose me as a leader as I am known to lead well.
16	I do not hold grudges; I forgive easily those who offend me.
17	I don't like to be the centre of attention and prefer others to shine.
18	I am careful and cautious; I can anticipate risks and problems of my actions and respond accordingly.
19	I manage my feelings and behaviours even in challenging situations; I generally follow rules and routines.
20	I am moved deeply by beauty in nature, in art (e.g. painting, music, theatre, etc.) and/or in excellence in many fields of life.
21	I express thankfulness for good things through words and actions.
22	I hope and believe that more good things will happen than bad ones.
23	I am playful, funny and use humour to connect with others.
24	I believe in a higher power and participate in religious or spiritual practices (e.g. prayer, meditation, etc.) willingly.

cumulative experience of such an empathic engagement can have deleterious effects on psychotherapists. These effects can manifest as emotional exhaustion, depersonalisation and a lack of personal accomplishment for therapists – causing burnout and compassion fatigue.[125,126] Exploring what sustains the wellbeing of psychotherapists, clinicians and counsellors and what makes them exemplary, Harrison and Westwood found an overarching positive orientation conveyed through an ability to maintain faith and trust in three attributes: (a) self as good enough; (b) therapeutic change process and (c) the world as a place of beauty and potential (despite and in addition to pain and suffering).[127] So a strengths-based approach has the potential to buffer therapists against burnout, compassion, fatigue and depersonalisation.

Who is PPT not suitable for?

PPT is not a panacea and will not be appropriate for all clients in all situations. As such, clinical judgment is needed to determine the suitability of PPT for individual clients. A therapist using PPT also should not expect a linear progression of improvement, because the motivation to change long-standing behavioural and emotional patterns fluctuates during the course of therapy. The progress of one client should not bias therapists about the likely progress (or their lack of) of another client. The mechanism of change in PPT has not been explored systematically, but inferring from change of mechanism uncovered by Lyubomirsky and Layous about positive interventions,[128] it can be argued that change brought by positive interventions could be moderated by level of symptoms severity, individual personality variables (motivation, effort), flexibility in completing and practicing the exercises and skills, and overall client-intervention fit. Nonetheless, therapists must also be aware that change may be due to expectancy effects. Finally, it is important to be aware of cultural sensitivities in assessing strengths. An emotive style of communication, interdependence on extended family members and avoiding direct eye contact may convey zest, love and respect.[129]

The central premise of PPT is that explicitly addressing positive resources can be an effective and perhaps more efficacious way of treating psychological concerns. Despite its name, PPT is not only about being positive. Without dismissing the severity of psychological distress or naively minimising clients' genuine concerns, clients are neither mere collections of symptoms nor embodiments of strengths. PPT systematically amplifies positive resources of clients, including positive emotions, character strengths, meaning, positive relationships and intrinsically motivated accomplishments (assessed through the PPTI measure described in Chapter 5). PPT neither suggests that other psychotherapies are negative nor aims to replace well-established treatment protocols. PPT is about refocusing rather than revamping therapeutic regimens. It is not a paradigm shift; it is simply an approach that seeks to balance the attention given to negative and positive life events in psychotherapy. For example, a clinician may balance discussion of some perceived slight or personal injustice with a discussion of recent acts of kindness shown to a client. Similarly, along with insults, hubris and hate, experiences of genuine praise, humility and harmony are deliberately elicited. Without dismissing or minimising the client's concerns, the pain associated with trauma is empathetically understood and recognised while the potential for growth is simultaneously explored. PPT involves a therapeutic reorientation to a *build-what's-strong* model that supplements the traditional *fix-what's-wrong* approach.[130] The ultimate goal of PPT, therefore, is to teach clients skills, which use their best resources to meet their toughest challenges.

So PPT, with character strengths at its core, may give the impression that it is prescriptive. Instead, it is a descriptive approach based on converging scientific evidence that certain benefits accrue when individuals focus on their positive experiences and attributes. Nevertheless, like any therapy, PPT may not be feasible for all clients or their concerns. First, its application must be guided by evidence. That is, it will be clinically imprudent to apply PPT with clients experiencing for example acute symptoms of panic disorder, selective mutism or paranoid personality disorder, as currently there is no evidence that PPT could be effective for these disorders. Still some clients may have a strong feeling that their symptoms, not strengths, ought to be the focus of treatment. They may fear that expression or articulation of their weaknesses may invoke judgment by the therapist. Others may have a deeply entrenched self-perception of being a victim, which they may be more accustomed to. For others, identification of character strengths may exaggerate narcissistic characteristics. Therefore, it is important that strengths are discussed in specific situational contexts and their nuances are discussed thoroughly. For example, some clients may not benefit from being kind or forgiving in some situations. Likewise, some may feel conflicted between being authentic and socially intelligent. Some may face the dilemma of solving a complex challenge either by being honest or empathic. Similarly, clients with a history of abuse and with a strengths profile of being humble, forgiving, and kind may not readily benefit from PPT until they develop the strength of perspective and critical thinking skills to understand situations more accurately and realistically. Clients with a history of unresolved trauma and symptoms of post-traumatic stress may respond better to symptom-focused treatments and may not be ready for PPT exercise on post-traumatic growth. In summary, PPT is not a panacea nor is it completely irrelevant for most clients. Its fit has to be explored and monitored continuously during the course of the treatment.

Despite convincing evidence that psychotherapy is effective, over and above placebo, a US study found that its usage is in decline and use of psychotropic medication is on the rise.[131] It could be argued that deficit-focused psychotherapy approaches may not cater to the needs of contemporary clients. Compared to the baby-boomer generation whose parents were scarred by traumas of World Wars, poverty and social inequalities, the current clientele of psychotherapy is likely to be the Millennial and Generation Z. These are young people who are largely urban, culturally diverse, ambitious, socially active and digitally and visual connected in real time with trends and twists of every moment. They may be less interested and invested in examining themselves with largely diagnostic lens. They already are active in running online campaigns against labels, which perpetuate stigma. Millennials are more interested in exploring their potential not only vulnerabilities.[132] They are likely to respond to de-stigmatising, innovative, mind-body integrated, focused, short-term treatments that are compatible with mobile and online interfaces. This may account for the growing popularity of positive psychology and the acceptability of PPT.

Mechanisms of change

There are several potential mechanisms of change in PPT.

1   PPT *broadens and builds* therapeutic resources, as do all other approaches to psychotherapy. For example, in traditional psychodynamic psychotherapy a client opens up her subjective world, and the therapist will interpret her associations to help the client achieve insight, thereby producing a broader perspective. Cognitive and behavioural therapies do the same by widening the client's behavioural and cognitive repertoires. PPT broadens the client's perspective by having him or her undertake activities that generate positive emotions. Although fleeting in nature, positive emotions broaden meaning, expand behavioural repertoires, help clients generate new ideas and facilitate reinterpretation of old and bitter memories. This broadening occurs at cognitive, affective and behavioural levels. Therefore, positive emotions in PPT are not simply indications of joy or happiness but more importantly, these emotions generate cognitive, behavioural and affective changes.

2   Clients seek psychotherapy because they are often troubled by negative emotions and negative memories. PPT exercises (e.g. bitter memories) help clients unpack negative memories and do a careful and thorough positive reappraisal using the specific strategies described above. The aim is to increase behavioural, cognitive and affective flexibility. This is usually done after clients complete their positive introductions and identify their character strengths – exercises that often produce positive emotions.

3   Experiential and skill building PPT exercises allow clients to develop their signature strengths. Symptomatic distress keeps these assets hidden, and clients coming for therapy are often unaware of their specific strengths. Unlike hedonic activities, which are short-cuts and rely on modern gadgets, PPT exercises are intentional activities that are time-intensive (e.g. first writing about and then completing a gratitude visit, devising a plan to use signature strengths, writing three good things in the journal daily, arranging a savouring date, giving a gift of time). Compared to sensory pleasures that fade quickly, these activities last longer, involve quite a lot of thinking and interpretation, and do not habituate easily. Clients from the onset of therapy are instructed that happiness does not simply happen, but rather it is something that they must *make* happen. PPT exercises change because any activity that taps signature strengths of clients can be engaging. For example, a client with the signature

strength of creativity was asked to think of something that would use her creativity. She selected pottery – something she always wanted to do but was never motivated enough to do.

4 PPT is about dealing with problems head-on. Some psychotherapies may be effective in bringing about therapeutic changes through venting of bottled up emotions or providing a place to express anger or resentment. PPT empathically attends to the concerns of clients, but it also actively teaches clients to function well despite their depressive symptoms. PPT exercises such as positive appraisal and using signature strengths to solve problems can ultimately help clients learn to be comfortable with some unavoidable and uncomfortable aspects of their personality or environment. Furthermore, the systematic identification of signature strengths allows clients to think more deeply about their positive qualities. If thinking about our weaknesses is likely to make them feel vulnerable, thinking about strengths, in a realistic way, is likely to bolster their self-confidence and prepare them to deal more effectively with their problems.

5 Finally, an overarching mechanism that helps clients change is *re-education of attention*. Most clients presenting for psychotherapy experience an elevated natural negative tendency, and they have learned to exaggerate it by focusing on and recalling negative aspects of their experience. Several PPT exercises aim to re-educate attention, memory and expectations away from the negative and catastrophic, and towards the positive and the hopeful. For example, keeping a *gratitude journal* can counteract the tendency to ruminate on the dissatisfying aspects of one's life (e.g. obstacles, disappointments) and orient clients towards events that enrich life and are vitalising (e.g. caring acts, goal attainment). Similarly, the gratitude visit may shift a client's memory away from the unfavourable aspects of past relationships to savouring the good things about interactions with friends and family. This re-education of attention, memory and expectation is accomplished verbally via journal writing. Participating in time-intensive positive activities does not leave time for clients to brood over their misery.

Effective psychotherapy requires the generation of ideas and actions to solve problems. However, this cannot be done unless the therapist establishes a strong therapeutic alliance. All major approaches to psychotherapy emphasise that therapist-client interaction should be positive, and characterised by empathy, warmth and genuineness. While this is achieved primarily through discussion of weaknesses within traditional psychotherapy, in PPT client and therapist talk about instances in which the parents meet the needs of the child, when the client transgressed but was forgiven, and when criticism was balanced by genuine appreciation. When this occurs, the focus on personal strengths is likely to be a more potent generator of change than a focus on personal weaknesses would have been. For example, low mood and a loss of interest in previously enjoyed activities were hallmark characteristics of one client who spent hours each day ruminating on her problems. Through PPT, she discovered that an appreciation of beauty and curiosity were among her signature strengths and, with the help of her therapist, she was able to design activities that tapped these strengths. After engaging in these activities, she reported a decrease in levels of unhelpful rumination.

PPT evidence base

PPT was initially validated with adult clients experiencing symptoms of severe depression.[133] This finding has been replicated in three independent studies.[134–136] Randomised controlled trials (RCTs) comparing PPT with no treatment show decreased depressive symptoms in students[137–140] and other non-clinical, community samples.[120,138,141] Traditional psychotherapeutic interventions have tried to treat psychopathology by understanding and curing symptoms and disorders. PPT offers a unique opportunity to expand the existing infrastructure of psychotherapy by integrating positives and negatives towards symptoms relief, buffer from their recurrence but also fostering systematically wellbeing – all leading towards enduring sense of recovery.

PPT is now being integrated within other interventions[142] and used with other client groups, for example, a small sample of smokers found benefits from PPT in combination with smoking cessation counselling and nicotine patch treatment.[143] Brain injury rehabilitation is another area that may benefit from modified PPT.[107,144] PPT has also been adapted for suicidal inpatients[145] and for physical health conditions.[146–148] More generally, positive interventions are being adapted for various populations, for example, people with developmental disabilities.[149] For a summary of studies using the PPT protocol, see Rashid.[150]

Wellbeing research has not been widely integrated within traditional treatment protocols for people with more severe mental health problems,[3] and so a further area that may benefit from modification is psychosis. There is preliminary evidence of applicability – an uncontrolled feasibility study of sixteen people with schizophrenia evaluated a 'positive living' intervention modified from a 6-session PPT.[151] The intervention was shown to be feasible and increased participants' wellbeing, savouring, hope, self-esteem and personal recovery.

In the next chapter, we describe how we developed theory to inform the modification of standard PPT for use with people living with psychosis.

CHAPTER 3

Theory base for Positive Psychotherapy for Psychosis

In this chapter, we describe two studies that together provide a defensible empirical foundation for research on wellbeing in psychosis. Fuller reports of both studies have been published. The first study was a systematic review to develop a conceptual understanding of wellbeing.[14] The second study used a qualitative design to develop a framework for characterising how wellbeing changes in people experiencing psychosis.[11]

Conceptual framework for wellbeing in psychosis

We undertook a systematic review to characterise the evidence base relating to wellbeing in people with psychosis.[14] The objectives were (1) to understand how wellbeing is measured in high-quality research studies involving people with psychosis, and (2) to develop an organising conceptual framework for wellbeing as used in these studies.

Method

We included randomised and non-randomised intervention studies investigating the effects of intervention compared with control on service users' wellbeing as the primary or secondary outcome, available in full-text in English or German language. Inclusion criteria for participants were (i) aged 16–65 years; (ii) having past or present diagnosis of a psychotic illness based on ICD-10 or DSM-IV or at least 70 per cent in a mixed diagnosis sample (interpreted to be over-inclusive when the diagnostic description was unclear) and (iii) use or have used mental health services.

Five sources of data were searched from inception to May 2012. Bibliographic databases (EMBASE, MEDLINE, PsycINFO, British Nursing Index and Archive, Applied Social Sciences Index and Abstracts, British Humanities Index, Sociological Abstracts, Social Services Abstracts, International Bibliography of Social Sciences, CINAHL and Cochrane) were searched using variants of 'wellbeing' and 'severe mental illness'. We also reviewed tables of contents from journals (*British Journal of Wellbeing, Journal of Positive Psychology, Psychiatric Rehabilitation Journal*) and special issues, searched the Grey Literature Network Service and charity websites (Mental

Health Foundation, New Economic Foundation, Young Foundation, Mind, Rethink), consulted eight experts and hand-searched reference lists of all included studies and of relevant reviews, opinion papers and guidelines.

The first 200 studies were independently rated for inclusion by two reviewers, achieving a concordance rate of 0.98. Disagreement was resolved by consensus. The remaining 19.137 studies were appraised by one review author. Data were extracted into an Excel spreadsheet developed for a previous systematic review with narrative synthesis.[152]

To meet Objective 1 (understand how wellbeing is measured in controlled trials with people with psychosis), we descriptively listed the measures and counted the retrieved studies in which they were used. After constructing the conceptual framework, we used vote counting to assess how frequently the individual framework dimensions were included in the used measures.

To meet Objective 2 (develop an organising conceptual framework for wellbeing), we used a modified narrative synthesis approach,[153] taking the measures of wellbeing from included studies as the units of data. We used the three domains of wellbeing and its determinants proposed by the UK Office of National Statistics (ONS) (individual feeling of wellbeing, factors directly affecting individual wellbeing, more contextual domains) as the initial organising framework.[154] We plotted the measures according to the ONS domains, detected common components across the scales and grouped them into higher order constructs. In an iterative process, the broad groups were repeatedly split into different categories and regrouped.

Results

Study selection is shown in Figure 3.1.

Objective 1: Measurement of wellbeing

The search resulted in 28 eligible articles. These used 20 measures to assess wellbeing, described in Table 3.1.

Objective 2: Conceptual framework of wellbeing in psychosis

The analysis of the content of included measures resulted in a conceptual framework of wellbeing that spans five domains: (i) non-observable, (ii) observable, (iii) proximal, (iv) distal and (v) self-defined. These domains can be understood as four layers of proximity to the person and one additional self-defined dimension.

The non-observable domain refers to intra-psychic phenomena such as self-perception, mood tone or meaning and purpose in life, which are not readily visible from outside. The observable domain comprises aspects of a person that are exhibited to the outside world, such as environmental mastery, resolution or physical health. The proximal domain describes factors that directly and immediately affect the individual. It includes what

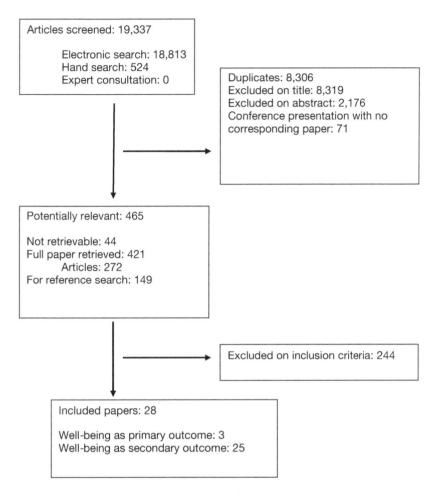

FIGURE 3.1 Flow diagram of studies included in the review

a person has or does, for example, various kinds of relationships, finances or occupation. Finally, the distal domain encompasses contextual factors that are not under a person's immediate influence, such as the wider environment or access to services.

In addition, some measures included a broad general question on overall wellbeing or overall life satisfaction, which we defined as a separate self-defined domain.

Table 3.2 shows the framework of wellbeing in psychosis resulting from our analysis in comparison with the generic framework of national wellbeing.[154]

The ONS framework of national wellbeing addresses the whole of society.[20] In contrast, the framework of wellbeing modified for psychosis focuses on the individual. Consequently, it places stronger emphasis on individual dimensions, while distal dimensions such as environment are less prominent.

Table 3.3 shows the scales used to measure wellbeing in the included studies according to their coverage of the conceptual framework of wellbeing in psychosis.

TABLE 3.1 Description of wellbeing measures with number of studies included in the review using them as primary or secondary outcome measures

Scale name	Brief description of constituent factors and domains	Established psychometric properties	Primary outcome measure (N studies)	Secondary outcome measure (N studies)
Subjective Satisfaction with Life Scale (SSLS)	Four domains: living situation, social relationships, work, self and present life	yes	0	2
WHOQOL-BREF	Four dimensions: psychological wellbeing (or health), physical health, social relationships, environment; plus overall quality of life	yes	0	2
Lancashire Quality of Life Profile (LQoLP)	Eight life domains: work, leisure, social involvement, finances, living situation, legal and safety, health and family relations; plus general wellbeing	yes	0	1
Yu Quality of Life for mental health scale (YuQoL)	Eight factors: life satisfaction, autonomy, health maintenance, family support, function, social activity, physical health, psychological wellbeing	no	0	1
Short Form (SF)	Six or eight factors depending on version: physical functioning, role limitations due to physical health problems, bodily pain, social functioning, general mental health, role limitations because of emotional problems, vitality, health perception	yes	0	1
Manchester Assessment of Quality of Life (MANSA)	Eight life domains: job, finances, friendships, leisure activities, accommodation, safety, physical health, mental health; plus general life satisfaction	yes	0	1
Lehman Quality of Life Interview (LQoL)	Eight life domains: living situation, family, social relations, leisure, work, safety, finances, physical health; plus general life satisfaction	yes	0	4
Quality of Life Enjoyment and Satisfaction Questionnaire (Q-LES-Q)	Five life domains: physical health, subjective feelings, leisure time activities, social relationships, general activities; plus overall life satisfaction	yes	0	2

Scale	Description			
Subjective Wellbeing under Neuroleptics Scale (SWN)	Five sub-scales: emotional regulation, mental functioning, self-control, social integration, physical functioning	yes	0	2
Psychological General Wellbeing Index (PGWI)	Six affective states equal six subscales: anxiety, depressed mood, positive wellbeing, self-control, general health, vitality	yes	0	2
Social Adjustment Scale II (SAS-II)	Eight subscales: work role, household role, parental role, external family role, conjugal and nonconjugal sexual roles, romantic involvement, social and leisure activities, personal wellbeing	yes	0	1
Ryff's Scales of Psychological Wellbeing (RSPW)	Six factors in the original scale (shorter version partly differ): environmental mastery, personal growth, self-acceptance, autonomy, purpose in life, positive relations with others	yes	0	2
Scale for the Assessment of Wellbeing (SAWB)	No sub-dimension, scale asks for 56 pairs of opposite feelings/ mental states	yes	0	1
Snaith-Hamilton Pleasure Scale (SHPS)	Four domains: interest/pastimes, social interaction, sensory experience, food/drink	yes	1	0
Personal Wellbeing Index (PWI)	Eight life domains: standard of living, health, achievement in life, personal relationships, personal safety, community-connectedness, future security, spirituality	yes	0	2
Life Satisfaction Index (LSI)	Five components: zest, resolution and fortitude, congruence among desired and achieved goals, a positive self-concept, mood tone	yes	0	1
Subjective Exercise Experiences Scale (SEES)	Three sub-scales: psychological distress, subjective positive wellbeing, fatigue	yes	2	0
Quality of Life Inventory (QOLI)	Satisfaction in eight areas: self-esteem, health, friends, relatives, money, work, play, love	yes	0	1
general life satisfaction (LS)	Single question	n.a.	0	1
enjoyment (ENJ)	Single question	n.a.	0	1

TABLE 3.2 Generic ONS framework modified for psychosis

ONS conceptual framework	Modified conceptual framework	Example domains
More contextual domains	**Domain 1: Distal**	
1 Natural environment	1 The environment	Area of residence, access to services, access to transport
2 The economy		
3 Governance		
Factors directly affecting individual wellbeing	**Domain 2: Proximal**	
1 Relationships	1 Connectedness	
	– General social connection	Social activity, relationships, social functioning, community, integration
	– Family connection	Family relations, family support, parental role, relationship with children and relatives
	– Emotional connection	Friendships, emotional ties
	– Romantic connection	Sexual roles, romantic involvement, love relationship
2 What we do	2 Activities	
	– General activity	Usual activities, daily activities
	– Professional activity	Work, job, professional role
	– Leisure activity	Leisure time activities, recreation
3 Where we live	3 Living conditions	
	– Housing situation	Living situation, standard of living, accommodation, immediate neighbourhood
	– Financial situation	Finances, economic function
	– Safety	Legal security, safety, personal safety
4 Personal finance	4 Mobility	

Domain 3: Observable

5 Health – mental and physical	1 Health – mental and physical	
	– Physical health and functioning	Physical health, physical activity, physical functioning
	– Physical self-care	Attention to physical health and care, self-care, health maintenance
	– General mental health and functioning	Mental functioning, cognition, concentration, role limitations due to emotional problems
	2 Participation	Learning, creativity, helping others, civic action
	3 Autonomy	Freedom, autonomy, environmental mastery
	4 Success	Achievement in life, desired and achieved goals, resolution, fortitude

Domain 4: Non-observable

	1 Bodily feelings/vitality	
	– Negative feelings	Fatigue, tiredness, apathy, exhaustion
	– Positive feelings	Energy, pep, vitality, zest
	2 Affect, mood tone	
	– Negative affect	Depression, anxiety, sadness, despair, anger
	– Positive affect	Feeling peaceful, happy, strong, great, terrific
	– Emotional regulation	
	3 Self-perception	Satisfaction with self, self-acceptance, self-concept, self-regard
	4 Self-control	Self-control, behavioural emotional control
	5 Life perspective	Meaning, purpose, spirituality, philosophy of life

Individual Wellbeing | Domain 5: Self-defined

Individual Wellbeing	1 People's own assessment of their own wellbeing	1 Overall wellbeing
		2 Overall life satisfaction

29

TABLE 3.3 Scales used to measure wellbeing and their coverage of domains of the applied conceptual framework of wellbeing in psychosis

Scale name	Coverage of conceptual framework domains				
	Distal	*Proximal*	*Observable*	*Non-observable*	*Self-defined*
WHOQOL-BREF	X	X	X	X	X
Yu Quality of Life for mental health scale (YuQoL)		X	X	X	X
Short Form (SF)		X	X	X	X
Quality of Life Enjoyment and Satisfaction Questionnaire (Q-LES-Q)		X	X	X	X
Lancashire Quality of Life Profile (LQoLP)		X	X		X
Lehman Quality of Life Interview (LQOL)		X	X		X
Social Adjustment Scale II (SAS-II)		X	X		X
Ryff's Scales of psychological wellbeing (RSPW)		X	X	X	
Subjective Wellbeing under Neuroleptics Scale (SWN)		X	X	X	
Quality of Life Inventory (QOLI)		X	X	X	
Subjective Satisfaction with Life Scale (SSLS)		X		X	X
Personal Wellbeing Index (PWI)		X	X		
Manchester Assessment of Quality of Life (MANSA)		X	X		
Snaith-Hamilton Pleasure Scale (SHPS)		X		X	
Scale for the Assessment of Wellbeing (SAWB)			X	X	
Life Satisfaction Index (LSI)			X	X	
Psychological General Wellbeing Index (PGWI)			X	X	
Single question on enjoyment (ENJ)				X	
Subjective Exercise Experiences Scale (SEES)				X	
Single question on general life satisfaction (LS)					X

Overall, fifteen measures included proximal, fourteen observable and fifteen non-observable dimensions. Distal dimensions were only mentioned once and self-defined wellbeing was asked for in nine scales. The emphasis placed on the addressed domains varied between the measures.

Discussion

This review characterised the evidence base relating to wellbeing in people with psychosis. The results offer detailed insight into the use of the concept of wellbeing in intervention research involving people with psychosis as well as explicit practical suggestions for a potential way forward in this scientific area.

Objective 1: Measurement of wellbeing

The twenty-eight studies included in our analysis used twenty different scales to assess wellbeing. These scales covered a wide range of conceptual backgrounds. There was no single agreed-on definition or framework for wellbeing and authors did not usually state why they chose a specific scale. This confirms the impression of wellbeing as an ill-defined concept. The most prominent conceptual overlap was found between wellbeing and Health-Related Quality of Life (HRQoL), although the decision by authors of whether to describe their scale as a measure of HRQoL or of wellbeing appeared to be arbitrary and was usually not justified. This ambiguity reflects academic debates as to how far wellbeing, HRQOL and other related constructs overlap or include each other.[40]

Objective 2: Conceptual framework

Our conceptual framework identifies five dimensions of wellbeing. The non-observable, observable, proximal and distal domains are conceptualised as layers of proximity to the person ranging from intra-psychic to contextual factors. In addition, the self-defined domain is based on the individual assessment of general overall wellbeing. Assessment of overall wellbeing or life satisfaction has been theorised to require respondents to reflect on their overall state of life including as many domains or components as are relevant to the respective individual.[54] Global ratings are thought to reflect a subjective valuation since different areas of life may be valued differently by individuals.[52] Such personally relevant factors do not necessarily overlap with a given scale's explicitly mentioned dimensions and an individual's personal view of what wellbeing means to them may be different to any aggregate framework.

The proposed conceptual framework of wellbeing in psychosis differs from the generic framework of national wellbeing developed by the ONS. Issues of inequality and social justice are not captured in the framework of wellbeing in psychosis. Instead the framework places stronger emphasis on individual rather than societal factors, and refers to a number of specific dimensions that may be particularly relevant to people with psychosis, such as mental health and functioning, but also participation, autonomy, self-perception or self-control. In the ONS framework, the domain of individual wellbeing represents the subjective part of the concept. In contrast, the new conceptual framework includes subjective experience more pervasively.

The new 'self-defined' domain adds an additional level of subjectivity, in that it captures a person's overall intuitive understanding of wellbeing.

So to summarise, our systematic review of studies on psychosis showed that 'wellbeing' was used within a range of theoretical perspectives, with an unclear distinction from concepts such as HRQoL, mental health, affect, life satisfaction, social adjustment and other psychological conceptualisations.[14] Interventions to increase wellbeing in psychosis were highly diverse and not based on a coherent framework of wellbeing. The systematic review developed a static framework of wellbeing, based on the measurement of wellbeing in research involving people with psychosis. This static framework differentiates four domains of factors relevant to wellbeing: observable (visible behaviours and characteristics); non-observable (internal emotional and cognitive processes); proximal (factors under partial individual control in the immediate physical and social environment) and distal (factors beyond individual influence, in the more distant environment), as well as a separate rating of individual's overall self-defined wellbeing.

The framework offers an empirically defensible organising structure for wellbeing research in psychosis, but does not illuminate the processes by which wellbeing is experienced or modified in this client group. This is important, because understanding processes of change will identify the most promising target points for evidence-based interventions.

Understanding wellbeing changes in psychosis

We therefore undertook a qualitative study to understand the processes involved in wellbeing change in psychosis.[11] The objectives were (a) to validate the static framework of wellbeing by applying it to a second data source for triangulation, and (b) to develop a dynamic framework of wellbeing to describe the process of changes involved in wellbeing.

A convenience sample of individuals with psychosis was recruited from community mental health teams in London in October and November 2012. Recruitment was conducted with the goal of theoretical saturation.[155] Inclusion criteria were 18–65 years of age, a diagnosis of psychosis, using or having used mental health services, sufficient fluency in English and ability to give informed consent. One researcher conducted all interviews, using a topic guide asking about the personal experience of wellbeing and its improvement. Participants were invited for a re-interview to validate the emergent dynamic framework. Interviews were audio recorded, transcribed and anonymised.

Transcripts were coded using NVivo9. We applied thematic analysis using a combination of inductive and theoretically driven techniques.[156] Analytical rigour was enhanced by using techniques taken from grounded theory including iterative inductive coding, line-by-line coding, constant comparison, the use of memos throughout the analysis process, as well as the use of summary tables to organise clusters of topics for each participant.[155]

Twenty-three participants were interviewed, of whom thirteen agreed to be re-interviewed. Characteristics of participants are shown in Table 3.4.

TABLE 3.4 Sociodemographic and clinical characteristics of participants (n = 23)

Age (mean years, SD)	44.6	9.3
Gender male (n, %)	15	65.2
Time since first illness onset (mean years, SD)*	16.5	10.5
Self-reported diagnosis (n, %)		
Schizophrenia	15	65.2
Psychosis	2	8.7
Schizoaffective disorder/Bipolar psychosis	2	8.7
Depression	2	8.7
Nervous breakdown	1	4.3
No mental health problems	1	4.3

* Two participants excluded due to invalid response

Objective (a): Validation of the static framework of wellbeing

The coding framework for influences on transition to an enhanced sense of self is shown in Column 2 of Table 3.5. The respondent validation identified no changes to the results.

The four elements of the static framework (non-observable, observable, proximal and distal) provided an adequate organising framework to allow full categorisation of the influences on the transition to an enhanced sense of self identified by participants. This transition represents a process of enhancing wellbeing, providing independent validation of the static framework.

Objective (b): Development of a dynamic framework of wellbeing

Participants described wellbeing as a desirable state that needed active input to be achieved and also to be maintained. Wellbeing was tied to participants' sense of self and involved transition from a current sense of self, described as deficient at least in some of its aspects, towards an enhanced sense of self. The attainment of this enhanced sense of self was perceived as increased wellbeing, and attributed to the successful transition. This process followed a common pattern that forms the dynamic framework of wellbeing. Three superordinate categories were identified in the coding framework: determinants of current sense of self (the participant's starting point at any given stage of development); influences on transition to an enhanced sense of self (the change process involved in improving wellbeing) and indicators of an enhanced sense of self (how wellbeing is experienced by participants).

TABLE 3.5 Coding framework for wellbeing

Category 1: Determinants of current sense of self	Category 2: Influences on transition to an enhanced sense of self	Category 3: Indicators of an enhanced sense of self
1.1 Personality	2.1 Non-observable influences	3.1 Good feelings
Character traits	Attitudes	3.2 Symptom relief
Personal values	Future thinking	3.3 Connectedness
Strengths	Reflection	3.4 Hope and optimism
Interests	2.2 Observable influences	3.5 Self-worth
1.2 Memories	Social interactions	3.6 Empowerment
Good memories	Support-seeking	3.7 Meaning and orientation
Bad memories	Self-care	
1.3 Health	Having a treat	
Mental health	Kindness	
Physical health	Spiritual practise	
Engaging in activities	2.3 Proximal influences	
	Basic needs	
	Relationships	
	Mental health services and staff	
	Antipsychotic medication	
	Psychotherapy	
	2.4 Distal influences	
	Societal values	
	Economy	
	Environment	

Specific factors identified as implicated in the transition – determinants, influences and indicators – varied across individuals both in quality and quantity. These factors were linked to personal values, and the values attached to specific factors differed between people and in an individual over time. Different areas of life were associated with a differing sense of self, that is, rather advanced stages in a specific area could coexist with poor sense of self in other areas.

Figure 3.2 shows the dynamic framework of wellbeing, illustrating the direction of change and the relationship between the three superordinate categories. It illustrates the interplay of factors on a person's trajectory towards wellbeing and the dynamic nature of the process. As soon as an

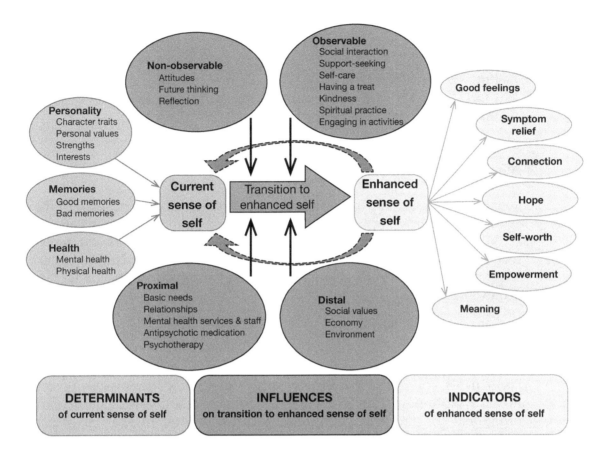

FIGURE 3.2 Dynamic framework of wellbeing

enhanced sense of self has been achieved, this becomes the new current sense of self allowing further development, for example, in other aspects of the self that are perceived as deficient, to start from there. This makes the striving for wellbeing in individuals an iterative and ongoing process, which can also suffer setbacks, for example, through relapse, and may then have to be picked up again at a lower level than before.

The coding framework is now described.

Category 1: Determinants of current sense of self

1.1 Personality

Personality was important for defining current sense of self. It also explained the nature of the desired enhanced sense of self and the perceived routes towards it. Personality was described as comprising character traits, personal values, strengths and interests. Values included things like having money, status symbols, a specific religious denomination, positivity, continuity or social responsibility. Acting on strengths and interests was generally perceived as rewarding.

> I'm a writer, I'm an author, and I like it when people like my books. I feel very good when I'm writing. I like all things about that. Writing makes me feel good. (#1)

1.2 Memories

Memories of personally important experiences shaped current sense of self. They included upbringing, country of origin, relationships, health care and activities. Good memories could provide hope or simply be an indulgence that yields positive feelings. While negative memories may damage current sense of self, they could also yield increased motivation for change and achievement.

1.3 Health

Participants connected physical health with their current sense of self. Illness symptoms or pain had a negative impact. Obesity was a particularly prominent concern. Being connected to antipsychotic medication, obesity was perceived as frustrating, conveying a sense of powerlessness and a negative self-image. Accepting obesity required great personal effort and losing weight was among the most frequently mentioned wishes in order to attain an enhanced sense of self.

> The problem of obesity it puts me down sometimes, it's not good for my wellbeing. There is no way I can reduce my weight because I have to keep on with the medication, and it started making me feel very sad and disappointed. (#13)

Mental health symptoms could interfere with any important aspect of life and impair the current sense of self. They impeded transition to an enhanced sense of self, for example, by impairing concentration or motivation. Mental health symptoms were even defined as the opposite of wellbeing, especially suicidality, threatening delusions or serious substance abuse.

> Because of the condition I just completely drop everything and I just give up and I lock myself inside for weeks and barely eat and forget to call my family, my parents, my kids, don't even look after myself properly. Sometimes I have passed weeks without showering and my house became a big mess. (#6)

However, one participant also reported goals of solving various world problems so as to enhance sense of self by providing meaning and self-worth.

Category 2: Influences on transition to an enhanced sense of self

The change process involved in improving wellbeing represented a 'transition to an enhanced sense of self'. The factors influencing the transition occurred on the four levels of the static framework: non-observable, observable, proximal and distal.

2.1 Non-observable influences

Internal change processes pertained to attitudes, future thinking and reflection. Examples of adaptive changes in attitudes included assuming more positive thinking styles, revising self-expectations, learning to acknowledge own abilities and engaging in downward rather than upward social comparison.

> I know they say 'compare to despair' but the opposite is true as well. So it's 'compare and be grateful for what you've got'. (#21)

Future thinking (both realistic and unrealistic) can facilitate transition. While goals provided a frame of references, an anchor for coping and achievement, dreams conveyed an imagined sense of normality and comfort, also leading to an enhanced sense of self.

> If I had a job, I'd work my hardest to get to the top and be the managing director of the company, if that was possible. For me it never was possible, so it's a dream. It's a dream that leaves me with hope. Once you got hope, you can keep the faith. (#4)

Reflection, for example through therapy, meditation, writing or chatting, was deemed indispensable for the transition to an enhanced sense of self. Positive effects included insight, new perspectives, orientation and motivation and better problem solving. It also helped to appreciate achievements, embrace limitations and find forgiveness. Forgiveness was a particularly complex topic, susceptible to conceptual confusion and difficult to achieve, but it held the potential to relieve tension, be empowering and help to move on in life. It was deemed positive especially when construed as forgiving oneself.

2.2 Observable influences

This category comprises visible behaviours and activities, such as social interactions, support-seeking, self-care, having a treat, kindness and spiritual practice. Re-establishing connections was challenging but an important and ultimately rewarding task. Related processes included overcoming social anxiety, practising social skills and finding activities with other people.

In particular, social interaction with non-service users seemed to facilitate transition. Proposed ways to receive support, feedback or acknowledgement were strongly tied to social contact and positive relationships, for example, with family, mental health professionals, or in faith communities, voluntary work or other spare-time activities.

> I get reassurance from family and the doctors and that keeps my well-being up, you know, I feel that I'm ok, so long as I get the reassurance from people. (#15)

Self-care included establishing a daily structure, personal hygiene and eating regular healthy meals, but also resisting alcohol, drugs or nicotine, or monitoring one's physical fitness and weight.

Having a treat went beyond self-care. For example, while healthy, regular eating was deemed part of self-care, indulging in the experience of good food may serve as a treat. It can be a 'bonus' to generate positive feelings, aid relaxation and enliven one's daily structure.

> You can listen to a happy song, you can blast the radio on and have a nice shower and wash your hair with the radio on. You can put moisturiser on, that's important as well. (#9)

Kindness, involving doing something for others, was perceived as rewarding, satisfying and profoundly enhancing of sense of self. Kindness, attention and care could be addressed towards anyone, but family members such as parents, children and grandchildren seemed particularly important.

> I look after my grandchildren, and I help other people. I always loved to help people. (#10)

Spiritual practice, such as church, mosque, private meditation or prayer, helped enhance sense of self through a number of pathways including the establishment of sympathetic social contact and feelings of comfort, security and orientation, improving insight and supporting personality development.

> Going to church I get to mix with my brethren, find people to talk to, not being on my own, listen to the lovely sermon, singing, you know, that gives me comfort. (#23)

Activities, if they matched needs and interests, also had a range of positive effects from aiding daily structure to directly increasing self-worth. Leisure activities were perceived as particularly positive when coupled with social connection. Among specific activities, having paid employment was most highly valued. However, most participants were long-term unemployed, so volunteering was considered the second most rewarding activity.

> I do voluntary work with older people. It makes me feel good that I'm doing something. (#22)

2.3 Proximal influences

This category comprises factors under limited personal control, including basic needs, relationships, antipsychotic medication, psychotherapy, and mental health services and staff. Having basic needs met, including a place to live, not being hungry and having sufficient money, was deemed essential for any positive development.

Relationships were particularly important to all participants. Supportive, validating, reciprocal relationships were ascribed a multitude of positive effects. Good relationships with family were paramount as family gave unconditional support.

> There's no substitution for family. Family do things that friends wouldn't do, sometimes friends initially also help you but family are always there and help you no matter what. (#5)

Identified sources of happiness included children and grandchildren and having a partner. An intimate life partner or sex life was intensely wished for, and often considered as something essential, potentially life-changing and boosting sense of self, both by those who had already experienced intimate partnerships as well as by those who had not.

There were conflicting views about antipsychotic medication. Participants talked about rejection, ambivalence, resignation and about a process of acceptance. While medication could be vital for functioning and the basis for positive development, it may also have debilitating side effects; and being able to live without medication was among the main visions for an enhanced sense of self.

Psychotherapy facilitated a multitude of positive adaptations leading to an enhanced sense of self. Group therapy or peer support additionally had the reassuring and identity enhancing effect of sharing problems with others who had similar experiences. Mental health services were perceived as a source of support despite possibly serious harmful effects on identity, for example, of involuntary treatment. Specific staff members, especially those conveying a sense of connection and mutual understanding, were described as a supremely positive influence on personal development.

> She just understands me and the way she talks to me is like, she doesn't seem like a therapist but more like a daughter. She talks to me very nicely and what I found with her, I just opened up; I never hold nothing back from her. (#11)

2.4 Distal influences

This category comprises factors beyond an individual's influence, including societal values, economy and environment. Societal values were described to facilitate the change process by providing options and opportunities, for example, access to leisure activities or education.

It's having these opportunities to do things because when one is unwell one doesn't see the opportunities that there are. (#17)

More generally, societal values provided a frame of reference and a sense of order and security. The economy was especially challenging for participants, many of whom were unemployed and dependent on social welfare, for example, disability allowance. The economic recession was mentioned as a source of insecurity. Experiencing the environment, for example, sunshine, a walk in the park or even television programmes about the natural wonders of the planet, may impact positively on mood and even create a sense of serenity.

When I see all of the beauty of nature, it makes me feel calmer in the inside. (#20)

Category 3: Indicators of an enhanced sense of self

Seven indicators of an enhanced sense of self were identified, as shown in Figure 3.2.

Good feelings or happiness in general were the most frequently mentioned indicators of an enhanced sense of self. Naming specific positive emotions was often difficult, but participants mentioned comfort, solace, calmness, relaxation, peace of mind, contentment and serenity. Positive bodily feelings, such as feeling well after exercise or feeling attractive, also indicated improved wellbeing, as did having fun.

Symptom relief was discussed by all participants as profoundly tied to an enhanced sense of self. It was often seen as the basis of wellbeing, or even as a basis of life. If symptoms remained, then improved coping was essential.

You're not letting the voices or paranoia control you, you're doing what you want to do. Wellbeing to me is, even if you're paranoid you still get on and do things. (#22)

Feeling connected with others, being a valued part of a relationship or group, and especially feelings of love amplified the sense of self.

When there are people asking for my service that makes me feel good, makes me feel worthwhile, and I get more connected with people from the project I am doing. These people need me and I have to provide for them. So there is this attachment, a strong bond which connects us. (#3)

Having hope and optimism was described as a further fundamental indicator of an enhanced sense of self. Hope was not only an important outcome, but also a trigger for further positive developments, a force that kept people going despite potential setbacks.

If you have hope you know you have a future, and only then your life has value. (#19)

Self-worth was characterised as feeling whole, a positive self-image, self-acceptance, self-esteem, self-confidence, a sense of achievement, satisfaction and a sense of normality.

When you've done your best and you're happy with it and you have accepted who you are and where you are going in life. (#14)

Empowerment was described as a sense of self-determination, control and freedom, as having inner strength, agency and being able to do what is important in life.

Wellbeing for me means doing things as an autonomous individual. (#7)

Having meaning in life was described as having a frame of reference, for example, a valued societal role or religion.

I'm a representative for the low support unit [. . .] It makes me feel good doing it, I feel a sense of comfort and purpose when I'm doing it because I'm not only doing it for me, I'm doing it for other people. Other people who don't want to speak, I can speak on their behalf; I convey it back to the council and see if we can come up with some suggestions that might help. (#12)

Dynamic framework for wellbeing

This study found that the process of improving wellbeing in people with psychosis was strongly tied to a sense of self. The current sense of self was determined by three influences: personality, memories and health. Improving wellbeing was an ongoing process in which the current sense of self undergoes a transition towards an enhanced sense of self. Influences that impact this transition could be categorised according to the domains of the static framework of wellbeing: observable, non-observable, proximal and distal.[14] Participants described an enhanced sense of self as equivalent to improved wellbeing. The indicators of an enhanced sense of self comprised good feelings, symptom relief, connection, hope, self-worth, empowerment and meaning. The enhanced sense of self may then facilitate transition in other areas in an iterative fashion. Factors involved in the process varied in quality and quantity, both across individuals and over time.

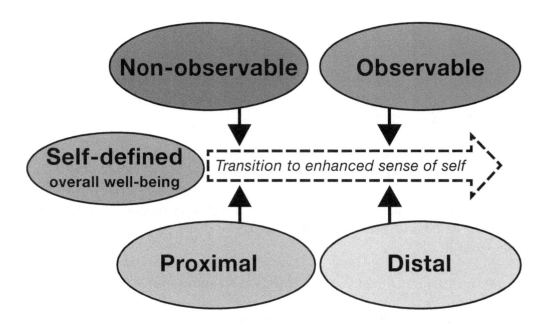

FIGURE 3.3 Comparing the static and dynamic framework of wellbeing

Objective (a): To validate the static framework of wellbeing

Factors influencing transition to an enhanced sense of self were consistent with, and therefore validated, the static framework of wellbeing. The results of the qualitative study also consolidate the findings from the systematic review by placing them in a framework applicable to individuals over time. Specifically, the layers of wellbeing factors identified in the static framework can be viewed as clusters of influences on wellbeing, which may be addressed in an intervention to improve wellbeing. Figure 3.3 shows the transformation of the static into the dynamic framework of wellbeing.

The static framework was based on assessment measures, which often contain items conflating factors that influence wellbeing and wellbeing itself. For example, the latest measure of population wellbeing developed by the ONS in the UK considers personal wellbeing, relationships, health, occupation, accommodation, income, education and societal indicators of economic productivity, natural environment and trust in government.[111] Other recent concepts of wellbeing have also combined what would be both influences on and indicators of wellbeing according to the results of our study, such as the PERMA model of individual wellbeing, which contains positive emotions, engagement, relationships, meaning and accomplishment.[157]

None of the existing measurement tools or interventions to improve wellbeing described in the literature span all influences on wellbeing. Interventions to improve wellbeing have been tested in various client groups, with a focus on one of the influences, for example, neighbourhood economic status,[158] physical exercise[159] or on specific combinations of some influences such as physical and activity, health behaviour and social engagement.[160]

Objective (b): To develop a dynamic framework of wellbeing

The dynamic framework indicates that context and personal effort can lead to an upward spiral of positive development and continuously increased wellbeing. A similar upward spiral has been found for the beneficial effect of positive emotions and a broad thought-action repertoire, which may amplify each other to counteract the detrimental effects of negative emotions and contribute to resilience.[161] While an upwards spiral is certainly not without a ceiling, especially given the likelihood of setbacks in the context of severe mental illness and the potential existence of areas resistant to positive change, the conceptualisation of wellbeing in the dynamic framework provides a strengths-oriented supplement to deficit-oriented approaches in mental health care. This places the framework in the context of positive psychology and resource-oriented approaches.[162]

The concepts of wellbeing and recovery do overlap.[163] For example, the CHIME framework recovery processes described in Chapter 3 mirror the *indicators* of the enhanced self. However, the indicators in the dynamic framework in addition include symptom relief and, most prominently, good feelings. Everyday sources of wellbeing – such as employment, friendship, exercise, sex or prayer – are as important for people experiencing psychosis as for any other group in society. Emphasising commonality in sources of wellbeing between people with and without psychosis may be more helpful than identifying diagnosis-specific sources of wellbeing.

The use of this theory base to develop an intervention to improve wellbeing in psychosis is outlined in the next chapter.

CHAPTER 4

Developing Positive Psychotherapy for Psychosis

In this chapter, we describe the modification of Positive Psychotherapy (PPT) into Positive Psychotherapy for Psychosis.

The adaptation is analogous to the modification of standard cognitive behavioural therapy (CBT) to CBT for psychosis (CBTp), and addresses some overlapping issues, including the importance of developing meaningful relationships. Positive Psychotherapy for Psychosis is consistent with 'third wave' cognitive psychotherapy approaches (e.g. acceptance and commitment therapy [ACT], mindfulness-based cognitive therapy [MBCT]) in emphasising strengths and values, and de-emphasising thought challenging.[164] It connects to an evolving understanding of wellbeing in psychosis[15] and the importance of a positive identity for recovery.[90]

Development of Positive Psychotherapy for Psychosis

We developed a manual for Positive Psychotherapy for Psychosis, by modifying 14-session standard PPT, and then developed an explicit and testable model that identifies the mediating processes and proximal and distal outcomes arising from Positive Psychotherapy for Psychosis.[7]

Development of the Positive Psychotherapy for Psychosis model comprised four stages. Stage 1 involved semi-structured interviews with staff (psychotherapists and care coordinators) and service users (patients with psychosis) to identify candidate modifications to standard PPT. Stage 2 involved consultation with expert therapists to refine the recommendations from Stage 1 and identify target areas of Positive Psychotherapy for Psychosis. Stage 3 involved the development of a manual and model. Stage 4 involved a review by clinicians and service users of the Positive Psychotherapy for Psychosis manual.

Stage 1 (Interviews)

Semi-structured interviews employed a topic guide that summarised standard PPT exercises[165] and sought feedback and suggestions for modification.

A total of twenty-three service users with a clinical diagnosis of psychosis (mean age: 44.6 years [SD 9.3], 35 per cent female, fifteen [65 per cent] with a diagnosis of schizophrenia) and fourteen staff (mean age: 36.5 years [SD 10.3], 71 per cent female, mean length of relevant experience: 11.6 years [SD 12.4]) were interviewed.

Four generic themes emerged as challenges: *attitudes, illness, engagement* and *interaction*. These four themes are different types of challenges that the interviewees felt may impact the utility of the intervention. These are outlined in Table 4.1.

Thematic analysis also identified PPT exercise-specific challenges and proposed solutions, for example, Satisficing vs Maximising and Altruism would be challenging and possibly unsuitable for service users with psychosis, so were removed. Identified issues and proposed solutions for all other sessions are outlined in Table 4.2.

Sessions were organised into three clusters, according to the perceived degree of challenge for people with psychosis: 'easiest' (Savouring, Three Good Things), 'intermediate' (Character Strengths; Signature Strengths, Signature Strengths of Others, Positive Communication) and 'most challenging' (Good vs Bad Memories, Gratitude, Forgiveness, Hope, Optimism and Posttraumatic Growth).

TABLE 4.1 Service user and staff generic views on standard PPT

Theme	Challenges	Proposed modifications
Attitudes	Positive approach may be rejected as 'unrealistic'	Make it realistic, validate negative feelings
Illness	Concentration/motivation may impact exercises	Use clear language; avoid theory, abstraction, didactic style; emphasise structure, flexibility; adapt tasks, use small concrete steps, assess group needs, tailor sessions to individuals
Engagement	Exercises may feel meaningless, negative memories of homework, lack of social/financial opportunities	Explain rationale/session-by-session outline, focus on meaningful life/values, identify realistic, personal goals, e.g. small tasks, gradually introduce/increase feedback, plan exercises in session, support and be aware of negative memories ('Don't call it homework'), use reminder phone calls/text messages, award certificates, afternoon sessions, breaks with refreshments, provide information to take away
Interaction	Difficulties with social contact, disclosure, self-confidence, group comparison, dominant group members, lack of interest in other people	Warm-up exercises; foster mutual acceptance/ equality, trusting environment, honest interest in others; therapist self-disclosure/humour to normalise experiences/integrate group

TABLE 4.2 Challenges and solutions identified in Stage 1 (interviews)

Standard PPT session	Challenges	Proposed modifications
1 Orientation	No specific challenges	No specific modifications proposed
2 Character strengths	Difficulties identifying strengths; strengths may be disputed; others may abuse one's strengths; strengths discussion is embarrassing; VIA questionnaire is too long; identification of three good things every night is too much; literacy issues; too formulaic or repetitive; difficult to remember as a daily task	Empower/assist group members: everyone has strengths; everyone is valued; encourage group support for identifying strengths ('other people can often see strengths that we can't'); 'Three Good Things' should be a separate session; emphasis on small good things; recording at flexible times; allow alternatives for writing (e.g. drawing, painting, collecting keepsakes); normalise experience of no good things on some days
3 Signature strengths	Difficulties identifying activities; unrealistic ideas; anxiety about lack of skills, abilities, or performance; unachieved goals may lead to negative feelings ('feeling like a failure')	Focus on realistic goals; have alternative, back-up goals; encourage teaching of strengths to others (including therapists); discuss strengths with others outside the therapy; in-session planning, follow up and recording of achievements
4 Good vs bad memories	Difficulties identifying good memories; focus on bad memories (unhappy childhood, trauma) and distress may accentuate negative appraisal; memory problems; belief that good memories are not deserved	Establish values and goals to stimulate memories; focus on recent memories; normalise positive and negative memories; emphasise self-kindness, help notice positive feelings ('good memories make you smile')
5 Forgiveness	May 'unlock' anger, trauma, shame and depression; feeling vulnerable or disempowered ('an invitation to be harmed again'); not ready to forgive; some events are 'unforgivable'; different interpretations of concept of forgiveness; difficult to achieve in short intervention	Avoid talking about trauma; construe as feeling 'let down by someone'; acknowledge forgiveness is a personal process that takes time; consider reasons for forgiveness; begin with small examples; therapist self-disclosure; emphasise connotations like 'lifting a burden', 'making peace', 'putting anger and bitterness behind you', 'moving on', becoming a 'better, stronger person'; be realistic: not all need be forgiven; those you forgive need not stay friends; consider forgiving oneself instead of/in addition to others
6 Gratitude	Difficulties identifying people or events; increased awareness of lack of positives; triggers negative thoughts or envy; disproportionate gratitude: being	Discuss people who deserve recognition; discuss appropriate level of gratitude; contextualise gratitude: emphasise reciprocal ('give and take') interactions;

Session	Challenges	Modifications
6 Gratitude	overly grateful for small things may be disempowering ('I'm always the one who is helped'); distribution of gratitude letter may be inappropriate; literacy difficulties; uncommon to express gratitude in some cultures	warm-up exercise to build up to writing a letter; discuss feelings of letter recipients, who should see letter, appropriate time to send; alternatives to letter, e.g. greeting card, making something, verbal thanks, writing letter to oneself
7 Feedback	No specific challenges	No specific modifications proposed
9 Hope, optimism and posttraumatic growth	Content may be distressing; evoke negative memories, disappointments, embarrassments, or serious ongoing problems (e.g. abuse, bereavement, harmful relationships); not everything has a positive side; might feel patronising, belittling, denying the problem, superficially positive	Avoid reactivating trauma: focus on recent 'disappointments', frame as 'learning from your mistakes'; begin with small examples; be realistic: some events might have little positive outcome; normalise negativity in experience; consider lessons learned and how to implement them in the future
10 Positive communication	Avoidance or fear of social situations; feel unconnected to people or groups; feeling inferior; difficult to transfer to real-life situations; psychotic misinterpretation of interpersonal communication, e.g. suspicion; takes too long to learn	Discuss valuing relationships and social interactions; discuss concerns over social settings; normalise social anxiety and negative experiences; use group to practice; therapist acts as role model; encourage small, meaningful interactions
11 Signature strengths of others	Difficulty finding meaningful tasks or others to collaborate with; no family or difficult family relationships, feel uncomfortable socialising; difficult to meet up with group members outside group; bored by long activities	Let group relationships and activities develop naturally; role-play in pairs; encourage small, accessible tasks; balance and alternate group pairings, encourage family participation but normalising relationship difficulties, identifying mediator to discuss family problems, nominate several possible family members or friends for involvement
12 Savouring	Difficulty concentrating, feeling positive emotions or 'letting go'; not valuing anything; negative feelings; frightened of good feelings; enjoyment 'cannot be learned', everyone enjoys things differently; 'pleasure' suggests superficial fun: may be harmful, e.g. substance abuse; food sensitivity, weight issues, eating disorders	Discuss and normalise enjoyment and values; let participants experiment; emphasis small pleasurable things (e.g. cup of tea, crossword); be conscious of participants with weight issues or eating disorders and pleasurable but harmful activities: avoid word 'pleasure'
14 The full life	No specific challenges	No specific modifications proposed

Stage 2 (Consultation)

The experts discussed the Stage 1 analysis and produced general and exercise-specific recommendations for Positive Psychotherapy for Psychosis. The four Stage 1 themes of *attitudes, illness, engagement* and *interaction* were used to guide general recommendations (indicated below) and Stage 1 exercise-specific challenges, and proposed solutions were used to guide the exercise-specific recommendations. A therapy title of Positive Psychotherapy for Psychosis was agreed, with an emphasis on aiming to improve wellbeing.

Informed by the generic theme of *illness*, session and exercise titles were modified to optimise clarity and accommodate psychosis-specific challenges, for example, Orientation to PPT, Positive Communication, and Hope, Optimism and Posttraumatic Growth were relabelled, in the latter case to avoid invoking the relationship between psychosis and trauma.[166,167] Positive Communication (active constructive responding) was relabelled as Positive Responding.

The experts devised a Celebration session where group members should be congratulated and awarded a certificate. This retained the integrative elements of The Full Life from standard PPT but increased focus on individual accomplishment, with a personal letter from therapists, which group members could choose to read aloud, or ask therapists to read aloud, to facilitate *engagement*.

Homework was integrated with the main session exercise and relabelled as an 'ongoing exercise', to address *engagement*. The experts decided ongoing exercises for Sessions 1–10 should begin in session, with planning and encouragement for group members to continue in their own time. Session 11 would reprise an earlier ongoing exercise. Ongoing exercises would be incentivised with gifts (e.g. Good Things Boxes), a journal, between-session phone calls and by including a previous session recap, all to facilitate *engagement*.

Exercises would be supported with clear, concise worksheets in lay language, to facilitate *engagement*, with colourful illustrations, to address *illness*. Writing exercises were deemed important and retained but literacy was de-emphasised by including options such as drawing, coloured pens/pencils and greeting cards, rather than letters for those with reading/writing difficulties, to address *illness*.

The experts agreed that exercises should be personal, experiential and interactive, to address *illness* and *engagement*. Small things should be valued and meaningfulness conveyed at every level, including facilitating the development of a meaningful narrative for each group member, therapist self-disclosure, therapist involvement in exercises, as well as appropriate choices of refreshments, venue and music, to facilitate *engagement* and *interaction*. Savouring of food and drink was included but with therapists asked to be mindful of negative symptoms and provide eating and drinking choices, to address *attitudes* and *illness*.

Three Good Things was reconceptualised as Good Things to reduce the burden of identifying three things, with Good Things Boxes and the Positive Psychotherapy for Psychosis journal used to allow flexibility when recording good things. Challenges identifying good things were addressed with group support and recapping previous good things, to facilitate *interaction*.

Personal strengths sessions were included but the experts agreed that the Values in Action Inventory of Strengths from standard PPT was too long and should be replaced by large pictures that display Character Strengths, to address *illness*. The experts agreed that a single personal strength should be identified, to address *illness*. Family involvement in Signature Strengths of Others was minimised, and the Family Strengths Tree and family gathering exercises were eliminated. Family involvement was broadened to include friends or staff, to facilitate *engagement*. Therapists referred to 'significant other or person' instead of family, to facilitate *interaction*.

Forgiveness was spread across two sessions, to address *attitudes*, and psycho-educational handouts were used, to address *illness*. Experts agreed that forgiveness should be conceptualised by using recent examples of someone who has let you down, thus reducing the likelihood that group members consider childhood trauma,[168] to address *attitudes*. Good vs Bad Memories was removed. The experts agreed its focus on bad memories and distress could accentuate negative appraisals. Instead it was combined with Gratitude, as in standard PPT, but also in One Door Closes, Another Door Opens and Forgiveness.

Experts agreed with the three Stage 1 clusters (i.e. easiest, intermediate and most challenging PPT exercises) but decided that sessions should culminate in positive themes. Therefore, Forgiveness preceded Gratitude, with One Door Closes, Another Door Opens in between. Mid-therapy feedback was eliminated to facilitate *engagement* and continuation.

Stage 3 (Manualisation)

Four key target areas of the Positive Psychotherapy for Psychosis model were identified from the systematic review,[14] dynamic framework[11] and Stages 1–2 findings: increasing positive experiences, amplifying strengths, fostering positive relationships and creating a more meaningful self-narrative. These components are intended to lead to improved wellbeing, defined as an enhanced sense of self according to the dynamic framework of wellbeing. The resulting Positive Psychotherapy for Psychosis model is shown in Figure 4.1.

A draft manual was then produced by researchers. Based on the initial session clustering from Stage 1 (i.e. easiest, intermediate and most challenging exercises) and Stage 2 modifications, a sequencing of Positive Psychotherapy for Psychosis sessions was finalised. This is shown in Table 4.3.

The Introduction of the manual discussed the model and the intervention, with generic advice for therapists. Positive Psychotherapy for Psychosis would be delivered by two therapists who would follow the manual. Therapist self-disclosure was encouraged and prompted in all sessions. Therapists would participate in exercises, to facilitate *interaction*.

Group members would not be prohibited from sharing distressing, unpleasant or negative states and experiences; any 'negative' statements from

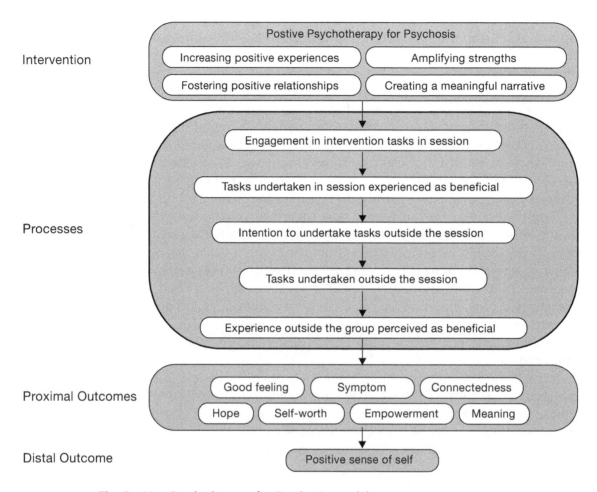

FIGURE 4.1 The Positive Psychotherapy for Psychosis model

group members would be validated, to address *illness*, but negative experiences would not become central to sessions. Instead therapists would establish a link between the negative experience and one or more target areas of Positive Psychotherapy for Psychosis, all to address *attitudes*. For example, if a group member would describe having been bullied at school but had also identified their strength as humour and playfulness, then the therapist could bring their attention to how they had been able to use humour to manage the situation. Therapists would be instructed to model and support positive responding, be accessible, support change and encourage experiential learning, to facilitate *engagement* and *interaction*.

Positive Psychotherapy for Psychosis would be provided regardless of current symptom severity and was designed for both community and inpatient settings. However, it was suggested to offer Positive Psychotherapy for Psychosis only to those who were cognitively able to follow the content, as determined by the relevant clinician.

Sessions would follow a generic structure: 90-minute sessions, with 5 minutes of savouring music at the beginning and end, and a 10-minute mid-session break with refreshments, to facilitate *engagement*. The overarching emphasis on continuity between sessions led to individual sessions beginning

TABLE 4.3 Positive Psychotherapy for Psychosis sessions

Session	Ongoing exercise	Content	Target area(s)
1 Welcome to Positive Psychotherapy for Psychosis	Positive introduction	Group guidelines, rationale, positive responding	Positive experiences, strengths
2 Savouring	Planned savouring activity	Mindful eating, drinking and listening exercises	Positive experiences
3 Good Things	Identify good things	Identify recent good things using the Good Things Box	Positive experiences
4 Identifying a Personal Strength	Identify a character strength	Identify one character strength using strengths pictures	Strengths
5 Using Personal Strengths	Strength Activity	Plan and carry out an activity using your strength	Strengths
6 Using Strengths Together	Strength Activity with Significant Other	Plan and carry out activity that uses strengths of both individuals	Strengths, positive relationships
7 Forgiveness 1	A Sea of Forgiveness	Focus on letting go of a grudge	Positive relationships, meaningful self-narrative
8 Forgiveness 2	Forgiveness letter	Identify a person to forgive and write them a letter	Positive relationships, meaningful self-narrative
9 One Door Closes, Another Door Opens	One Door Closes, Another Door Opens	Identify positive conclusions from negative experiences	Meaningful self-narrative
10 Gratitude	Writing a gratitude letter	Identifying a person you have never properly thanked and write them a letter	Positive relationships
11 Celebration	Positive responding	Celebrate achievements	Positive experiences

with a welcome, recap and warm-up exercise, to facilitate *engagement*, before introducing the main ongoing exercise. The more theory-laden content of standard PPT was shifted towards greater experiential tasks, with warm-ups and role-plays, to address *illness*. The Positive Psychotherapy for Psychosis manual contained session-by-session guidance, example scripts and therapist tips for all sessions. Positive Psychotherapy for Psychosis used additional supporting materials, including the journal, session handouts, strengths pictures, Good Things Boxes and music. The journal included pages for all sessions, which summarised the content, rationale and ongoing exercise of each session, used accessible language and colour coding for the session to which they apply. At each session, group members would receive worksheets that fasten in the journal, all to address *illness* and facilitate *engagement*. Music was selected by researchers in collaboration with musicians. The eleven tracks were all instrumental to optimise savouring and chosen to correspond in pitch, pace and ambience to session topics, in order to facilitate *engagement*.

Stage 4 (Review)

Nine therapists reviewed the draft manual and suggested minor modifications to warm-up exercises and Positive Psychotherapy for Psychosis components. One expert, who had experience providing wellbeing interventions to the general population, reviewed the handouts. Six service users and service user researchers from the Service User Advisory Group reviewed the draft manual and identified four key issues (attitudes, illness, behaviour change and confidentiality) and further modifications. Their review is summarised in Table 4.4.

TABLE 4.4 Service user advisory group feedback on Positive Psychotherapy for Psychosis

Theme	Challenges	Modifications
Attitudes	Positivity may appear inauthentic/patronising: 'it can be hard to think that there might be light at the end of the tunnel'	Emphasise being genuine and realistic
Illness	Problems/symptoms may feel unacknowledged	Emphasise that negatives are not being ignored
Behaviour change	Relapse in psychosis must be acknowledged: 'benefits may last only as long as the therapy'	Ongoing exercises encourage behaviour change; recaps/celebration session encourage continuation of exercises; journal/worksheets given to group members to keep
Confidentiality	Concerns for confidentiality in group setting	Confidentiality highlighted in Positive Psychotherapy for Psychosis manual; example script given for Session 1

Following these revisions, the Positive Psychotherapy for Psychosis manual was finalised.

Summary of changes

Overall, six components of standard PPT were adapted for people with psychosis: positive responding, savouring, personal strengths, gratitude, forgiveness and a session looking at identifying positives from negative situations. Four standard PPT components were not included: altruism, satisficing and maximising, a mid-therapy feedback session and a session focussing on leading a 'good life'. Finally, four components were developed that are not found in standard PPT: mindful listening to music at the start and end of each session, emphasis on therapist self-disclosure, between-session phone calls and a celebration session that corresponds to some extent with the original 'good life' session.

In the next chapter, we describe how the intervention was evaluated and refined.

CHAPTER 5

Evaluating and optimising Positive Psychotherapy for Psychosis

The Positive Psychotherapy for Psychosis intervention was then evaluated in a pilot randomised controlled trial (ISRCTN04199273). The trial protocol was published,[12] and full reports of outcome evaluation[8] and process evaluation[9] from the trial have been published elsewhere. A target sample size of thirty complete data sets in each trial arm was chosen according to recommendations for pilot trials,[169] with an anticipated 25 per cent dropout. The obtained sample size allowed effectiveness at a medium effect size (Cohen's $d = 0.5$) to be detected with 90 per cent power at a 5 per cent significant level, taking into account 20 per cent attrition.

Inclusion criteria were: aged 18–65 years; primary clinical diagnosis of psychosis defined as schizophrenia and other psychoses including schizo-affective and delusional disorder but not depressive psychosis or psychosis due to substance misuse; current use of adult mental health services; fluency in English; and ability to give informed consent and participate in group therapy in the opinion of the key clinician.

Control and intervention group participants received standard care, comprising systematic assessments of health and social needs, formation of a care plan, appointment of a key worker to monitor and coordinate care, and regular reviews to adapt the care plan. Care is provided by multi-disciplinary mental health teams, and treatments may include medication, social or psychological interventions. Intervention group participants in addition received eleven weekly 90-minute sessions of Positive Psychotherapy for Psychosis in a closed group format.

The primary outcome measure was the 14-item Warwick-Edinburgh Mental Wellbeing Scale (WEMWBS).[63] Two alternative wellbeing measures were also used: the 25-item Positive Psychotherapy Inventory (PPI) measures a PPT-specific concept of wellbeing[170] and the 12-item Manchester Short Assessment of Quality of Life (MANSA) measures quality of life framed as satisfaction with life as a whole and with specific life domains.[28] Six indicators of wellbeing, as identified in the dynamic framework,[11] were also assessed: Savoring Beliefs Inventory (SBI) assesses the ability to derive pleasure through anticipating upcoming positive events, savouring positive moments in the present and reminiscing about past positive experiences;[171] Integrative Hope Scale (IHS) assesses hope;[172] Rosenberg Self-Esteem Scale (RSES) assesses self-esteem;[173] Rogers' Empowerment Scale (RES) assesses empowerment;[174] Sense of Coherence Scale (SCS) assesses orientation to view

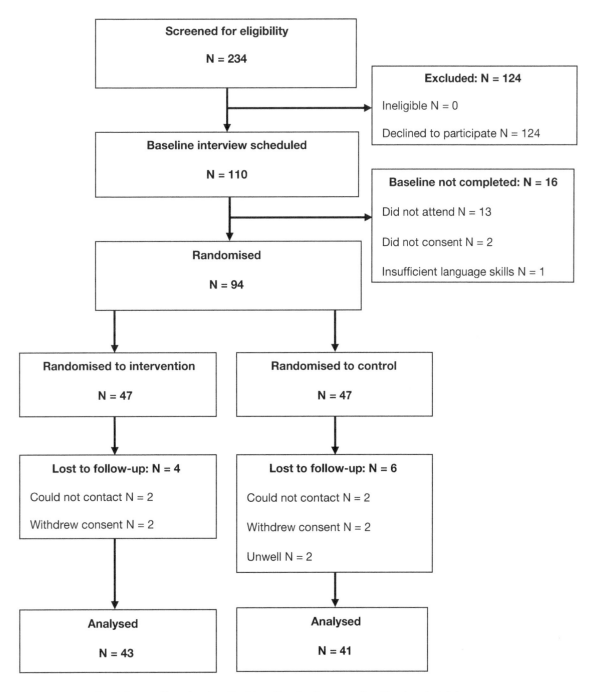

FIGURE 5.1 Participant flow in the Positive Psychotherapy for Psychosis trial

their environment as comprehensible, manageable and meaningful;[175] Short Depression-Happiness Scale (SDHS) assesses affect on a bipolar continuum between depression and happiness.[44] We also used the Health of the Nation Outcome Scale (HoNOS) assessment of social disability[176] and the Brief Psychiatric Rating Scale (BPRS) assessment of symptomatology.[177]

Participants were recruited between April and August 2013 from eight teams in one mental health trust (service provider) in South London, UK.

TABLE 5.1 Sociodemographic and baseline clinical characteristics (n = 94)

		Intervention	Control
		Mean (SD)	Mean (SD)
Age		43 (11.0)	42 (11.5)
		n (%)	n (%)
Gender	Male	26 (55.3)	30 (63.8)
Ethnicity	White	21 (44.7)	23 (50)
	Non-White	26 (55.3)	23 (50)
Birth place	UK-born	29 (61.7)	27 (57.4)
Accommodation	Owned	8 (17.0)	4 (8.5)
	Rented	27 (57.4)	34 (72.3)
	Other	12 (25.5)	8 (17.0)
Relationship status	Single	39 (83.0)	42 (89.4)
	in Partnership	8 (17.0)	5 (10.6)
Qualifications	None	5 (10.9)	2 (4.3)
	Secondary education (11–16 years)	11 (25.6)	16 (34.8)
	Further education (16–18 years)	11 (25.6)	12 (26.1)
	Higher education (18+)	12 (26.1)	10 (23.3)
	Relevant professional training	7 (15.2)	6 (13.0)
Employment	Working or studying	10 (21.3)	10 (21.3)
	Not working	37 (78.7)	37 (78.7)
	Mean (SD)	Mean (SD)	
Years using mental health services		13 (11.0)	14 (11.0)
Warwick-Edinburgh Mental Wellbeing Scale (WEMWBS)		3.19 (.76)	3.00 (.89)
Manchester Short Assessment of Quality of Life (MANSA)		4.05 (.85)	4.14 (1.01)
Positive Psychotherapy Inventory (PPI)		3.58 (.73)	3.44 (.80)
Brief Psychiatric Rating Scale (BPRS)		30.70 (8.81)	33.57 (8.42)
Short Depression-Happiness Scale (SDHS)		2.29 (.69)	2.48 (.76)
Integrative Hope Scale (IHS)		4.02 (.79)	3.72 (.85)
Rosenberg Self-Esteem Scale (RSES)		2.24 (.64)	2.09 (.66)
Savoring Beliefs Inventory (SBI)		4.80 (1.22)	4.48 (1.02)
Rogers Empowerment Scale (RES)		2.74 (.32)	2.71 (.32)
Sense of Coherence Scale (SCS)		4.18 (1.05)	3.81 (1.11)
Health of the Nation Outcome Scale (HoNOS)		7.29 (5.05)	9.62 (5.19)

After giving informed consent and completing baseline measures, they were randomised by the independent King's Clinical Trials Unit in groups of 8–20 participants (as block randomisation representing multiples of two and four people). Follow-up interviews took place within two weeks of the intervention finishing.

The flow diagram for the ninety-four study participants is shown in Figure 5.1.

Baseline participant characteristics are shown in Table 5.1.

Positive Psychotherapy for Psychosis was provided to six groups, and each group had an average of eight (range 4 to 10) participants. The median number of sessions attended was seven.

No adverse events were reported. Given the low rate of missing items in questionnaires with only one necessary exclusion of the IHS, reporting of all eighty-four participants with follow-up assessments is possible for all other scales. Raw data on change for all assessed variables are presented in Table 5.2.

TABLE 5.2 Changes from baseline to follow-up (n = 84, except for IHS n = 83)

Measure	Group	Mean difference (CI)	p
WEMWBS	CONTROL	0.15 (–0.10–0.41)	n.s.
	INTERVENTION	0.26 (0.06–0.45)	0.010
MANSA	CONTROL	0.11 (–0.07–0.30)	n.s.
	INTERVENTION	0.34 (0.11–0.57)	0.004
PPI	CONTROL	–0.02 (–0.15–0.11)	n.s.
	INTERVENTION	0.20 (0.06–0.35)	0.000
BPRS	CONTROL	0.78 (–1.16–2.72)	n.s.
	INTERVENTION	–2.51 (–4.70—0.32)	0.026
SDHS	CONTROL	–0.07 (–0.22–0.09)	n.s.
	INTERVENTION	–0.24 (–0.45—0.03)	0.028
IHS	CONTROL	0.19 (–0.02–0.41)	0.080
	INTERVENTION	0.21 (0.00–0.42)	0.048
RSES	CONTROL	0.05 (–0.07–0.18)	n.s.
	INTERVENTION	0.19 (0.04–0.34)	0.016
SBI	CONTROL	0.05 (–0.16–0.27)	n.s.
	INTERVENTION	0.08 (–0.15–0.32)	n.s.
RES	CONTROL	0.01 (–0.07–0.08)	n.s.
	INTERVENTION	0.07 (–0.01–0.16)	0.079
SCS	CONTROL	0.17 (–0.03–0.36)	0.088
	INTERVENTION	0.24 (0.01–0.46)	0.040
HONOS	CONTROL	–0.37 (–1.91–1.18)	n.s.
	INTERVENTION	0.03 (–1.38–1.44)	n.s.

TABLE 5.3 Intention to treat analysis (n = 84, except for IHS n = 83)

Scale	Follow-up mean (s.e.)			Effect size
	Control	Intervention	ANCOVA	
n	41	43		
WEMWBS	3.24 (0.10)	3.36 (0.10)	F(1,81) = 0.8, p = .37	.15
MANSA	4.21 (0.10)	4.42 (0.10)	F(1,81) = 2.3, p = .13	.21
PPI	3.48 (0.07)	3.72 (0.07)	F(1,81) = 5.9, p = .02	.30
BPRS	33.23 (.98)	29.37 (0.96)	F(1,81) = 7.8, p = .006	.42
SDHS overall	2.34 (0.09)	2.13 (0.08)	F(1,81) = 3.0, p = .09	.29
SDHS happiness	2.91 (.10)	3.03 (.10)	F(1,81) = 0.6, p =. 42	.16
SDHS depression	2.60 (.10)	2.29 (.10)	F(1,81) = 4.7, p = .03	.38
IHS	4.04 (0.10)	4.11 (0.10)	F(1,81) = 0.3, p = .62	.08
RSES	2.21 (0.07)	2.37 (0.07)	F(1,81) = 2.9, p = .09	.23
SBI	4.65 (0.11)	4.75 (0.10)	F(1,81) = 0.4, p = .53	.09
RES	2.73 (0.04)	2.80 (0.04)	F(1,81) = 2.0, p = .16	.22
SCS	4.12 (0.10)	4.26 (0.10)	F(1,81) = 1.0, p = .32	.13
HONOS	8.53 (0.68)	8.14 (0.66)	F(1,81) = 0.2, p = .68	.07

Intention-to-treat (ITT) analysis found no significant effect of intervention group on the primary outcome of wellbeing (WEMWBS) at follow-up after adjusting for baseline scores (p = .37), and the effect size was small (Cohen's d = .15). Table 5.3 summarises ITT analyses for all measures.

Adjusting the model for therapy group minimally increased effect sizes for the BPRS (F(1,76) = 8.7, p = 0.004, ES = 0.43), and SDHS depression (F(1,76) = 4.9, p = -.03, ES=0.41) but did not lead to any more outcomes falling below the p = 0.05 significance level. In both models, the highest effect sizes were found for symptom severity (BPRS) and depression (SDHS depression), followed by wellbeing as measured by the PPI.

CACE analysis showed a non-significant positive association between the intervention and WEMWBS scores at follow-up (b = .21, z = 0.9, p = .4).

Process evaluation

We also investigated the experience of receiving Positive Psychotherapy for Psychosis.[9] Participants from the six groups run in the trial were alternatingly allocated to interview (three groups) or focus group (three groups) for the end-of-trial process evaluation. A semi-structured topic guide investigated the experiences of the components of Positive Psychotherapy for Psychosis. It included questions probing what participants enjoyed and found useful, and what they found difficult or challenging. Non-directive prompts were used to stimulate in-depth discussion. Three experienced researchers, none of whom was involved in providing the therapy to the respective participants, conducted the focus groups and interviews. All data were collected within two weeks of the last session of therapy, between August and October 2013. Participants received £20 for participation. Interviews lasted between 5 and 100 minutes, and focus groups between 75 and 105 minutes. All assessments except for three interviews were audiotaped and transcribed verbatim. Feedback from three participants was captured with notes taken by the researcher due to lack of consent for audio recording.

Feedback was obtained from thirty-seven (95 per cent) of the thirty-nine people meeting inclusion criteria for this study. Four participants had attended between one and three sessions, eight between four and six sessions, twelve between seven and nine sessions and thirteen participants between ten and eleven sessions. Reported diagnoses: 38.5 per cent schizophrenia; 33.3 per cent bipolar disorder and 28.2 per cent psychosis/psychotic depression. Participants had a mean age of 45.6 years (SD 10.3); 51 per cent were male and most were of White British (40 per cent) or Black British African (24 per cent) background.

Three superordinate themes were identified: general experiences, views on standard PPT components and views on specific components. Responses provided by interview and focus group did not noticeably differ.

Category 1: General experiences

Almost all participants reported that the intervention helped them to focus on the positive things in life rather than ruminating on the negative, helping them to become more confident and to develop their strengths to increase enjoyment of life. The supportiveness of the therapists and the breaking down of the 'them and us'[10] divide in sessions was also cited by over half the participants as being a significant factor in the enjoyment and subjective success of the therapy.

Two participants reported that, as a result of Positive Psychotherapy for Psychosis, they were able to enter voluntary employment, and stated that their positivity and belief in their strengths had supported them through the process. Approximately a quarter of participants valued the opportunity to draw images to represent their thoughts rather than using text. About half of the participants respectively found the support and feedback from other participants helpful in generating an atmosphere of acceptance with the same number reporting value in having the more positive components of the course before the more negative and challenging topics such as gratitude and forgiveness. Critical comments from participants included that the number of sessions were too few, that some topics brought up difficult negative emotions and a concern that they would not be able to maintain improvement after cessation of the sessions.

Category 2: Core components of standard PPT

Feedback on specific exercises was obtained.

Savouring exercises

Savouring was one of the most enjoyed sessions and one that nearly all participants reported as being useful. These participants found the savouring session helpful in encouraging them to give more time to doing things they enjoy, with one participant commenting that he had applied the concept of savouring to his relationships with people and was better able to enjoy the company of his friends. Another participant attributed starting to play the violin again to his learning of the savouring concept, as it encouraged him to get back to playing the violin, a previously loved hobby. Several participants reported that it would have been helpful if there had been a stronger emphasis on using the savouring process outside of the sessions for experiences other than eating and drinking.

Good Things exercises

This component was also enjoyed and considered useful by nearly all participants. Thinking about a positive thing that had happened that day was reported by the majority to have helped to reduce negative rumination and that opening their good things box improved their mood. One participant said that reviewing their good things box helped them to realise the things that were meaningful and that they truly valued in life. Also referred to as helpful by nearly half of participants was the element of the session that asked people to reflect on what they had done to make the positive experience happen, which was intended to make participants develop a more internal locus of control when it comes to generating positive experiences for themselves.

Personal Strengths exercises

Over half the participants reported being surprised at the strengths that they identified and those suggested by other group members. Several commented that they would not ordinarily have recognised these as personal strengths, but the sessions helped them to see how valuable these were in their lives. Several participants also reported that identifying and developing their strengths helped them to overcome obstacles without depending on others, which made them feel more able to cope with symptoms. Planning an activity that used individual strengths was considered useful by nearly all participants, with around a quarter reporting that it aided their appreciation that there were a number of things they needed to do to facilitate carrying out the activity, for which they had not given themselves credit before. Nearly half also said it was helpful to realize that overuse of strengths can compromise wellbeing.

Forgiveness exercises

Forgiveness was one of the components that nearly all participants reported to be very helpful, but nearly half also found difficult in terms of eliciting difficult emotions. Several participants particularly emphasized how useful it was to appreciate that it may not always be necessary to forgive and that it was possible to forgive even if you can't forget. One participant explained that he found forgiveness a difficult area, especially for people with mental health problems, but said that the sessions gave participants the foundations to understand and apply the concept. Nearly half the participants reported that it was useful to consider the positive qualities of people they found difficult to forgive, and not just consider them as a 'bad' person. The forgiveness letter was considered by nearly all participants to be challenging but useful, with one participant saying he was really inspired by hearing another participant's forgiveness letter. However, several participants found the exercises too difficult to complete because of the bad memories they had generated.

Gratitude exercises

This was a component that nearly all participants enjoyed but several reported as a difficult and emotive session. Nearly half particularly valued that it was not about just feeling grateful but about considering the positive consequences. The gratitude letter participants were asked to write to a significant person in their life received favourable comments from nearly all participants; however, around a quarter found it challenging to write. One participant said they could not continue with the exercise since it brought back unwanted emotions.

One Door Closes, Another Door Opens
(seeing the positives in negative situations) exercises

Participants initially found this a rather challenging session but useful in terms of introducing the concept, and were able to identify with the feeling that lots of doors had closed on them. Participants also felt that the session made them more hopeful that they could see positives when faced with a difficult life event.

Category 3: Specific components

Participants also gave feedback on specific components of the intervention.

Therapist participation/self-disclosure

Therapist participation in the exercises was reported by nearly all participants as being very helpful, both to demonstrate how to undertake an exercise and also as a way to engender an atmosphere of normalization. Over half the participants also said that it was helpful to see the therapists getting something out of the exercises as well, which they felt helped participants to engage in and bond with the group and made the exercises appear more relevant.

Between-session telephone calls

These calls were generally considered helpful, not only to remind participants about attending the next session and the topic that would be covered, but also to support them with their ongoing exercise. Others said it was encouraging to have people show an interest in them, which made them feel appreciated as individuals rather than as part of a group. However, a couple of participants doubted the calls were necessary, or even found them disturbing, and therefore asked not to receive them.

Savouring of music at beginning and end of each session

This was an extension of the savouring component of standard PPT. It was reported to be very enjoyable and helpful by nearly all participants, aiding concentration and relaxation at the start, allowing participants to focus on the content of the session, and as a winding down exercise at the end.

Celebration

The celebration session was reported to be excellent – both enjoyable and useful, by nearly all participants. The main comment was that the therapists had really learned about the participants' personality and positive attributes, and that therefore the letters given to participants to mark the end of the group were very helpful in highlighting their strengths and what they had brought to the group.

Optimisation of Positive Psychotherapy for Psychosis

The outcome evaluation showed a non-significant result for the primary and most secondary outcome measures, except for the BPRS, SDHS depression and PPI, which showed significant improvements in the intervention as compared to the control group at moderate effect sizes. No significant effect of group was found on wellbeing as the main outcome. However, a significant improvement on the researcher-rated BPRS was found, with a moderate effect size in the ITT analysis comparable to effect sizes found for CBT in this client group.[178] Equally strong effects were found on the patient-rated SDHS depression sub-scale. The evaluation therefore provides initial evidence on the likely feasibility and acceptability of Positive Psychotherapy for Psychosis in the client group of people with psychosis. More work is needed to maximise its effectiveness. Positive Psychotherapy for Psychosis may be particularly suitable for reducing overall symptom severity and specifically depression. Comorbid depression is a known challenge in the treatment of people with psychosis, affecting about 40 per cent of people at risk of psychosis[179] and about 50 per cent of people with schizophrenia.[180]

The positive impact of Positive Psychotherapy for Psychosis on depressive symptoms needs to be evaluated further, with specific attention to including research diagnoses and establishing the causal pathway of action. Ways of supplementing the effect on symptoms in general are worth considering in future research, including for example, a choice or combination of Positive Psychotherapy for Psychosis and brief CBT intervention.[181]

The process evaluation identified particularly useful components, informing changes to the intervention manual:

1 The order of activities may affect responses to the intervention. In particular, it was useful to cover the more positive topics prior to the more challenging topics, such as forgiveness.

2 Additional session(s) focusing on maintenance of gains and maintaining a positive focus after treatment has finished are recommended.

3 While enjoying the savouring concept, some participants wanted more emphasis on the savouring of processes other than food and drink. Future interventions could therefore increase attention to other savouring experiences and activities, for example, savouring friendships.

4 Therapists should be mindful of the complex and potentially painful and lengthy processes involved in forgiveness, which may not be adequately supported in a brief therapy. Forgiveness was approached from the perspective of letting go of a grudge, thereby thinking about smaller things to forgive to develop an understanding of the process and how it can feel to forgive. This was achieved by a group discussion about what forgiveness is, its benefits and how it feels. A 'tug of war' group exercise was used as a metaphor of the benefits, illustrating the idea of embodiment: that just as our mind can influence bodily actions, our motor system – for example, bodily movements – can have an impact on cognition and the way we think. Future approaches to addressing forgiveness in the context of a brief therapy might present the topic as a process of 'letting go of grudges' and focusing on the subjective benefits of forgiving. Moreover, there is evidence of a dose-effect relationship in forgiveness interventions.[182] It may therefore be helpful to focus on forgiving transgressions that are not too serious in nature, to give participants the opportunity to start to learn and practice forgiveness in a relatively safe and confined context.

5 The positive feedback on the between-session calls suggests they are a promising and versatile therapy component. While some therapies use reminder calls about appointments and/or conduct therapy over the telephone, to our knowledge, use of between-session calls as in Positive Psychotherapy for Psychosis has not yet been reported. Such calls may be helpful with respect to memory problems or lack of motivation found in people with psychosis, and also applicable to other clinical populations with similar difficulties. Since some participants did object to the calls, clinicians should consider the acceptability and usefulness of such calls on an individual basis.

We also obtained feedback on the handouts. The issues identified were very small font size, too many examples/words/boxes, unclear title, ambiguous images and lack of space for free-text comments.

Therapist and research team experience, outcome and process evaluation from the randomised controlled trial, and newly published research were used to refine the Positive Psychotherapy for Psychosis manual to the final version contained in this book.

In the next chapter, we provide some of the experiential learning accrued from giving the intervention, and guidance on how it can be adapted.

CHAPTER 6

Positive Psychotherapy for Psychosis

Therapist questions (and answers!)

In this chapter, we provide guidance for therapists about the issues we have found emerge in running Positive Psychotherapy for Psychosis groups, and identify modifications for providing the intervention through different modalities or to other clinical populations. We briefly review theory, summarising the material covered in Chapters 2 to 5. We then outline the general structure, facilitator skills and session-specific issues to consider, followed by a discussion of various adaptations.

What is the rationale for Positive Psychotherapy for Psychosis?

Positive Psychotherapy for Psychosis is a strengths-based intervention, differing from many traditional therapies that tend to be deficit- or problem-based. As a result, it includes exercises that look at identifying and developing personal strengths, noticing and remembering positive experiences, and topics such as gratitude and forgiveness. It also contains practical tools to aid understanding of the different topics, and to support maintenance of gains when the programme has finished.

Positive Psychotherapy for Psychosis is primarily informed by Positive Psychotherapy (PPT), a positive psychology intervention that was originally developed for depression and is based on the premise that optimal treatment for depression involves 'directly and primarily building positive emotions, character strengths, and meaning' (p. 775)[183] rather than simply targeting negative symptoms, faulty cognitions and difficult relationships. PPT exercises focus on mindful savouring of enjoyable experiences, positive responding, identifying, developing and using character strengths, finding positives in negative events and also includes areas such as forgiveness and gratitude. The evidence base for PPT was described in Chapter 2.

We adapted PPT for use with people with psychosis. The theory base for the new intervention – called Positive Psychotherapy for Psychosis – was described in Chapter 3. In Chapter 4, we describe how we developed Positive Psychotherapy for Psychosis. Chapter 5 describes how we modified the intervention, based on outcome and process evaluation in a randomised controlled trial.

Who is Positive Psychotherapy for Psychosis for?

Positive Psychotherapy for Psychosis is for people with a diagnosis of psychosis. It has been used in community and rehabilitation in-patient settings.

How is Positive Psychotherapy for Psychosis provided?

This manual describes a 13-session group-based intervention. It may also be provided:

- as an individual therapy;
- as an adjunct (e.g. by incorporating specific techniques) for other psychotherapeutic approaches; and
- for other clinical populations.

At the end of this chapter, we offer advice on these adaptations.

How frequent are the sessions?

When we evaluated Positive Psychotherapy for Psychosis, we delivered each of the sessions to a group once a week. Each session was scheduled to last 90 minutes. We would recommend this frequency for out-patients, since it enabled a balance to be achieved between ensuring continuity and not overloading clients (both socially and cognitively). However, this may be altered to suit the needs of the clients, and resources of the facilitators. For example, for in-patients or day patients, it may be useful to adapt sessions for delivery twice a week.

Depending upon the client group and context of delivery, an alternative to between-session phone calls may be the inclusion of a joint additional reflection session on homework progress. Such between-session homework reflection sessions might be guided more by group members than by facilitators, potentially over the course of the therapy leading to an informal mutual self-help group emerging. This could be very helpful for maintenance and empowerment and will most likely be possible in a setting in which participants meet every day anyway.

How many clients can attend a group?

In addition to the facilitators, we found that groups could be run successfully with a minimum of three and a maximum of eight clients per group.

Who can facilitate Positive Psychotherapy for Psychosis groups?

Having two co-facilitators for groups was useful for a number of reasons. It

- provided different perspectives on exercises;
- facilitated the normalising of different views and experiences;
- offered more individualised support for clients who needed it; and
- ensured continuity in case one therapist was absent.

However, Positive Psychotherapy for Psychosis can be delivered by only one facilitator where necessary.

It is advisable for at least one facilitator to have experience of providing therapy, in particular for clients with psychosis. However, due to the comprehensive guidance provided in this book, such experience is not essential. Facilitators must have a good understanding of the underlying principles of Positive Psychotherapy for Psychosis, and how the ethos of the therapy influences both the content and the style in which it is provided. We therefore recommend facilitators be very familiar with the contents of this book. The session-by-session descriptions in the manual provides detailed delivery guidelines, including therapist tips and case examples. These can help facilitators deliver exercises and deal with the specific challenges that will arise by building on the existing experience in the delivery of Positive Psychotherapy for Psychosis.

Training and supervision capacity for this new therapy is limited, but increasingly psychologists and other psychological therapists are incorporating elements from positive psychology into their practice. We therefore recommend identifying local experts (e.g. some universities provide positive psychology courses), or developing peer supervision arrangements.

The role of the facilitator

A core tenet of Positive Psychotherapy for Psychosis is the reduction, as far as possible, of any perceived 'them and us' divide between facilitators and clients, and the establishment of an equal working partnership. A key way to do this is for facilitators to be actively involved and participate in all exercises, including ongoing exercises and subsequent reviews of progress. There is therefore an emphasis on facilitator self-disclosure, to model learning points for clients and to reiterate the understanding that the principles of Positive Psychotherapy for Psychosis can be useful in order to improve well-being in everyone, not just those with psychosis. Facilitators should, however, ensure that their examples remain short and relevant, so clients and their experiences remain the focus of the group.

Key facilitator skills

The following are core skills for facilitators to use during sessions.

Support positive responding

Notice and praise every success. Be a role model in sessions for this interpersonal skill. Support practice through demonstrations, role play and working in pairs. Encourage discussions that value relationships and social interactions. Address rather than ignore concerns about social situations if they arise, with the aim of validating and normalising social anxiety and negative experiences.

Be accessible

When speaking to clients, avoid theory, abstraction and didactic style. Use clear, understandable language and agree (with reminders) on simple guidelines and ground rules for the group. Emphasise organisation and structure but be flexible. It is important to assess and reflect on clients' difficulties and needs, and adapt sessions if necessary. Emphasise mutual acceptance and equality of clients (and therapists) to create a safe, trusting environment.

Support change

Where useful, talk about your own experiences to normalise the exercises and the feelings they may generate. Focus on meaningfulness and values. Notice and use any personal interests that people mention. Ensure goals are realistic and that people find them meaningful. Support people to find opportunities, to break down activities into small concrete steps, and to anticipate and address challenges. Give affirming feedback. Avoid the word 'homework' as some people may have had difficult experiences at school.

Encourage experiential learning

Openly discuss what to expect, and anticipate negative feelings. Promote honesty and authentic curiosity about others. Provide direct individual support where necessary, but as far as possible, involve all people and create an inclusive group where everyone has some voice. Listen to and remember key themes in each person's story, and use these in later sessions to promote continuity and learning. Be empathic and non-judgemental in your understanding, and avoid awkward personal questions. Encourage people to talk to family, friends and staff about the exercises and their impact.

What are the main challenges for facilitators and clients?

Strengths-based approach

Clients may find the strengths-based approach difficult initially, if they associate therapy with discussing and solving problems. This may make it difficult for them to understand the ethos or benefits of a more strengths-based approach to therapy. This can be addressed by the facilitators providing a clear rationale for positive psychology interventions at the start of therapy (as included in Session 1), clarifying that this therapy is not primarily about discussing the problems of clients, but is designed to develop a positive attitude and to provide tools and ways of thinking that help to deal with difficult situations in the future. Rehearsal of this message during other groups will be helpful. When difficulties are discussed, facilitators can validate the concern but redirect clients to consider the positive learning experiences from the difficulty being discussed.

Exercises

Some clients, particularly those with some degree of cognitive impairment, may find completing some exercises challenging. Positive Psychotherapy for Psychosis has been designed with this in mind. For example, there are options for clients to draw or paint images rather than write their responses, and therapist tips are given for how to manage challenges associated with specific exercises.

Facilitator self-disclosure

Positive Psychotherapy for Psychosis encourages facilitator self-disclosure, in the form of active participation in exercises, as a way of both modelling activities and reducing the power differential between facilitator and client. The approach taken in Positive Psychotherapy for Psychosis to self-disclosure is therefore different from the majority of traditional psychotherapies, in which self-disclosure is not recommended, and where opportunities for it are fewer. As a result, facilitators may find it challenging at first to adapt to this mode of delivery. The key point to remember is that there is good rationale for this re-balancing. Self-disclosure is traditionally advised against because of concerns that the therapist will be meeting their own needs from therapy; it may 'confuse' the client by mimicking a social relationship (raising unmeetable expectations that the therapist will be the client's friend), or it may take the focus off the client's needs. All of these concerns still of course apply, but emerging research shows that authentic encounters with health professionals, in which the client experiences being treated as a person not a patient, can lead to profound turning points in the client's life.[184,185] So the re-balancing is towards more use of the facilitator as a source of recovery support, by normalising the challenges of life, modelling struggle and success with the therapeutic tasks, and being genuine and honest in the group. Therapist tips within each session plan can help guide facilitators with this.

What ground rules should be set for the group?

i   Attendance: Clients will get more out of the group with regular attendance.

ii   Punctuality: It is important to try to arrive on time so all clients get to benefit from the whole session running to schedule.

iii   Confidentiality: Stories, personal details and experiences shared in the group should stay in the room.

iv   Listening: It is important to listen to others when they are speaking.

v   Consideration: Be considerate to other members of the group.

What is the structure of each session?

This book provides session-by-session agendas for the thirteen 90-minute sessions of Positive Psychotherapy for Psychosis, each containing exercises, worksheets and therapist tips for delivery. Sessions begin and end with the mindful savouring of music, to help clients relax into and focus on the session at the start, and to provide a short period of relaxation and calm at the end. We provide suggested music to use, subject to copyright restrictions. Sessions typically continue with a warm-up exercise, followed by an exercise to complete during the session and the introduction of an ongoing exercise to be completed before the next session. There is a scheduled break of 10 minutes and a further 10 minutes of contingency time, both of which can be changed as relevant.

What are the ongoing exercises for?

An ongoing exercise is introduced in the second part of each session, and in most cases is started during the session. Progress and reflections on the exercise are reviewed and discussed at the beginning of the next session. Facilitators should empathise with difficulties, and time is given in the first session for facilitators to outline the idea of ongoing exercises and for explaining why completing the exercises will be beneficial. Facilitators should be non-judgmental, notice every success however small (e.g. 'I thought about doing the exercise'), normalise common challenges and encourage clients to see stumbling blocks in terms of learning opportunities. Therapist tips and case examples in the individual chapters in this manual describe some challenges encountered in practice and suggest some possible ways to address them.

What is the journal?

Positive Psychotherapy for Psychosis makes use of a journal-type tool called the Positive Psychotherapy for Psychosis Journal. This can take different forms. Our approach was to use a small ring-binder, containing lined and plain paper for writing, a contents page and a pre-printed summary of what is covered in each session. We encouraged clients to personalise their Journals if wanted, and to add completed worksheets to their Journals.

What is the Good Things Box?

In Session 4, the concept of a Good Things Box is introduced and is a key theme returned to during the course of the sessions. Clients are given a box in which they can keep mementoes of good things that have happened to them. Clients can then open the box and remind themselves of these when things are difficult. Consciously thinking about what is going well in life, as well as taking small steps to encourage recollection of these events in the future by collecting mementos and storing them in the Good Things Box can protect against low mood and can help engender a more positive outlook. There is evidence that thinking about good things can increase happiness and decrease depressive symptoms. We provided our clients with simple, small, lidded boxes (approximately 25 cm wide) in this session, and encouraged them to use these as their Good Things Boxes. However, clients could be encouraged to use similar boxes/containers that they have at home. Templates are also provided for Good Things Cards – these are cards on which clients can write short notes about good things that have happened, and include these in their Good Things Boxes. Clients can be given several copies of Good Things Cards for use during the sessions and in the future.

What are the between-session telephone calls for?

We offered brief telephone calls between sessions, during which clients were encouraged to talk about their progress on the ongoing exercises, and help was provided where relevant. These calls were optional for clients. Depending on the delivery context, time and resources available, these calls can be offered as part of Positive Psychotherapy for Psychosis. It is recommended that these are delivered by the facilitators, so the calls are with people familiar to the clients. The calls were usually around 5 minutes long, depending on how much help a client wanted and how talkative they were. In in-patient or day-patient settings, such calls could be replaced with brief face-to-face conversations.

THERAPIST QUESTIONS (AND ANSWERS!)

What are the end-of-session letters?

These letters are a key part of the final session. In advance of the final session, facilitators prepare a letter for each client, outlining their progress and achievements through the sessions, and positive experiences that they have shared with the group. Facilitators should therefore ensure they maintain notes from each session to help inform these letters and include examples of what clients have said over the course of the sessions. Letters should be as personal as possible, and written in simple language to enable clients to easily understand and to read their letters to the group if they wish to. While these entail some work by the facilitators, they should be written with care and attention since they are a key component that clients will remember after the therapy.

To inform these letters, and as a general support for maintaining the development of a positive narrative by clients over time, we recommend that facilitators make brief notes at the end of each session, summarising examples provided by clients, their responses to exercises and where relevant, each client's plans for the ongoing exercise. Where there is more than one facilitator, it is helpful to take these notes jointly, and in PPT style, focusing on strengths and achievements. This will enable facilitators to help clients to remember their progress in future sessions and will provide useful information on which facilitators can draw when writing the end-of-session letters for each client.

Booster sessions

We did not include booster sessions in our testing of Positive Psychotherapy for Psychosis, but results from the process evaluation suggest that these may be useful. Timing and frequency will usually be resource-dependent, and we would suggest at least one booster session a few months after the last session, perhaps extending to two or three booster sessions spread over 6 months. Ideas for these may include:

- asking each client to bring their Good Things Box with them and share things they have added;
- telling a new story of a time clients have been at their best since the last session; and
- going through some of the key topics again, with additional exercises.

Can Positive Psychotherapy for Psychosis be provided as an individual therapy?

Positive Psychotherapy for Psychosis has been evaluated as a group therapy. However, there might be reasons to provide it as an individual therapy:

- Some clients may prefer individual sessions.
- Individual sessions may fit in more easily with the structure of therapy provision in the locality.
- The therapist may have more experience in individual therapy.

Therapists will need to modify some elements of Positive Psychotherapy for Psychosis as presented in this book, in particular the group-based warm-up exercises.

Can Positive Psychotherapy for Psychosis be integrated into other psychological therapies?

Facilitators may prefer to incorporate one or more components of Positive Psychotherapy for Psychosis into traditional therapies, depending on the needs of the client group. Should facilitators wish to do this, it is recommended that they read the full content of all sessions to ensure that clients have the necessary guidance and knowledge to fully engage with the session. Facilitators should also be aware that the Positive Psychotherapy for Psychosis sessions are ordered in a specific way, that is, to have positive and resource-building exercises earlier on and more challenging exercises later. The later sessions draw on the skills learned in earlier sessions, for example, using personal strengths to help clients to forgive or how to decide who to be thankful to in a way that makes the exercise empowering and strengths-enhancing, rather than disempowering. While the first sessions may serve as stand-alone sessions/exercises, it may be necessary to do some preparatory work in order to use later sessions in a different context.

Can Positive Psychotherapy for Psychosis be provided to other clinical populations?

Positive Psychotherapy for Psychosis was developed and evaluated for people with psychosis, and delivery to other clinical populations may well be feasible, particularly for experienced psychological therapists. It will be important to consider areas that might need more sensitive handling. For example, forgiveness and family work were key areas of modification for people with psychosis, as discussed in Chapter 3. It may be worth asking patients and therapists to review the content of sessions, in order to identify potential issues such as topics, frequency and duration of sessions, and any disorder-specific issues (e.g. mobility in the warm-up exercises). We also recommend formal evaluation of the intervention when used with different clinical populations.

CHAPTER 7

Intervention manual

Overview

Positive Psychotherapy (PPT) is a psychological therapy that focuses on strengths and positive experiences in order to promote wellbeing. Research shows that PPT has increased wellbeing for healthy recipients and for people with common mental health problems such as depression. It has not been evaluated in people with a diagnosis of psychosis.

Positive Psychotherapy for Psychosis is an adaptation of PPT, for people with psychosis. Positive Psychotherapy for Psychosis targets four areas:

- Increasing positive experiences
- Amplifying strengths
- Fostering positive relationships
- Creating a more meaningful self-narrative

Positive Psychotherapy for Psychosis is a 13-session group-based intervention, with sessions covering:

- Welcome to Positive Psychotherapy for Psychosis
- Positive experiences
- Savouring
- Good things
- Identifying a personal strength
- Personal strength activity
- At my best
- One door closes, another door opens
- Forgiveness (1)
- Forgiveness (2)
- Gratitude
- Looking back, moving forward
- Celebration

This is the intervention manual. It contains a description of the theory, structure and content of the Positive Psychotherapy for Psychosis Intervention.

Theory

This is the intervention manual for Positive Psychotherapy for Psychosis. It is adapted from a standard PPT for use with people with psychosis. Standard PPT is based on the assumptions that difficulties in mental health can occur when we struggle to be fulfilled and happy, that positive emotions and strengths should be valued and that therapy should be built on personal strengths and positive experiences. The aim of PPT is to promote wellbeing. Martin Seligman is one of the originators of PPT and, according to his 'PERMA' theory, wellbeing is understood to have five dimensions: Positive emotions, Engagement, Relationships, Meaning and Accomplishment[157].

Standard PPT exercises identify and amplify a person's psychological assets, such as character strengths, meaning and positive relationships. This process involves systematic and sustained therapeutic work with these resources, in order to open a client's mindset beyond the innate propensity for negativity, with the goal of helping the person to establish a life worth living. Initial results from standard PPT demonstrate that people not only want to be less miserable but also want lives that are filled with pleasure, engagement and meaning.

Research shows that standard PPT has increased wellbeing for healthy recipients and for people with common mental health problems such as depression, but it has not been evaluated in people with a diagnosis of psychosis. Positive Psychotherapy for Psychosis is a modification of PPT for use in psychosis. The modifications are based on a systematic review,[14] qualitative research,[11] expert consultation,[7] and evaluation of outcome[8] and process[9] in a pilot randomised controlled trial.

The systematic review synthesised the findings from controlled trials of interventions investigating wellbeing in people with psychosis. The twenty-eight studies meeting inclusion criteria for the review used twenty different measures of wellbeing. Using narrative synthesis, five dimensions of wellbeing were identified from these measures: non-observable, observable, proximal, distal and self-defined. These are shown in Figure 7.1.

The **non-observable** domain refers to intra-psychic phenomena such as self-perception, mood tone or meaning and purpose in life, which are not readily visible from outside. The **observable** domain comprises aspects of a person that are exhibited to the outside world, such as environmental mastery, resolution or physical health. The **proximal** domain describes factors that directly and immediately affect the individual. It includes what a person has or does, for example, various kinds of relationships, finances or occupation. Finally, the **distal** domain encompasses contextual factors that are not under a person's immediate influence, such as the wider environment or access to services. In addition, the separate **self-defined** domain refers to a broad and overall individual perception of wellbeing according to what wellbeing means to the person.

This static framework of wellbeing for people with psychosis offers an evidence-based conceptual framework of wellbeing, which can provide an empirical basis for organising wellbeing research in psychosis.

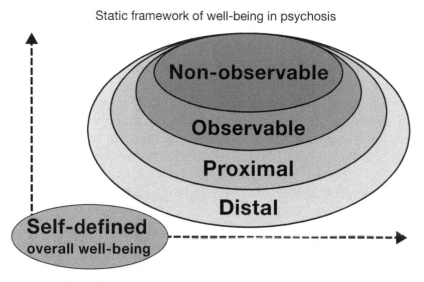

Static framework of well-being in psychosis

FIGURE 7.1 Static framework of wellbeing

A subsequent qualitative study aimed to validate the static framework of wellbeing through triangulation from a second data source, and to develop a dynamic framework of wellbeing that also takes into account the processes involved in improving wellbeing. It involved twenty-three semi-structured interviews with service users with psychosis, of whom thirteen were re-interviewed for respondent validation. Clients were asked about their personal experience of wellbeing and of improving wellbeing. Analysis found the static framework to be a valid organisational structure embedded in the newly developed dynamic framework of wellbeing. Clients described wellbeing as a desirable state that needed active input to be achieved. Wellbeing was tied to clients' sense of self and involved transition from a current sense of self, often described as deficient, towards an enhanced sense of self. In the resulting dynamic framework, the non-observable, observable, proximal and

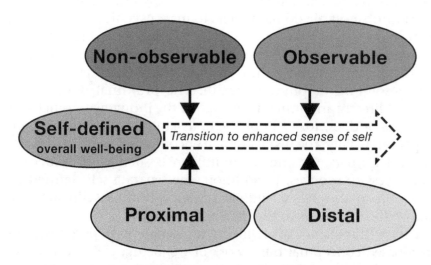

FIGURE 7.2 The static and dynamic framework of wellbeing

distal domains from the static framework form influences on the process of improving wellbeing, that is, an enhanced sense of self. This connection is shown in Figure 7.2.

Attainment of this enhanced sense of self was perceived as increased wellbeing, and attributed to the successful transition. This process followed a common pattern that underpins the dynamic framework of wellbeing. Three superordinate categories were identified in the framework: determinants of current sense of self (the participant's starting point); influences on the transition to enhanced sense of self (the change process involved in improving wellbeing) and indicators of the enhanced sense of self (how wellbeing is experienced by clients). The full dynamic framework of wellbeing is shown in Figure 7.3.

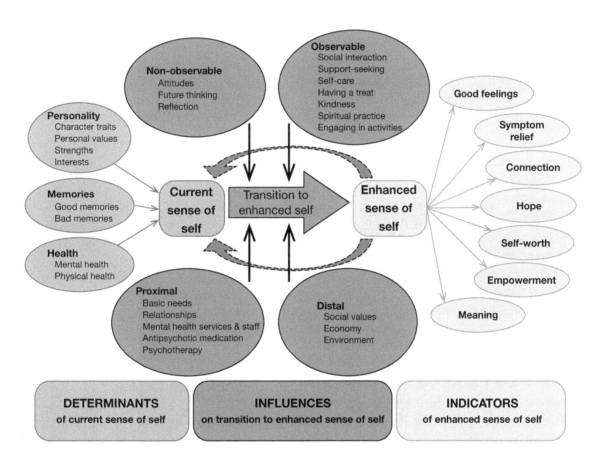

FIGURE 7.3 The dynamic framework of wellbeing

Specific factors identified as implicated in the transition, that is, determinants, influences and indicators, varied across individuals both in quality and quantity. These factors are variables with values, and the values attached to specific factors may differ between people and within an individual over time. The dynamic framework represents an iterative process. As soon as the enhanced sense of self has been achieved, this becomes the new current sense of self allowing further development.

The next stage of development of Positive Psychotherapy for Psychosis involved an expert consultation using semi-structured interviews with twenty-three service users and fourteen staff members. In these semi-structured interviews, the components of original PPT were introduced and suggestions for adaptations and improvements for people with psychosis were obtained. The qualitative data generated in these interviews were then presented to a panel of experts including therapists, researchers and NHS policymakers in a joint meeting. Suggestions derived from the semi-structured interviews were discussed and a consensus was reached on adaptations to the original 11-session intervention.

The 11-session group intervention was then tested with ninety-four people with psychosis in a randomised controlled trial (ISRCTN04199273). Assessments occurred pre-randomisation and post-therapy. Analysis showed significant positive effects on wellbeing, symptoms and depression. Suggestions derived from the semi-structured interviews conducted at the end of the intervention with clients and therapists were discussed, and a consensus was reached on final adaptations to the Positive Psychotherapy for Psychosis manual, including increasing the intervention to thirteen sessions. This development process led to the final Positive Psychotherapy for Psychosis manual (this document).

Positive Psychotherapy for Psychosis targets four areas:

• Increasing positive experiences
• Amplifying strengths
• Fostering positive relationships
• Creating a more meaningful self-narrative

These target areas of the intervention are intended to lead to an enhanced sense of self. Figure 7.4 shows the Positive Psychotherapy for Psychosis model, describing how the intervention leads to the processes and intermediate outcomes, which contribute to better wellbeing – defined as an enhanced sense of self.

Positive Psychotherapy for Psychosis is a group therapy delivered in thirteen weekly sessions. Each session contains exercises focussing on one or more of the target areas, as shown in Table 7.1.

Each Positive Psychotherapy for Psychosis session lasts for 90 minutes, comprising 5 minutes of savouring at the beginning and end of each session, 60 minutes of session-specific content, 10 minutes for a mid-session break and 10 minutes contingency time. Each session introduces an ongoing exercise that clients are encouraged to continue in their own time. Describing the exercises as 'ongoing' may help clients to expect and plan to carry it out on in their own time. Individually chosen exercises should be small, achievable, personal, meaningful, specific, pleasurable and understandable. The generic structure for a session is shown in Table 7.2.

Clients are given a Positive Psychotherapy for Psychosis journal in the first session. The journal is used by clients in various exercises throughout the therapy to record experiences. Clients should be encouraged to personalise the journal, and to bring it to each session.

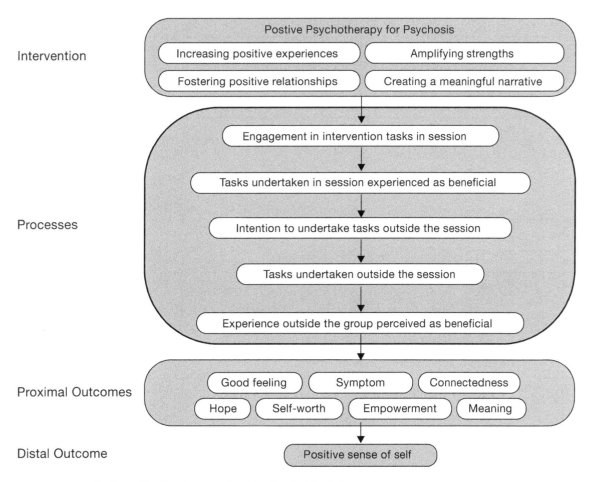

FIGURE 7.4 Positive Psychotherapy for Psychosis Model

Our qualitative research with staff and service users suggested that the following four issues may be important to keep in mind when facilitating Positive Psychotherapy for Psychosis:

1 Support positive responding

Notice and praise every success, however small it may appear. Be a role model in sessions for this interpersonal skill. Support practice through demonstrations and between-therapist role play. Encourage discussions that value relationships and social interactions. Address rather than ignore concerns about social situations if they arise, with the aim of validating and normalising social anxiety and negative experiences.

2 Be accessible

When speaking to clients, avoid theory, abstraction and didactic style. Use clear, understandable language and agree (with repeated reminders) simple

TABLE 7.1 Positive Psychotherapy for Psychosis exercises and active ingredients

Session	Exercise	Target area(s)
1	**Welcome to Positive Psychotherapy for Psychosis**	
	– Introductions, ground rules	– Positive experiences
2	**Positive Experiences**	
	– Positive responding	– Positive experiences
		– Strengths
		– Positive relationships
3	**Savouring**	
	– Consciously enjoy moments or activities	– Positive experiences
4	**Good Things**	
	– Identify good things that happened that day	– Positive experiences
5	**Personal Strengths**	
	– Identify a personal character strength	– Strengths
6	**Personal Strength Activity**	
	– Use a personal character strength	– Strengths
7	**At My Best**	
	– Overview session of progress so far	– Meaningful self-narrative
	– Strengths	
8	**One Door Closes, Another Door Opens**	
	– Negative experience with positive outcome	– Positive experiences
9, 10	**Forgiveness**	
	– Identify a person to forgive, write a letter	– Meaningful self-narrative
	– Positive relationships	
11	**Gratitude**	
	– Write a letter to someone you are grateful to	– Positive relationships
12	**Looking Back, Moving Forward**	
	– Recap, maintaining progress	– Meaningful self-narrative
	– Positive experiences	
	– Strengths	
13	**Celebration**	– Positive experiences
		– Positive relationships
		– Strengths

TABLE 7.2 Generic session structure

---

1 ENTER WITH MINDFUL SAVOURING (MUSIC PLAYS)

Invite clients to come in and sit down. Suggest they actively listen to and savour the music.

Guide clients through the exercise: slow and regulate breathing, relax, try to let go of the previous part of the day and what had captured your attention, arrive in and focus on the present and mindfully listen to the music. Content and detail of guidelines to be appropriate for client group.

---

2 WELCOME (AND RECAP)

Gain feedback on ongoing exercises, especially the exercise started in the previous session. Encourage people to share experiences. Ask for examples of what people have put in their Good Things Box and have added to their journals. Respond to stories using positive responding. Try to elicit achievements, strengths and general 'good things'. Praise small and large achievements.

---

3 WARM-UP EXERCISE

---

4 EXERCISE(S)

Introduce the rationale for the present session's exercise and explain. Distribute handouts as required.

---

5 BREAK

---

6 EXERCISE(S) (CONTINUED)

Encourage discussion after, rather than before, the exercise.

---

7 ONGOING EXERCISE

Prepare for exercise to be completed outside of session. Support action planning (When? Where? What is needed? Potential obstacles and ways around them?). Problem-solve likely barriers and express curiosity and enthusiasm.

---

8 END WITH MINDFUL SAVOURING (MUSIC PLAYS)

Invite clients to take the last moments of the session to listen to the music, and actively enjoy and savour the sounds. Provide guidance as appropriate. When the music has finished, close the session and ask clients to leave when they feel ready.

---

guidelines for the group. Emphasise organisation and structure but be flexible. It is important to assess and reflect on clients' difficulties and needs, and adapt sessions if necessary. Be personable as a therapist and share own experiences and views. Emphasise mutual acceptance and equality of all clients as well as therapists to create a safe, trusting environment.

3 Support change

Where useful, talk about your own experiences to normalise the exercises and the feelings they may generate. Focus on meaningfulness and values. Notice and use any personal interests that people mention. Ensure goals are realistic and that people find them meaningful. Identify *new* meaningful and achievable goals, that is, not things people would have done anyway, to counter avoidance behaviour among clients. Support people to find opportunities, to break down activities into small concrete steps and to anticipate and address challenges. Give affirming feedback. Avoid the word 'homework' as some people may have had difficult experiences at school.

4 *Encourage experiential learning*

Openly discuss what to expect, and anticipate negative feelings. Promote honesty and authentic curiosity about others. Provide direct individual support where necessary, but as far as possible involve all people and create an inclusive group where everyone has some voice. Listen to and remember key themes in each person's story, and use these in later sessions to promote continuity and learning. It has proven practically useful to take a brief note on each participant's story, strengths and achievements after each individual session. Be empathic and non-judgemental in your understanding, and avoid awkward personal questions. Encourage people to talk to family, friends and staff about the exercises and their impact.

Implementation

Based on our experience in implementing Positive Psychotherapy for Psychosis, we can make some recommendations for implementation.

Therapist supervision

Positive Psychotherapy for Psychosis therapists should receive regular peer supervision sessions facilitated by an experienced group therapist with at least an understanding of positive psychology principles. The aim of peer supervision is to support therapist reflection and experiential learning about the four target areas of Positive Psychotherapy for Psychosis, so that through parallel processes their development transfers into and informs their facilitation of PPT groups. The facilitator should therefore use questions that mirror the four target areas of Positive Psychotherapy for Psychosis. Example facilitator questions include:

- [Positive experiences] What are you enjoying in running your group? What was the most positive experience?
- [Strengths] When are you at your best in the group? When did you really have a chance to show your facilitation skills?
- [Relationships] Is there anything different about your relationships with clients compared with other therapy groups? When do you have the best connection with clients?
- [Narrative] Is running the group just like any other therapy group? Have you ever found yourself slipping into talking too much about symptoms?

Therapist engagement

A brief note on each participant's story, strengths and achievements should be taken after each individual session, preferably jointly by both facilitators. This can serve as a reminder to return to in later sessions and as the basis for the certificate clients receive in the last session. The process evaluation in the pilot RCT showed that clients particularly valued the sense of attentiveness and interest in the individual this conveys. Joint notes in PPT style also help to reinforce a focus on the positive, thus countering therapeutic drift.

Client engagement

Optional between-session calls are made to remind people about subsequent sessions and to check how they are progressing with their ongoing exercise. Clients are invited to reflect on the previous session's content and on their experiences with the ongoing exercise. Support with obstacles and barriers can be offered and motivational problems can be addressed. This should always be carried out using validating and motivational interviewing-based language, emphasising the gains and the learning already achieved by clients irrespective of whether they have completed their planned exercise. Pressure or critique should be avoided. This not only supports attendance and engagement; it also serves as an additional means of reflecting on content, learning and rehearsing.

The RCT process evaluation showed that between-session calls were most highly valued by clients if conducted by the main therapist. However, it is also feasible to employ a secondary therapist to conduct these calls, allowing the client to practise social interaction with a different person.

Skill maintenance and transference

Each session starts with a recap of what was covered in the last session, together with prompts where appropriate for participants to share things they have added to their Good Things Box, or to identify a successful savouring experience. To further reinforce change, it may be of benefit to offer optional ongoing booster sessions (e.g. bi-monthly or monthly for 3/6 months).

Each session is now described in detail. Timings for each part of the session are shown, and use of handouts is indicated using the symbol:

Therapist tips are included where relevant; these are found in the boxes following each exercise.

Detailed session-by-session guidelines are now given.

SESSION GUIDE

Session 1: Welcome to Positive Psychotherapy for Psychosis

Rationale

This is a session to describe Positive Psychotherapy for Psychosis to clients, and outline its main concepts and ideas. Since PPT is strengths-based, it is likely to be quite different than other more problems-based therapies that clients may have experienced. It is therefore important that time is spent in this session explaining Positive Psychotherapy for Psychosis and what clients can expect from rationale of the therapy and future sessions. Specific emphasis should also be given to the way negative experiences and emotions will be addressed and dealt with throughout the therapy, in order to counter clients' potential concern that they might be discouraged to share or address negative issues.

Time is given to an ice-breaker exercise, to enable clients to get to know each other and feel more relaxed. This is intended to encourage bonding within the group at an early stage, and make clients feel more comfortable sharing things with others in the group. Anxiety, especially social anxiety, is explicitly addressed and normalised, as are motivational problems and difficulties with concentration or drive that may be frequently encountered in this client group. Further barriers to engagement are elicited in group discussion, and the goal of the therapy to counter them in a positive and fun way is emphasised. The goal is to maximise the intention to attend future sessions.

The Positive Psychotherapy for Psychosis journals are distributed and their purpose explained. The journal is included as part of Positive Psychotherapy for Psychosis as a means of giving clients the chance to write down their thoughts, to keep a record of the exercises they complete and their progress, and to provide a reference for the content of sessions. It is brought by clients to each session.

Aims

This session aims to:

- introduce Positive Psychotherapy for Psychosis and introduce and distribute the journal; and
- increase future attendance and engagement through
- explicitly addressing concerns and unrealistic expectations about the therapy;
- giving clients the opportunity to get to know each other and the therapists and thereby reduce anxiety;
- addressing and normalising frequently encountered barriers to attendance and engagement in the client group (e.g. concentration problems, lack of drive).

Session summary

- Mindful savouring
- Warm-up: Pass the ball
- Introduction to Positive Psychotherapy for Psychosis
- Expectations
- Introducing the journal
- Ongoing exercises and questions
- Exercise: Pass the ball
- Mindful savouring

Materials needed

- Music
- Ball
- Journals containing all pages in Appendix 1
- Handout 1
- Pens and pencils

Session plan

1 ENTER WITH MINDFUL SAVOURING   5 MINUTES

Welcome clients into the room and invite them to take a seat. Explain briefly that the session will start with some relaxation time while listening to music. The following example script may be a useful starting point for therapists.

> **Example script**: 'Come in and take your time to arrive. Actively listen to and savour the music.' Pause. 'Take a breath and relax. Let go of the previous part of the day and of whatever has captured your attention before, just listen to the music: Close your eyes if you want to. Just listen to the music and let go of all other thoughts.' Pause. 'If any thoughts appear in your mind, gently let them go again and focus your attention back on the music. It is normal for our mind to wander, random thoughts come up in everybody's mind. Just remember to gently let them go again and focus on enjoying the music.' No introduction or rationale. Begin as the music stops and people settle. Discuss positives and challenges of savouring music and explain that this will be discussed in more detail in Session 3.

2 WARM-UP: PASS THE BALL   10 MINUTES

Invite clients to form a circle. Explain that this is an exercise in which people are going to get to know each other, and learn the names of others in the group. Therapists should briefly introduce themselves first. Describe the exercise: in summary, a ball game where each person passes the ball to another, and as they do so, they should say their own name aloud. Clarify that the ball can be passed along the circle or gently thrown to someone on the other side of the circle. As clients get comfortable with this, introduce a new element – instead of people saying their own name as they pass the ball, they should try to say the name of the person to whom they are throwing the ball.

> Clarify that clients can pass the ball rather than throw it. Make explicit reference to the difficulties that people may have remembering names: normalise and reiterate that it is fine to not remember.

3 INTRODUCTION TO POSITIVE PSYCHOTHERAPY FOR PSYCHOSIS   15 MINUTES

Welcome clients to the group and to Positive Psychotherapy for Psychosis. Explain what Positive Psychotherapy for Psychosis is, and how it differs from traditional psychotherapies, focusing on the fact that it is strengths-focussed rather than problems-focused. Include the focus on people's psychological assets such as character strengths, engagement, meaning and positive relationships, rather than focussing on any problems they might be experiencing.

> Emphasise that this does not mean clients cannot bring their problems to the group – it more means that the emphasis will be based at how people can use their strengths to help solve problems, and how to take positive experiences out of seemingly negative events.

 Explain that by focussing on positives rather than problems, each client can improve their overall wellbeing. Circulate and go through Handout 1.

Negative issues

Discuss how negative issues will be dealt with. Sessions 1 to 7 focus on positive things in our lives and ourselves. For example, clients identify strengths and positive resources, practice their ability to better notice the good things and to better enjoy positive experiences. Sessions 8 to 11 start to introduce more negative issues, disappointments and frustrations and use the positive strategies and strengths learnt in the earlier sessions to address these negative issues. Hence, Positive Psychotherapy for Psychosis does not prevent clients from talking about negative issues – these are even explicitly elicited in some of the sessions – but it focuses on using more positive strategies to deal with them.

Group rules

Discuss the key group rules, as appropriate for the client group and context. This may include confidentiality and its limits, group guidelines (e.g. regular attendance, punctuality, mutual respect, not interrupting people, switching off mobile phones, etc.), roles (e.g. each client to play an equal role), responsibilities (e.g. being kind to other group members and therapists) and importance of engaging with ongoing exercises.

4 BREAK   **10 MINUTES**

5 EXPECTATIONS   **15 MINUTES**

This is an opportunity for therapists to ask clients if any of them had or have any worries about the group. Frequently mentioned concerns may include social anxieties, worries about self-disclosure, concentration and motivation problems. Explicitly normalise these concerns, for example, the experience of anxiety about starting a new programme, such as those of having a weekly commitment, meeting new people, learning new things. Ask clients to share their worries, if they feel comfortable, so the group can discuss how they can deal with each of them to make the programme more enjoyable and to make attendance easier. Help clients to work through each worry together, and ask if anyone else shares the same or a similar worry to encourage normalisation and bonding.

It is likely that clients will be at different stages of their recovery. Some will find the content demanding and suffer from more illness-related obstacles, while others may find some of the content relatively easy. The past and current experiences of clients will also vary – and sometimes this can make it difficult for clients to connect with the rest of the group. Since this is a PPT group, clients are also explicitly encouraged to use their strengths and practise social skills to help and learn from each other. Therefore, emphasise that everybody can contribute positive and valuable things – we just need to give it a chance and notice it. At some points, a client may be challenged; at another point the same person may be the one who helps another client to understand something or get on with an exercise. Emphasise this mutual help as being a reason to attend rather than to drop out from the group due to differences in recovery stage.

Explicitly address potential barriers to attendance. Openly ask clients what problems they expect to encounter and discuss solutions. Barriers likely to come up in addition to the above concerns include transport problems, memory difficulties and illness-related issues (e.g. paranoia, hallucinations). Discuss how these challenges can be addressed and remember to refer back to successfully solved problems in the following sessions, for example, praising clients for remembering to come or for successfully countering their paranoid ideas. If relevant, note that the term 'psychosis' in Positive Psychotherapy for Psychosis was used in developing the approach, but doesn't require people to use or 'buy' the diagnostic label – the focus will be on living well, not on diagnosis.

6 INTRODUCING THE JOURNAL   10 MINUTES

Distribute the journals to clients. The rationale for using the journals should be discussed.

Research has shown that recording positive experiences is good for emotional and physical health.[186] Hence, the group, including the therapists, are encouraged to use the journal as much as they can, to record their experiences and engage with the exercises. Gain from the exercises will be larger the more reflection and repetition clients engage in. This means that writing down experiences in the journal will help clients to gain more from the therapy. Encouraging clients to experience a sense of ownership may also increase engagement and personal learning gains. Hence, clients are encouraged to personalise their journal and view it like a diary – as their private resource – and not like a schoolbook.

Emphasise that the journals are for each client to keep, and that they can write or draw in it to record their experiences, as they want to. Ensure that clients understand that whatever they write, draw or include in their journals is for their eyes only and is not intended to be shown to anyone else. Therefore, clients should not hold back when they express themselves and write about their experiences – since the more they open up, the more benefits they are likely to feel. If after recording their experiences, they decide they want to share them with someone close to them, they are of course encouraged to do that. Encourage clients to continue to work in their journals in their own time. Remind clients that they should bring their journals to each session, since they include the plans for each session (which they can read in advance if they wish to), and also contain their record of experiences.

> Ask clients at the end if they have any questions in relation to the use of their journals. Remind clients that they can ask the therapists at any time if they have any queries about how to best use their journals.

7 ONGOING EXERCISES AND QUESTIONS   5 MINUTES

Briefly introduce the idea of ongoing exercises and how they will be used in Positive Psychotherapy for Psychosis. Explain that the concept of ongoing exercises will be discussed more fully in the following session.

Ask clients if any of them have any questions. As the ongoing exercise for this session, invite clients to write down their thoughts about Positive Psychotherapy for Psychosis, the first session and any other questions that may come up over the following week so they can be discussed at the next session.

8 EXERCISE – PASS THE BALL   5 MINUTES

Repeat the 'Pass the Ball' exercise. Normalise any difficulties of not remembering others' names.

9 END WITH MINDFUL SAVOURING   5 MINUTES

After each session description, we follow two case studies, illustrating how fictional clients – Sally and George – responded to the session. Both case studies incorporate experiences with many real clients, and demonstrate therapist strategies.

Case studies

Sally

Sally appeared quite withdrawn and anxious when she arrived at the group, but seemed to settle down into the mindful savouring exercise well. Sally found the remembering the names of people in the group quite difficult in the warm-up exercise Pass the Ball, and was a little agitated. However, after some reassurance from the therapists that everyone was bound to find it difficult, she joined in enthusiastically.

When asked about specific worries in relation to the group, Sally said she was worried that sometimes she may not be able to complete some of the exercises and that would make her anxious, and that sometimes she may not manage to attend because of her psychotic symptoms making it difficult for her to leave the house. The therapists comforted her that the group was a supportive environment where everyone would learn together. They said that some people would find some exercises easier than others, and that this was likely to differ between people. They reassured her that she could always ask questions if things were not clear. With regard to Sally's concerns about attendance, the therapists normalised the worries about psychotic symptoms making attendance difficult at times, and said this was something they appreciated. They suggested she discuss this during each between-session telephone call so that the therapists could try to support her to attend the next session.

In the second Pass the Ball exercise, Sally was pleased since she had remembered nearly everyone's names! She seemed to engage with the mindful savouring exercise and said she was looking forward to coming to the next session since most of her worries had been allayed.

William

William was jovial when he arrived to join the group and seemed to be comfortable talking to the other clients and the therapists. He was quite restless during the mindful savouring exercise and despite encouragement to close his eyes and listen to the music, he spent most of the time looking around the room and jiggling his legs. William joined in the Pass the Ball warm-up with enthusiasm, and although he didn't get everyone's names correct, he laughed when he got it wrong, which created a good-humoured atmosphere within the group.

William said he didn't have any particular concerns now that he had joined the group, but that he had previously been anxious about attending the first session. He listened intently to the other members when they voiced their concerns. He said the only thing that may hinder his attendance was his lack of organisation, and that sometimes he forgot about arrangements he had made. The therapists asked if a call the day before and a reminder during the between-session call may be of help in this respect. He agreed and this was noted.

William seemed proud that he had remembered everyone's names in the second Pass the Ball exercise. He appeared more relaxed in the mindful savouring exercise although seemed to struggle with concentrating on listening to the music.

Session 2: Positive Experiences

Rationale

Positive responding teaches clients to respond in an active and constructive manner to good news from friends and family. Studies have shown that positive responding (also known as active constructive responding) benefits both the individuals in the conversation and the relationship between these people.[187] Responding positively to someone elicits a positive response back from other people. This can increase positive feelings for each other and can help build relationships over time. However, the other three response styles are negatively related to wellbeing for both the person with the good news and your relationship with the individual.

The idea of clients sharing a time at which they were at their best helps to remind clients of their strengths, their values, what they enjoy, and things they are good at. This can foster a positive sense of self, which can be useful in managing mood, by elevating self-esteem, fostering self-kindness and providing a basis for better social relationships. However, it should be remembered that such an exercise can also provoke difficult feelings, especially when done the first time. This can be a powerful way of realising that self-respect is something one has to get used to. It is common for people to feel strange when publicly praising themselves – but it is something that can be practised and that can lead to a more positive outlook.

Aims

This session aims to:

a   understand the concept of positive responding;
b   start to practise seeing oneself in a positive light by thinking about a time when they have been 'at their best';
c   introduce ongoing exercises.

Session summary

- Mindful savouring
- Warm-up: One Thing about You
- Introducing positive responding
- Exercise: At My Best
- Introducing ongoing exercises
- Mindful savouring

Materials needed

- Music
- Flipchart (prepared as set out below), pens and scissors
- Blu-Tack
- Handout 2
- Pens and pencils

Session plan

1 ENTER WITH MINDFUL SAVOURING   5 MINUTES

2 WELCOME AND RECAP   5 MINUTES

Invite clients to share any question or concerns they noted down about the group after the last session and briefly discuss.

3 WARM-UP: ONE THING ABOUT YOU   10 MINUTES

Bring the flipchart into the group, having divided the sheet as follows before the session:

NAME	PICTURE

Explain that this is an exercise where the group gets to know a little bit more about each of the members. Invite each person to write their name in one of the boxes on the left side of the sheet, draw a picture of something that describes something about themselves in the box to the right and briefly explain to the group what they have drawn and what it says about them. Emphasise that the pictures are not intended to be accurate or detailed – just an outline is fine! Therapists should complete the exercise first, and ensure that the pictures they choose are small, accessible and capable of being drawn (and recognised!) easily for example, a cat if they like cats, a cake if they like cakes or a football if they enjoy playing or watching football. Once all members of the group have participated, the therapists should quickly cut down each of the boxes so there is a pile of names and a pile of pictures. One at a time, the therapists should select a picture, fix it to the flipchart with blue-tack and ask the group to remember to whom this picture belongs. When this has been guessed correctly, the name should be stuck next to the picture and the exercise continued until all pictures have been correctly associated with a member of the group. End by congratulating all members on sharing something about themselves, and that you hope everyone feels they know everyone a little bit better now.

Therapists should normalise the experience of finding it difficult to draw an image, and humour may be included as an important part of this exercise!

4 INTRODUCING POSITIVE RESPONDING   10 MINUTES

Describe the concept of positive responding, and explain that the way we respond to other people in a conversation is important for how we feel about the other person and also about ourselves. Therapists should role-play the various ways in which people can react to another in a conversation. See over for guidelines.

Discuss what clients think about positive responding in the group. It is likely that some people will find it demanding, while others will find it trivial. Present this as an opportunity to learn from each other. Normalise the fact that sometimes apparently small or self-evident things can change a lot.

Explain that positive responding is encouraged as the mode of responding to each other throughout the course of the therapy. This will serve to internalise and practice positive responding. Therapists do a role-play of different ways to respond when a friend tells you that he/she has managed to get some part-time voluntary work:

Passive constructive	*That's nice, that you are volunteering*
Passive destructive	*Oh. Remind me again when we are going to the cinema next week?*
Active destructive	*But if you start volunteering, I won't be able to see you as much.*
Active constructive	*That is wonderful! I am so happy for you. You will be an excellent volunteer! What will the work involve?*

Give out Handout 2 and discuss the different ways of responding to good news.

5 EXERCISE: AT MY BEST   20 MINUTES

This is an exercise where clients share with the group a time when they have felt pleased or proud of something they have done or something that has happened. People may tend to remember negative events and emotions more than positive ones, because bad events signal the need to change and therefore are remembered, whereas pleasurable events give little incentive to advance and therefore are more easily forgotten. This preferential memory for negative events has an adverse impact on how we feel and consequently on how we relate to other people. The group is going to do an exercise that encourages everyone to move away from negativity and think about things positively – that is, to notice the good instead of the bad things about ourselves. Ask each person to spend a few minutes thinking about a time they were 'at their best' – a time when they felt proud of themselves. Therapists should clarify the idea further by giving a personal example of an experience about a time when they were 'at their best' to guide clients about the types of things they could think about. In doing so, therapists should also acknowledge that it can be very difficult to tell a purely positive story about oneself and normalise this experience.

> Therapists should keep their stories and responses brief and use small, accessible examples.

---

6 BREAK   5 MINUTES

7 EXERCISE: AT MY BEST *continued*   20 MINUTES

After the break, invite people to feed back their stories to the entire group. Encourage clients to describe what the positive story tells about themselves, for example, in terms of strengths. Encourage feedback from the other group clients using positive responding.

Allow as many stories to be told as is possible within the timeframe.

Therapists should respond to people positively and emphasise strengths that arise from clients' stories. If clients find this challenging, therapists may find it helpful to ask them to consider what others might say about them.

8 INTRODUCING ONGOING EXERCISES   5 MINUTES

Explain that coming to the group, listening and taking part in the exercises are all great things to do and will help to increase clients' wellbeing. However, it should be emphasised that in order to make an even bigger difference to their lives, clients are encouraged to carry on some of these exercises outside of the group. Briefly describe the purpose of ongoing exercises, and explain that there will be an ongoing exercise for each session, which will usually be started together in the session, with an opportunity for clients to continue it in their own time.

The ongoing exercise for this week is to note down a positive story 'at my best' in the journal. People can use the same example as used in the group or think of a new one. Those who haven't had a chance to tell their story to the group will be invited to do so in the following week's recap session. Emphasise that drawing or painting is also invited in case somebody doesn't want to write – or indeed any other form of artwork that enables the person to remember and tell the story next week. Also emphasise that nobody will be forced to tell their story, but simply encouraged to do so if they wish.

9 END WITH MINDFUL SAVOURING   **5 MINUTES**

Case studies

Sally

Sally seemed to really enjoy the 'One Thing about You' exercise – showing a talent for drawing. She decided to draw some flowers – and said this represented the fact that she really enjoyed being in her garden. Others in the group complimented her on her artistic skill. She recalled other people's drawings easily and seemed more comfortable speaking in the group.

Sally was quiet when the therapists introduced positive responding, and didn't seem to have any questions. When probed, she said she thought it was a good idea but something she would do naturally anyway. The therapists said that it may well be the case that some people do this instinctively, and commended her for this.

For her example of when she had been 'at her best', Sally provided an example, which suggested that she didn't fully understand the concept. She talked about a time when she had been in hospital and there hadn't been any beds left for her. As a result, she had a horrible time because she had to move beds every day for a week, which she found hard. However, she said after a week the hospital found her a bed and she was very happy about this. The therapists encouraged her to see a positive in the story and to reflect more on it from the perspective of a time she was proud of – that despite the challenges she faced at a time when she was ill, she believed in herself and focussed on getting better, which would be a time when she was 'at her best'.

William

William was enthusiastic about the 'One Thing about You' exercise – and drew a picture of a lots of stick people, of different sizes. He explained this represented the fact that he was part of a large family, three brothers and two sisters, and that he loved them all very much. When the therapists asked if he saw them often, he said he wasn't very good at seeing them because he often forgot arrangements he had made to meet them. The therapists suggested that maybe that was something he could work on during the course of the sessions, and William agreed.

William seemed to understand the concept of positive responding, and after seeing the therapists role-play the different responses, said that it really made him happy when other people showed interest in what he was saying and responded positively. He said he would try to do more of this.

William's example of a time when he had been 'at his best' was when he was able to put into practice a skill he had learnt, of taking a step back in difficult situations and not automatically confronting people. He said this was a time a few months ago when his ex-wife was being argumentative, which frustrated him. He said he decided to let her say what she wanted to, acknowledge he had heard it and wanted a few days to think about what she had said. He recognised he had become more mature in this way. The therapists asked if this had been difficult for him – he said it had been since there had been lots of things he had wanted to say in response, but he reflected on it after and was happy he had not said those things and had instead given himself a chance to 'cool off'. The therapists and several clients praised him for his efforts.

Session 3: Savouring

Rationale

This session focuses on a technique called 'savouring'. Savouring involves consciously and actively enjoying experiences or activities. The concept of savouring overlaps with that of mindfulness: the former concentrating on positive experiences in the past, present and future, and the latter focussing on only the present. Research has shown that noticing and thinking about positive events in our lives increases positive emotions, wellbeing and optimism for the future. Stresses of life can affect everything from our health, diet and work, to our communities, relationships and the environment. As a result, we might feel anxious and tired. Research shows that when people are in a relaxed state, the brain moves into a deeper, richer, mode of thought. Savouring can help us to shift gears and slow down a little. As a result, we are better able to more consciously enjoy the things we encounter. Encouraging relaxation lowers your heart rate, slows your breathing rate and reduces cortisol levels (stress hormones). It can also improve concentration and mood. Relaxation has also been linked to physical health gains, including medical symptoms, sensory pain, physical impairment and functional quality of life.[188] Further, increasing relaxation can in turn increase concentration and academic achievement.[189]

Isen and colleagues found that not only does positive affect generate more expansive cognitive thinking but such thinking may be responsible for the finding that positive affect facilitates memory and creative thought.[190] Further, Fredrickson's Broaden-and-Build Theory,[191] developed on the basis of the findings by Isen and colleagues, states that positive emotions broaden people's momentary thought-action repertoires and build their enduring personal resources. Fredrickson and Losada also demonstrated that positive affect can lead to human flourishing, suggesting its influence on subjective wellbeing.[192] Bryant found that beliefs about savouring were positively correlated with present happiness, intensity and frequency of happiness and affect intensity.[171] As people savoured more experiences, negative affect and social anhedonia decreased.

Aims

This session aims to help clients:

a understand the idea of savouring and its values for mental health; and
b practise savouring of food and music.

Session summary

- Mindful savouring
- Recap of experiences
- Introducing savouring
- Exercise: Mindful eating
- Ongoing exercise: Savouring in your own time
- Exercise: Mindful listening

Materials needed

- Music
- Handouts 3 and 4
- Pens and pencils
- Food: Popcorn, chocolate (small pieces, e.g. bar broken into cubes), grapes or other fruit in small pieces
- Drinks: cups of fizzy drinks, juice or water

Session plan

1 ENTER WITH MINDFUL SAVOURING   5 MINUTES

2 WELCOME AND RECAP   10 MINUTES

Encourage clients to share their 'at my best' stories and how they felt about thinking about the stories writing them down, and about telling them in the group. Elicit problems that were encountered, ask the group to respond to them, normalise and praise achievements.

Therapists should not pressurise clients into contributing, and ask for and encourage volunteers only. Be aware that some participants may only find negative stories or only negative aspects in their story. Therapists should normalise this experience and try to find positive achievement worthy of praise in apparently negative stories.

3 INTRODUCING SAVOURING   10 MINUTES

Since savouring is a central theme in Positive Psychotherapy for Psychosis, spend some time explaining the concept to clients. Introduce the aims of the session as above and discuss the idea of savouring. For example, savouring means consciously and actively enjoying experiences or activities.

Explain how savouring can be useful in everyday life, and briefly describe how research supports this notion.

Savouring can be experienced using each of the five senses (sight, hearing, taste, smell and touch) and give examples for each, for example, sight – looking at a beautiful sunset, hearing – listening to a favourite piece of music, taste – eating a delicious piece of cake, smell – smelling a bunch of flowers and touch – stroking a cat.

There are some easy guidelines that clients can use to support their savouring experiences and circulate Handout 3. Discuss each of the guidelines and the examples. Also explain that it is often easier to savour small things to start with, to get a feel for what savouring feels like and how it can be useful.

Finally, explain that in this session we will focus on savouring food and also music. Other areas in which savouring can be applied will also be discussed. Ask if clients have any questions about the concept of savouring.

Therapists should anticipate that some clients may experience inner barriers against enjoyment and may also find the concept of savouring difficult to understand. Therapists should seek to normalise both positive and negative emotions. Emphasis should be placed on the understanding that enjoyment can be very personal.

Some participants may be averse to specific foods, on special diets, or have eating problems. Make sure you offer a range of foods so that at least one thing is likely suitable for everybody.

4 EXERCISE: MINDFUL EATING   15 MINUTES

This is an exercise that aims to encourage people to think about how to savour items of food. The exercise starts with the clients and therapists savouring some food together. Make it clear that clients do not have to eat the food if they don't want to, but they can still follow the savouring instructions. Introduce the foods that are going to be savoured, for example, popcorn, chocolate and grapes, and therapists should place the food on a table in the middle of the group (if they didn't choose to place the food here at the start of the session). Emphasise that what is important is that clients very slowly and consciously enjoy this experience. Invite clients to pick one piece of food and put the food in their hand and concentrate on it. Ask clients to observe the texture and notice the way it feels in their hands. Suggest that clients look at the difference between light and shade, the structure, surface, smell, their own reaction to the food (e.g. salivation).

Therapists could use the following script to help guide this exercise:

Slowly lift it towards your mouth. Focus on slowing down your pace and doing everything gradually. A gradual slowing down of pace is better than screeching to a halt. Start with a small decrease and gradually reduce it. Observe the way this feels. Are you salivating? Put it in your mouth. Observe how it tastes and how it feels. How does it feel on your tongue? How does the texture change? Be mindful of every step. You don't have to eat it if you don't wish to – just observe the way it feels and looks in your hand. How does the light and shade look in the palm of your hand? Feel the weight of it.

Therapists should ask clients to share how they felt about savouring their item of food. They should ask if anyone found the process difficult and also what people were able to take away from the process. Discuss how savouring food – or at least some bites of a meal – might change the experience of eating for clients. Ask clients how the exercise may have changed the way they feel and think about food and themselves.

5 BREAK   10 MINUTES

6 ONGOING EXERCISE: SAVOURING
(MINDFUL DRINKING)   15 MINUTES

Either continue by inviting participants to choose another type of food, or change to mindful drinking. Example script: 'We are going to think about applying the savouring skills we learned in the first part of the session to drinking. We have fizzy drinks, juice, and water.' Hand out drinks. 'Again, you do not have to drink. You can just observe the way the cup feels in your hand or notice how the light reflects on the liquid. If you wish to drink, notice how the liquid feels in your mouth and observe the differences between the liquid and the solid food. Does it taste sweet or sour? Is it cold? Can you feel bubbles?' Repeat if time allows.

7 ONGOING EXERCISE: SAVOURING
(MINDFUL LISTENING)   15 MINUTES

Example script: 'We have had some food and drink. Now we are going to think about applying savouring to other things. Let's all be very quiet and concentrate on the quietness and try to enjoy it. Or if we hear sounds, let's listen to what they are. What can we hear? What are the sounds in this room? Can we hear sounds from outside? If you we hear any sounds, let's try to take them as they are, mindfully, without naming them but try to savour and enjoy them, just as you did with the food and drink. Is the sound high or deep? Does it vibrate? Does it change in intensity? Does it have a pattern? Can you enjoy the experience of hearing it? Is it a nice sound? And if your thoughts wander off, or if you don't enjoy the sound, just take your mind gently and slowly back to the room and to the listening.' Pause for reflection. Savouring in your own time. Distribute Handout 4.

'I would like you to think about other potential savouring experiences you may enjoy in your own time. Pick one or two areas where you usually hurry through and slow those areas down. This could be eating the first three bites of a meal slowly and mindfully. Focus on peaceful experiences. This might be when you are in the garden, out walking the dog, following floating clouds with your eyes, watching the sunset, feeling the breeze blow, hearing and enjoying the sound and feel of the wind, drinking a cup of coffee in the morning. Try to think about savouring these experiences in a slow, mindful way. Make a note of savouring plans and experiences in your Handout. You might like to pick a particular sense to attend to, for example, touch or sounds. How does it feel when the water touches your skin in the shower? What do the birds sound like when you are walking in the park? Make a reminder note of any planned savouring activities in your journal.' Discuss possible savouring opportunities.

Some people may be sensitive about food (e.g. weight issues, eating disorders, paranoia). People may find it challenging to concentrate for long periods so offer breaks. Ask people to suggest examples that they might enjoy. Let people 'find out' what they enjoy. Identify 'common tastes' in the group. Emphasise small pleasurable things (e.g. cup of tea, crossword, the sunshine). Be aware of pleasurable but harmful activities (avoid word 'pleasure'). Some people may find hearing voices challenging during mindfulness of sounds.

8 END WITH MINDFUL SAVOURING   5 MINUTES

Case studies

Sally

Sally got on well with the recap. She wrote about a time when she had been 'at her best', which was different from the example she had used during the session. She wrote about a time a few weeks ago when she had bought her daughter a delicious cake from the market, and walked it around to her even though it was pouring with rain. Sally said this showed how generous she was and how much she made an effort to do something nice for her daughter. Several clients spoke about how nice this was of Sally, and the therapists suggested that Sally add to her account what it had taught her about herself (i.e. that she was generous and willing to make a considerable effort to do something nice for someone).

She seemed curious about the concept of savouring and clearly understood the concept, contributing some useful examples at the beginning of the discussion. Sally chose a grape for the mindful eating exercise, and followed the instructions well. When asked how the experience of savouring a grape had been for her, she said she had really enjoyed it and it made her realise that she usually just ate while doing other things and didn't take the time to really notice the taste and textures. She said it tasted sweeter than she would have thought and noticed the mottled colouring on one area of the grape. Sally chose a piece of popcorn for the second part of the exercise, and said she hadn't realised how much like polystyrene the texture of popcorn was! She also noted that popcorn made a 'funny' noise when she bent it and that she realised she didn't particularly like the taste so wouldn't be having it again!

Sally appeared to have a good grasp of the concept of savouring, and was happy to contribute her ideas for what she could savour that week. She said she would really savour the experience of having a long bath, with bubble bath, and think about the feeling of the water and the bubbles, as well as the smells. She also said she really enjoyed baking, so would savour the experience of baking some biscuits, the texture of the mixture and the smell of the biscuits cooking.

She recognised the fact that savouring needs to be practised regularly to have a beneficial effect – but right from the start, she was able to see the benefits, which for her would be a calming down and blocking out her voices in a positive way. The prospect of this elevated her mood.

William

In the recap, William explained he had written about his example that he had given in the previous session, about when he had been 'at his best'. When prompted, he said writing it down had made him realise how far he had come and how proud he was of putting a skill into practice. He also noted other occasions where he felt he had benefited from taking a step back. The therapists encouraged him make a note of his reflections and how they made him feel.

William contributed enthusiastically to the discussion on savouring guidelines and examples of savouring activities. He thought savouring could be easily applied to basically any aspect of life. His openness, enthusiasm and his striving to enjoy life seemed to resonate very well with the concept.

William chose a piece of chocolate for the mindful eating exercise, however within a few seconds he had eaten the chocolate, even before the activity had properly started! He was asked if he wanted to take another piece of chocolate and hold it in his hand and follow the mindfulness exercise along with the therapists. Even though it was hard for him to resist the urge to just eat the chocolate, he followed the instructions successfully. Afterwards, he found it difficult to describe how the savouring of the chocolate had felt for him. With some probing from the therapists and after hearing the thoughts of other group members, William offered some relevant insights into how savouring the chocolate had felt for him. He said while difficult to start with, he really felt he had tasted the chocolate and didn't usually notice the flavour but that he did during this exercise. He said he also really appreciated the smooth texture and how it melted when he had left it in his mouth. William then chose a grape, and followed the savouring process well, making some perceptive remarks about the different textures of the skin and the inside of the grape, and the sound made when he squeezed it.

William initially appeared to misunderstand the concept of savouring and instead suggested a list of activities he enjoyed, rather than experiences which he could necessarily savour. His bubbly and energetic nature made it difficult for him to understand the value of slowing down and being mindful of every aspect of an experience, however small it may be. However, after further discussion and with help and feedback from the rest of the group, William seemed to understand the concept and provided some interesting examples: enjoying a walk through his local park, looking at and smelling the new flowers that had been planted and spending ten minutes in the morning listening to the birds from his bedroom window.

William seemed to engage more with the mindful listening exercise than with the food, and closed his eyes and appeared to visibly relax his body. In the following weeks he said he really enjoyed savouring music, and had in fact started to do it more at home. He said he sometimes drifted off and started thinking about other things, and found the therapists' directions to bring your mind back to the music very helpful.

Session 4: Good Things

Rationale

The theory underlying the assumed mechanisms of PPT maintains that humans are predisposed to attend (both cognitively and affectively) to threat alert. This is thought to confer evolutionary advantage – as earlier and more prominent awareness of threat leads to higher likelihood of survival. The tendency to attend to negative experiences, such as threat, loss and trespass, may explain why negative things attract human attention and memory more easily than positive ones. In consequence, humans are biased towards the negative.[138] The theory that depressed individuals exaggerate this natural tendency has also been proposed by other influential researchers.

This tendency to notice negative things rather than positives has been called the cognitive bias of depression by Aaron Beck who developed CBT for depression,[193] and this cognitive bias is connected to feeling low about the past, in the present and with respect to future expectations. However, nowadays – from an evolutionary perspective – it is not necessary for our survival to expect the worst at any time because we are reasonably safe. So the protective effect is lost and just the depressive view of the world and ourselves remains and has a negative impact on mood and on our relationship with other people.

People often spend far more time thinking about things that have gone wrong than they do in enjoying what has gone right. Such a way of thinking can discourage positive thinking and can instead lead to a cycle of rumination. Rumination in psychosis has been associated with negative symptoms and therefore reducing rumination and encouraging thinking about positive things in life may help to reduce negative symptoms such as anxiety and depression. Consciously thinking about what is going well in life, as well as taking small steps to encourage recollection of these events in the future, can protect against low mood and help engender a more positive outlook.

There is evidence that thinking about good things can increase happiness and decrease depressive symptoms. In one of Seligman's first experiments, he tested the efficacy of a 'three good things' exercise.[120] Clients were asked to log onto a website daily for seven days and list three things that went well on that day and why they happened. Clients showed an increase in happiness and decrease in depressive symptoms over six months post-intervention. Replications and adaptations of the 'three good things' exercise in later research has also yielded favourable results.[145,194]

Success has been seen in other therapies that include the collecting of items that reflect positive things in a person's life, to act as a memory aid when things are difficult. For example, similar to the Good Things Box introduced in this session, cognitive therapy sometimes uses a Hope Kit – which can contain pictures of loved ones, reminders of positive experiences.

Further, Positive Psychotherapy for Psychosis also focuses on clients recognising what they have done themselves to make the good thing happen.

Doing so can help reduce depressive feelings of hopelessness and helplessness and give clients a sense of their independence. When clients realise that they have taken an active role in making something positive happen (even if this is just 'pulling myself together, getting dressed and leaving the house'), this can foster a higher internal locus of control and motivation. This motivation to take on activities is very important for people with psychosis who experience negative symptoms.

Aims

This session aims to:

a help clients appreciate how helpful it can be to think about and record good things that have happened to them and look back on these in the future (to try to counter any negative thoughts); and

b introduce the idea of the Good Things Box and Good Things Cards as resources that can be used not only during sessions but can continue to be used going forward.

Session summary

- Mindful savouring
- Recap of experiences with savouring and journal
- Warm-up: Stand up who . . .
- Ongoing exercise: Good things
- Mindful savouring

Materials needed

- Music
- Handouts 5 (one copy per client) and 6 (two copies per client)
- Pens and pencils
- Choice of Good Things Boxes

Session plan

1 ENTER WITH MINDFUL SAVOURING	5 MINUTES

2 WELCOME AND RECAP	10 MINUTES

Encourage clients to feed back examples of savouring and discuss their experiences and how they got on with their journal.

Therapists should probe examples of savouring given by some clients, ensuring that examples are not just of experiences that clients have enjoyed, but are also those where the client has consciously made an effort to slow things down and really think about how they felt at that time. Many clients may also have chosen to savour food or drink, since this is often an experience with which people are more familiar. Encourage clients to continue with savouring other things (e.g. a walk in the park) during the course of the sessions and note down their experiences in their journal.

3 WARM-UP: STAND UP WHO . . .   20 MINUTES

This is an exercise that aims to encourage people to think about the pleasant things that they like doing.

Part 1

Introduce the warm-up exercise as a way of familiarising everyone with the concept of thinking about pleasant things that people like to do. Explain to clients that one of the therapists will start off by saying 'Stand up who . . .', and that if the statement applies to them, they are invited to stand up (or raise a hand if they can't send up for physical reasons). Give some examples comprising activities, not personal strengths, for example, 'Stand up who . . . has ever been to the seaside . . . enjoys sitting in the sun on a spring day . . . likes football . . . enjoys being with friends . . . enjoys going to the museum', etc. Check that everyone understands before commencing.

Therapist examples during the exercise should focus on good things, and should begin and end as inclusively as possible, with more specific, individualistic statements occurring in the middle and should be mindful to ensure that all clients have at least one example which applies to them.

Part 2

Encourage clients to repeat the exercise by standing up themselves in turn and coming up with their own examples and others who identify with the statement can stand up too.

Therapists should also take part in this exercise, and use this opportunity to provide examples that they feel some clients will identify with. Therapists should encourage all clients to suggest their own examples. Therapists should conclude briefly by asking clients for feedback as to how they found the exercise, being mindful that some clients may have found coming up with their own examples very challenging and may need support to do so.

4 BREAK   **10 MINUTES**

5 ONGOING EXERCISE: GOOD THINGS   **30 MINUTES**

This is an exercise in which we start to look at some of the good or positive things that happen, what clients have done to make these good things happen and how helpful it can be to remember these in the future.

Introduce the rationale for this session to the clients, and link this with the warm-up exercises and the previous session in which savouring positive experiences was looked at. Explain that both the warm-up exercise and the ongoing exercise can help clients identify specific examples of things they enjoy doing, that is, good things. This helps to avoid defensive thinking styles and aids clients who may have trouble finding something they enjoy. Noticing what they have actively contributed themselves to make the good thing happen increases clients' sense of empowerment and a more internal locus of control. This can increase motivation and confidence, and help people get more active. Therapists should each talk about a good thing that has happened to them recently, using positive responding.

> Therapist examples should be small and accessible, for example, 'I started/ finished reading a book last evening' or 'I enjoyed having coffee with a friend at the weekend'.

Good Things Boxes and Good Things Cards

Introduce the Good Things Boxes and explain to clients that these are being given to them to keep as a place to put reminders of good things that happen to them. Invite the clients to pick a box that they want. Describe how the box can be used: clients can collect objects that represent a good thing that has happened (e.g. a picture from a paper to represent that they have enjoyed reading something, a sugar bag from a café to represent that they have enjoyed having a cup of tea there). They are free to personalise the boxes as they wish. Introduce the Good Things Cards using Handout 5.

Explain that these can be used to make a short note of a good thing that has happened to you that day as an alternative to putting an object into the box. Make clear the rationale for using the Good Things Box – as a reminder of positive experiences so the boxes can be opened, prompting recall of past positive events, which can lift mood and encourage hope and optimism. It also acts as a reminder of their own power to make good things happen. So it is important to write down briefly what they did themselves to make the good thing happen. Remind clients that it is important to put a little note on collected items to remind about when, where and why they were chosen – this will help them remember the good thing later. Give out copies of Handout 6 to each client for their Good Things Box.

Ask clients to try to think of at least one good thing that has happened to them in the past few days. Emphasise that good things can be small (such as going for a nice walk or enjoying a meal) as well as being bigger (such as enjoying a birthday gathering with some friends). Ask clients to fill out a Good Things Card for each good thing they come up and to put these in their Good Things Box. Explain the importance of also thinking about what clients have done to make these good things happen. For example, meeting a friend for a coffee would mean a client has likely made contact with the friend, agreed to go for coffee, been motivated enough to leave the house, arranged how to get to where they are meeting and have spent time with their friend. Emphasise how important it is that clients do not underestimate how much they have done to make each good thing happen and that they note this down on all Good Things Cards they complete, together with the date that good thing happened. Make it clear that any piece of paper can be used instead of a Good Things Card. They should also be encouraged to do the same for items they put into their Good Things Box, and can do this in their journal.

Using Good Things Boxes and Good Things Cards going forward

Discuss how clients can make the best use of their Good Things Box and Good Things Cards going forward. Explain that this is not something just to be continued during the therapy, but the intention is that clients continue to use their Good Things Box going forward after completion of the therapy. Encourage clients to set some time during each day (maybe at the same time each day to make it a habit, e.g. just before bed) during which they can spend a few minutes reflecting on good things that have happened that day and either add an object to their Good Things Box or fill in a Good Things Card. Suggest that keeping the Good Things Box in a prominent place may make remembering to think about good things a bit easier, and that for some people it may be beneficial to enlist the help of friends or family to remember good things and add to the Good Things Box.

Say that there will be a short discussion at the beginning of the next session where clients can share with the group some of the things they have put in their Good Things Box over the last week, and that some time at the beginning of each session will be spent seeing how people are getting on with their Good Things Box. Tell clients that they will also be invited to bring their Good Things Box to the last session to show the group some of the things they managed to add to their boxes.

> Therapists should try to normalise the experience of having no good things on some days but invite people to continually look through their journal and in their Good Things Box to remind themselves of good experiences they have had. Explain that it is often difficult at the start to think about good things each day. People often have high expectations, but big things happen only rarely. The goal of this exercise also is to notice the small good

things that make our every days better and more positive – such as using the savouring skills they learned last session. Encourage people to be creative in recording good things, especially for those who may find reading and writing challenging (e.g. using more objects, drawing and painting, cutting out pictures). Be sensitive to clients having difficult personal or home lives. Be aware that some clients may require more support than others to identify good things and that for some clients, remembering good things may also be depressing. This dialectic of positive and negative should be acknowledged and clients supported to embrace the positive side of an experience even though sadness or disappointment may also come with it.

6 END WITH MINDFUL SAVOURING   **5 MINUTES**

Case studies

Sally

Sally found this a difficult session to engage with. A naturally shy person, she seemed to find the warm-up exercise daunting, especially at the beginning where she did not stand up very often in response to suggested examples of activities people may like doing. She appeared to find it helpful when one of the therapists explained during the course of the exercise that it was normal for people to not have participated in a lot of the activities before, and that people should not feel bad if they had not stood or put their hands up very often. After this, her demeanour changed to be a lot more positive. When the exercise moved on to clients suggesting their own examples of things they liked doing, it took a lot of encouragement for Sally to contribute her own examples. When the difficulties for clients thinking of their own examples were discussed, Sally said that she didn't feel like there was anything she really enjoyed doing. After further support from the therapists, explaining that often these were very small things, rather than big events, and giving some examples, for example, watching a favourite TV programme, Sally offered a few of her own examples and seemed pleased when other clients stood up and agreed that they found such activities enjoyable.

Sally was excited about the prospect of having a Good Things Box and chose her box happily. When one of the therapists asked everyone to think about a good thing that had happened over the last few days, Sally ventured that she couldn't really think of anything. With some prompting and on listening to examples of other clients, she wrote briefly about how much she enjoyed seeing a friend who came around for dinner. She struggled to make the link between the good thing and how she had made that happen. The therapist normalised this by saying often people under-emphasise the things they had done to make that good things happen. One of the therapists suggested that Sally had actually had to do many things to make this good thing happen: contacting a friend, buying the food and preparing the dinner, and not cancelling the meeting even when she didn't feel like seeing her friend. Sally embraced these suggestions and agreed that she had taken steps that had made the good thing happen. Sally seemed happy to carry on the activity at home.

William

William approached the warm-up activity with enthusiasm. He stood up in response to a lot of examples, and was happy to offer appropriate examples himself when asked. He also followed the lead of the therapists and responded positively to many of the clients when they came up with their own examples.

He picked a Good Things Box and quickly completed four Good Things Cards in the session. When invited to share what good things he had chosen for his Good Things Cards, it became apparent that William was picking examples of what he had done or accomplished over the last few last few days (for example, making dinner or going shopping), rather than thinking specifically about something which was good or pleasurable. The therapists initiated a brief group discussion about the differences between activities that people simply get done and those 'good things' that enrich one's life. The therapists acknowledged that accomplishing tasks and activities obviously may take an effort and getting things done warrants self-praise, satisfaction and pride. However, 'good things' are those things that you can consciously think about as a positive experience and one that you enjoyed. These may be small things, but they may be larger things, such as a birthday party. The therapist probed as to which of William's examples he had really enjoyed doing and could be something he could remember in the future to remind himself of a good thing that had happened. On reflection, William chose one activity – going to a painting class at his local day centre. He changed what he had done to make the good thing happen from 'going to the class' to 'checking the timetable for classes, getting organised to go, getting on the bus and arriving on time, being sociable with other people in the class'. William seemed pleased and even proud when he thought about what he had done in order to go to the painting class, and said he would carry on the activity at home.

Session 5: Personal Strengths

Rationale

Simply identifying your key strengths is said to be able to help an individual develop a more strengths-based, positive identity.[195] This helps people to separate their sense of self from negative events in their life. Further, awareness of one's strengths also helps people to develop goals congruent with their strengths – therefore doing what people naturally do best.[196]

Research shows that strengths enable us to act in ways that contribute to our wellbeing and the wellbeing of others. Character strengths (e.g. kindness, teamwork, zest) are distinguished from talents and abilities. Athleticism, photographic memory, perfect pitch manual dexterity and physical agility are examples of talents and abilities. Strengths have moral features, whereas talents and abilities do not. Increasing awareness of strengths encourages people to more effectively apply themselves at work and at play by approaching tasks in a way that better uses their abilities. In turn, doing better at things can lead to an upward spiral of engagement and positive emotion. Positive emotion can encourage optimal functioning and enhanced social openness.[197] Research suggests that initial positive emotional experiences predict future positive emotional experiences, by broadening cognition, positive coping repertoires and increasing interpersonal trust.[198]

Using your strengths can put you in a 'flow state' – where you are absorbed and interested in the task at hand and it is appropriately challenging but not too difficult. Flow is characterised by intense concentration, loss of self-awareness, a feeling of being perfectly challenged (neither bored nor overwhelmed) and a sense 'time is flying'. Flow is intrinsically rewarding; it can also assist in the achievement of goals (e.g. winning a game) or improving skills (e.g. becoming a better chess player). Anyone can experience flow, in different domains, such as play, creativity and work. Flow is achieved when the challenge of the situation meets one's personal abilities and therefore using your strengths can put you in a slow state. This can encourage the feeling of achievement and satisfaction and help to give meaning in life.

However, overusing strengths can also be detrimental. It is important to see that some of the negative things in our life actually stem from overusing a strength. For example, overusing the strength of curiosity can turn into nosiness and provoke rejection from other people. Realising this and viewing critique in a more positive way (that is, as an overuse of a strength) can make it less hurtful and easier to change (positive reframing). For example, there may be a way to more constructively use curiosity. Overusing strengths may also have negative consequences; for example, kindness may lead to exploitation by other people. Viewing the feeling that others always take advantage of oneself as an expression of your strength rather than your weakness can be empowering and make it easier for people to, for example, assert themselves better. This session will explain why it is important that clients know, realise and practise their strengths but at the same time do not overuse their personal character strengths.

Aims

This session aims to:

a   explore character strengths and why recognising them is beneficial;
b   discuss how overuse of strengths can have a negative impact; and
c   help clients identify a personal character strength they possess and find a way to further develop it.

Session summary

- Mindful savouring
- Recap of experiences with Good Things Box
- Warm-up: The Last Roll
- Exercise: Personal Strengths
- Ongoing exercise: Identifying a personal character strength
- Mindful savouring

Materials needed

- Music
- Handout 7
- Strengths pictures (shown in Appendix 3)
- Rolls of toilet paper
- Pen and pencils

Session plan

1 ENTER WITH MINDFUL SAVOURING   5 MINUTES

2 WELCOME AND RECAP   5 MINUTES

Discuss experiences of collecting good things in the Good Things Box and filling in the Good Things Cards.

3 WARM-UP: THE LAST ROLL   10 MINUTES

This is an exercise that encourages people to share things about what they think they are good at and for people to get to know each other better – there are likely to be some laughs as well!

Pass around the toilet paper roll and ask each person to tear off as many sheets as they normally use, then pass it to another member of the group and ask them to do the same. Don't explain the purpose at this point – it just adds to the mystery! Continue until everyone in the group has torn off some paper.

Once the roll has been around to everyone, explain the next part. For each piece of paper torn off, everyone must reveal one thing they think they are good at. Clarify that the thing they are good at can be simple, for example, being kind to people or being punctual. Therapists should start the exercise with their own examples. If some people have taken many pieces of paper and others few, invite people to share their collection of paper if they wish.

Therapists should try to link people's examples with possible strengths and promote discussion.

4 EXERCISE: PERSONAL STRENGTHS   15 MINUTES

This is an exercise that starts to link good things with personal strengths, and aims to help clients identify a personal character strength.

109

Discuss the rationale for including sessions on personal strengths in Positive Psychotherapy for Psychosis, and make the link from the last session when people were encouraged to think about good things that have happened. When a good thing happens, this can show people one of their strengths and often good things in life happen because of our strengths. Further, research shows that strengths enable people to act in ways that contribute to our wellbeing and the wellbeing of others. Distinguish character strengths (e.g. kindness, teamwork, zest) from talents and abilities (e.g. being able to run fast, having a photographic memory). Emphasise that strengths also have moral features, whereas talents and abilities do not. Explain that the session will help increase clients' awareness of their strengths and promote positive emotions. However, highlight that this does not mean that problems are forgotten or not acknowledged: sometimes, there will still be problems but that identifying and using strengths can be one method to cope with problems.

Ask clients to think about strengths that may be associated with some of the good things in their Good Things Box. Encourage discussion about specific strengths that each good thing could indicate and support clients in giving praise to each other. Try to foster an understanding that human strengths are as real as human weaknesses.

Therapists should also take part in this exercise and suggest strengths that are indicated by a good thing in their Good Things Box. Therapists should facilitate group interaction: therapists and clients should support one another to identify, articulate and believe in strengths. Therapists should normalise strengths: 'everyone has strengths', 'everyone is valued'. Therapists should also encourage positive responding by role-modelling. For example:

'I went out for a run yesterday despite the fact that it was drizzling.'

'What made it so worthwhile for you?'

'Well, I didn't like it when I started but I did it anyway because I knew I would really feel good about myself later. And actually, while I was running, I sort of enjoyed the slight cool rain in my face.'

'What did that show you about your character strengths?'

'I think it showed that I am persistent and also, though this may not be a character strength, that if you conquer your inner resistance there are always things you can enjoy, even a bit of rain.'

Overuse of strengths

Explain that sometimes overusing a strength can be a potential problem. For example, if someone's strength is kindness, but they are so kind to people that they get taken advantage of, then this overuse of a strength can be problematic. Another example is the strength of curiosity – if this is overused it may be perceived as someone being nosy rather than curious. Similarly, a strength of bravery may be detrimental if overused, if this leads to risk-taking and putting yourself in dangerous situations. Therapists should also seek to use this way of thinking in this session and future sessions if appropriate with respect to any examples or situations a client shares. For example, therapists can encourage clients to reframe problems or negative experiences using the concept of overuse of strengths, and to help them find positive ways of approaching their problems.

5 BREAK   10 MINUTES

6 ONGOING EXERCISE: IDENTIFYING A PERSONAL STRENGTH   30 MINUTES

Distribute the character strengths pictures around the room (e.g. on free chairs, noticeboards, the floor). Explain that these pictures may make the group think of certain character strengths. Suggest everyone walks around the pictures and thinks about which strength(s) may be associated with each one. Therapists should separate and speak to clients individually as they are walking around the pictures and encourage them to share which strength(s) they identified. Clients should be encouraged to try to identify with the pictures and strengths and explain why they identify with it. Further, clients should be asked to think about how the strength manifests in their lives.

Encourage each client to pick two pictures that represent their strengths, and return to sitting in the group. Therapists should then ask each client in turn to explain why they identify with their pictures, and to describe how the strength manifests in their lives. Feedback from the group using positive responding should again be encouraged. Therapists may find it helpful to start with their own examples.

After each client has had a chance to share their thoughts on the two pictures they have chosen, ask everyone to spend some time over the next week writing in their journal about each picture and the strengths they identified.

Therapists should empower and assist clients to identify strengths, recognising some clients will find this a challenging exercise.

An example of a client's thoughts about a picture in relation to their strengths is as follows:

'I quite like the picture with the autumn leaves. For me personally this shows an appreciation of beauty as one of my strengths. Beautiful things and moments are something I value very much. I like flowers, and the park, and the ducks in the park, and beautiful pictures and so on. Probably I don't give myself the opportunity to enjoy beauty enough. I think I will have to focus more on this in daily life.'

Therapists could also prompt clients to think about what friends or family would say the client's strengths are.

Ask clients to notice how their chosen strength manifests itself in their life and to make notes of that in their journal.

Circulate Handout 7 as a reminder of the strengths pictures.

This activity can be started during the session if time allows. Encourage clients to discuss their strengths with their friends and family.

7 END WITH MINDFUL SAVOURING   **5 MINUTES**

Case studies

Sally

Sally shared that she had put a photo in her Good Things Box of her friend's dog. This represented a day last week when she had taken a walk in the sun with her friend and her dog. She had really enjoyed catching up with her friend and throwing the ball for the dog in the park. Sally hadn't made a note of the date this happened or what she felt she had done to make this happen. When prompted, Sally was unsure about what she had done in this respect. One of the therapists asked Sally if she had made the arrangement with her friend beforehand, and Sally replied that her friend had called her up the day before and asked if she wanted to join her walking her dog the next day. The therapist then suggested that perhaps Sally had to do quite a few things in order to make the event happen: set an alarm and get up in time, check bus times and be on time for the bus, and meet her friend as arranged – thereby honouring a commitment. She also spent a couple of hours with her friend, not always talking or properly following what her friend said because of her voices in the background, but still keeping up a conversation, and she timed her return to catch a convenient bus. Sally said she hadn't really thought about it like that, but began to appreciate that even seemingly small things do require quite a lot of effort.

Sally only took two pieces of toilet paper, and said that she thought she was good at listening to people. Other group members responded positively, saying that they agreed. Sally struggled for another example, but after some prompting said she thought she was quite good at baking cakes and it was something she enjoyed. The therapists modelled positive responding, which was mirrored by other members of the group. Sally agreed to note these examples in her journal.

Sally chose a picture of the man running up the steps and the picture of one 'happy' face among many 'sad' faces. She gave an excellent account of the first picture: she thought the picture represented the strength of perseverance and she said she identified with it because she had been through so many difficult things in her life but had kept going and managed to overcome them. She said this strength had been of real use to her and that she will continue to use it in the future. Her good thing story also reflected this strength in several ways. When prompted to ask what overuse of this strength might look like, Sally suggested that if she really needed support but unrealistically hoped things would be fine without and she carried on, this may be ultimately detrimental to her health. She therefore said that she had to remember to keep this strength in balance and not to overuse it, that is, also ask for help if needed or give herself a break if things got too tough. Sally identified with the second picture because she said she had a strength of often being happy while other people were sad. One of the group members suggested an alternative interpretation – that of optimism rather than happiness. Sally liked this idea and said she identified with this as well, in that she had learnt that optimism can help challenge negative thought processes and keep on going.

William

William had not put any objects in his Good Things Box, but had written eight Good Things Cards! He shared some of the good things he had noted; however it appeared that he had written down each activity he had done every day, rather than thinking about a good thing that had happened, for example, he went to the shops to buy some lunch. The therapists worked to help William understand this, and to discuss some of the activities he had done from the perspective of good things that happened to him. William suggested that a good thing that had happened was that his mother had come around and taken him for a coffee and to the cinema. William had really enjoyed catching up with his mother and also the film that he watched, and the therapists supported him in noting this on a Good Things Card. The therapists asked William to think about what he had done to make this good thing happen. He said he had got himself dressed and ready to leave on time when his mother came around, and he had really made an effort to have a conversation with her and ask her about what had been going on for her recently. The therapists reminded him to make a note of this on his Good Things Card.

William took four pieces of toilet paper. He said that he thought he was good at managing his anger now he had worked on it, playing with his children, chatting with friends and small home repair projects. The therapists encouraged him to talk in more detail about one of his examples and what he think it showed about him. He said last week when he saw his children, he organised a day of activities and had saved money for them to go on their favourite rides at the fair. He was proud that they had really enjoyed their day and thanked him. The therapists suggested that this may show William has a strength of being a loving, caring and fun father. William smiled and agreed with this, and wrote down the examples in his journal.

William chose a picture of many ants together lifting a branch and one with colourfully dressed children jumping. He said he identified with the picture of the ants since he thought that one of his strengths was helping people. One of the therapists asked if he liked working with other people, since there were quite a few ants 'working' together. William said he really enjoyed working with others and had been commended on this in a recent volunteer placement and decided that the picture reminded him of both of these strengths. He said that the children jumping reminded him of his strength of his attitude to life – that he was usually approached things with enthusiasm.

Session 6: Personal Strength Activity

Rationale

Once people have identified some of their own personal strengths, research has shown that putting these strengths into action can yield positive benefits. For example,[120] Seligman showed that 'signature strengths' showed positive changes at six months post-intervention. They defined 'signature strengths' as those strengths that are typical for a person and that truly represent the constitution of a person – and that they are strengths pursued as a result of inherent motivation. Clients were asked to use their top five strengths in a new way. Mitchell and colleagues conducted a similar study of signature strengths-interventions and found an increase in subjective well-being at a three month follow-up, compared to a placebo control.[199] They also used a variation of this intervention and asked their clients to choose their perceived top three strengths from a list. Clients were then instructed to share these strengths with a friend and to incorporate them in their daily lives. Emmons and McCullough[208] found that a strengths-based intervention showed positive effects on happiness and depressive symptoms compared to control group.[200] Gander and colleagues also found positive effects of activities involving using personal strengths.[194]

Aims

The aim of this session is to plan and carry out a personal strength activity using the character strength identified in Session 5.

Session summary

- Mindful savouring
- Recap of identifying personal strengths
- Warm-up: Playing to your strengths
- Exercise: Identify a personal strength activity
- Ongoing exercise: Plan and carry out a personal strength activity
- Mindful savouring

Materials needed

- Music
- Handout 8

- Flipchart
- Pens and pencils

Session plan

1 ENTER WITH MINDFUL SAVOURING   **5 MINUTES**

2 WELCOME AND RECAP   **10 MINUTES**

Therapists start by going around the group and asking people if they can remember the strengths they identified in the last session. If anyone has difficulty in remembering, prompt them, along with the rest of the group to encourage them to remember. Therapists should use positive responding to understand how clients usually use their strengths in daily life to tune them in to possible activities. Also ask about one example of a good thing that has happened and if anybody wants to feedback on something they have actively savoured.

3 WARM-UP: PLAYING TO YOUR STRENGTHS   **10 MINUTES**

Explain that the group will be split into two (assuming a minimum total group number of four) and they will each be asked to spend five minutes thinking of a short poem that they will present to the group. Suggest that tasks that can be assigned could be: ideas for the poem, reading out to the group, writing out the poem on a flipchart. Separate the group, give them pens and paper and set a timer for five minutes. Encourage the groups to have each member say which bit they think they would be best at, and to share around the tasks in this way. Each therapist should work with a group and make sure they explicitly assign the tasks in this way. At the end of five minutes, ask the groups to come back into a circle and present the poem (using as many people to present as they want to, using the flipchart as well).

Conclude by explaining that this was a challenging exercise but that people identifying and using their strengths meant that in a short time, the groups were able to accomplish their aims. Encourage positive responding. Discuss how this made people feel, especially focussing on positive feelings.

4 EXERCISE: IDENTIFY A PERSONAL STRENGTH ACTIVITY   10 MINUTES

This is an exercise in which clients identify and plan an activity that uses one of their personal strengths.

Introduce the exercise by linking it with what was discussed last session: identifying personal character strengths. Reiterate that strengths usually serve us best when life is difficult. For example, when one is depressed, having and using strengths may enable strong family, and social support, or they may help to have positive emotions to work against negative feelings. Emphasise that everyone possesses strengths and they can be considered part of the 'real me'. Explain that this session is designed to encourage the group to start to practise those strengths, to explore them and to find out how good it can feel to do meaningful things that correspond both with one's interests and strengths. Doing this will build on the personal strengths identified in the last session as well as on the savouring skills to maintain focus on the chosen activity.

Explain that in this session, everyone is going to think about an activity that corresponds to one of their personal strengths. Emphasise that it is often difficult to decide what we want to do at all, even though we know our strengths. Also note that often we do not always have the luxury to do what we really, really want as there are things outside of our control. Very often, things we like doing naturally coincide with our strengths. That doesn't mean that we are necessarily doing a lot of this activity. Initiate a discussion within the group about possible activities for each client, and therapists should also join in with their suggested activities. Guide the group to start the discussion by thinking of their personal strengths and then activities that may be associated with those strengths (for example, a strength of sociability could link to an activity of meeting a friend at a day centre for a volunteer group). Encourage each client to explain how the activity links to one of their personal strengths.

Example personal strength activities to guide therapists are included in Appendix 3.

Therapists should emphasise choice as well as a meaning in the activities. Therapists can refer back to what clients have said in previous groups, and suggest they think about what is in their Good Things Box if they need some inspiration. Clients could also be asked if there is anything they did previously that they really enjoyed that they would like to get back into doing again.

Therapists should discuss potential barriers to identifying activities and be realistic about potential activities. Therapists should also be mindful that clients are not suggesting activities primarily because they enjoy doing them – and that they are thinking about their personal strengths and choosing an activity that uses such strengths.

Therapists may also suggest that clients complete an activity with a friend or family member, or another member of the group if appropriate. Other possibilities may be to involve a care-coordinator or support worker.

---

5 BREAK   10 MINUTES

6 ONGOING EXERCISE: PERSONAL STRENGTH ACTIVITY   20 MINUTES

This exercise builds on the personal strength activities suggested in the previous exercise, and helps clients to plan and carry out one of their activities over the coming week.

Explain to the clients that this next exercise involves planning and carrying out one of the personal strength activities that they each developed earlier in the session. Continue the discussion about personal strength activities from before the break until everybody has chosen a suitable activity. Encourage everyone to feed back their chosen activity to the group and say how it corresponds with their strength and why they have chosen it. Help clients find an alternative activity if the one they picked seems unsuitable, unrelated to strengths or unrealistic to be achieved.

Emphasise that the reason for planning an activity ahead is to try to avoid the common situation where people have ideas of what they would like to do, but do not ever carry them out. For example, we often have good intentions, for example, want to spend more time with loved ones, self-care or creative pursuits, but our behaviour is not consistent with our good intentions. This may be the case if we spend more hours in front of the computer or television. Clarify that it is therefore important to consider, when planning an activity, to think about any potential barriers that may stop you doing what you want to do, and how these may be overcome. Clients should also be explicitly encouraged to choose an activity that they don't usually do rather than something they are used to doing.

Ask clients to think about one of their personal strength activities and discuss the key areas that should be considered when planning this activity: including goal-setting, things needed, specific steps, expected difficulties, ways around difficulties and any other concerns. Encourage each client to share their idea for a personal strength activity and any thoughts they have about the key planning areas.

> Therapists should take care to ensure that suggested activities are (i) relevant (reflect an identified personal strengths), (ii) realistic and possible, (iii) not an activity that the client usually does. Where it appears that a suggested activity does not meet one or more of the above, therapists should explore the potential problems more thoroughly and suggest other activities if appropriate.

Therapists distribute Handout 8 and ask clients to complete it as fully as possible, in light of what the group has just discussed.

Encourage clients to be open with any questions or problems they may have with planning or carrying out the exercise. Allow time to go through the worksheets together. Therapists move around and check what people are writing, discuss individually for some minutes while other group members are working on their own. Make sure at the end, everybody has a realistic plan. Ask clients to carry out their personal strength activity before the next session and to record their experiences in their journal.

> Therapists should briefly discuss how clients can approach the activity if a barrier arises that has not been anticipated; for example, are there any ways around this problem? If there are not, can I change the activity slightly or consider a different activity? Therapists should also normalise feelings of anxiety when approaching the selected activity and recognise that in some instances, clients may not be able to complete the activities. In this case, in the next session, the group will help to think about how those clients can be helped to overcome these barriers.

8 END WITH MINDFUL SAVOURING   5 MINUTES

Case studies

Sally

Sally remembered her strengths of perseverance and optimism that she identified in the last session. She also offered a good thing that she had put in her box: a ticket she kept from going to the cinema with a friend, which she said she had really enjoyed. When asked what she had done to make it happen, she said she had saved enough money, made a commitment and followed it through.

Sally was quiet in the warm-up exercise and was reluctant to speak up about which part of the task she could be good at. One of the therapists prompted her and another member of the group to suggest a part they thought they could do. Sally said this would probably be helping to generate ideas for the poem and writing it, as long as someone else did it too. Another member offered to do this with her, and the remaining members took the other tasks. Sally worked well with her partner and produced a very comical short poem, which was very well received by the group. Sally said it was quite challenging and she felt quite pressurised and anxious, but it was a great feeling to have spoken up about what part she felt comfortable taking on and to have received such great feedback. She noted this in her journal.

Sally found identifying a personal strength activity quite difficult. She couldn't really find anything she wanted to do that was related to her strengths. The therapists encouraged her to think about other strengths she might have as well. After some prompting, Sally said she would go to an arts and crafts class that was offered at her local community centre: it was something she always wanted to try but felt shy because she didn't think her art skills were good enough. So she said she would use her strength of perseverance to try out one session and see if it was something she enjoyed doing. Sally was happy to put down a day and a time to do this since the classes only run once a week. She identified a major barrier as being her anxiety on the morning of the class may make her feel negatively about going and make it more difficult for her to leave the house. The group helped Sally to think about ways to tackle this barrier in the event it was a problem: have a plan for the day, deep breathing and positive thoughts if anxiety levels increase, calling a friend before the class, and making her favourite sandwich to take with her. Sally was smiling at the end of planning her activity and seemed optimistic about the prospect of carrying it out.

William

William recalled one of the personal strengths he had identified in the last session, enthusiasm, but had to be prompted to recall his strengths of helping people and working with others. He gave a big smile when the group reminded him. He said he had savoured his tea every morning – he realised it was something he missed when he didn't have it, so really tried to take the time to sit down and think about its flavour, consistency and temperature.

William offered to read out the poem, saying that he quite liked amateur dramatics so if other people didn't mind, he could do that part of the task. He still helped other members with their parts of the task and was a good team player. He read out the poem very well and was congratulated by the group. He said he felt really pleased he had done such a good job and that this would encourage him to put himself forward for more things in the future.

For William's personal strength activity, he suggested that he went along to his community centre and helped people learn how to use the computers. This was something he had mentioned in earlier sessions that he did as a mentor to new joiners. For this reason, the therapists congratulated him on having the skills to do this, but encouraged him to try to think of another way of using one of his strengths that he hadn't done before. William said there had been an opportunity to join a gardening club and meet as a group once a week to design a small plot and then work together with a small budget to build a garden. He said he was very interested in doing this but was worried he had no experience. The therapists suggested this may be a really good idea that was aligned with his strengths of working with others and enthusiasm. William seemed pleased with this idea, and wrote down that he would find out when the group was and sign to start up that week. William was encouraged to think about how we could overcome any potential barriers to going to the gardening club. He said not getting ready early enough to get the bus, but said he could set his alarm and make an effort to be there earlier to give himself some time for delays. He wrote this down on his handout and said he would complete the rest with the dates when he had found out when the club was on.

Session 7: At My Best

Rationale

This session addresses the need for repetition and rehearsal of what clients have learnt. Cognitive impairments in people with psychosis can mean that repeating material and giving time to practice what has been learnt are important, both in the session and at home. This is a key part of Positive Psychotherapy for Psychosis – ensuring that gains are maintained by giving clients the chance to talk about their ongoing exercises, Good Things Box and savouring experiences, as well as including two sessions specifically intended to go over what clients have learnt to far and discuss how they can maintain these gains (this session and Session 12).

The session also introduces the second half of Positive Psychotherapy for Psychosis, which focuses on how negative experiences, disappointments or difficulties can be dealt with using the positive strategies learned during the earlier sessions. Our experiences showed that some clients find this transition difficult, so this session addresses the change: plans for the next sessions and discussions about clients' concerns.

Aims

This session aims to:

a   show clients how giving and receiving compliments can be enjoyable and beneficial;
b   give clients the opportunity to share what they have collected so far in their Good Things Box;
c   allow clients to think about and share another time at which they have been at their best; and
d   discuss ways in which learning and progress made across the sessions can be maintained.

Session summary

- Mindful savouring
- Recap of experiences with personal strength activity
- Warm-up: Compliments
- Recap of good things
- Exercise: When I'm at my best
- Ongoing exercise: Maintenance of gains
- Introduction to next sessions
- Mindful savouring

Materials needed

- Music
- Handout 9
- Pen and pencils

Session plan

1 ENTER WITH MINDFUL SAVOURING   5 MINUTES

2 WELCOME AND RECAP   10 MINUTES

Therapists should go around the group and ask clients to feed back their experiences of their personal strength activity. Encourage positive responding and acknowledge the things that each client had to do to make these activities happen. For those clients who were unable to complete their personal strength activity, respond encouragingly, appropriate to the circumstances; for example, highlight their strengths in choosing that activity and planning well, suggest changes that may enable the client to carry out the activity in the following week, or acknowledge sometimes things are hard to carry out but that doesn't mean the client should get despondent.

> Ensure clients are encouraged to develop further strengths other than the ones they picked and used in their personal strength activity.

3 WARM-UP: COMPLIMENTS   10 MINUTES

This is an exercise that encourages people to see how it feels to receive and accept compliments and how to give them to someone else. It aims to enhance a positive view of the self and one's role in the group, and practices the social skill of positive interaction with others.

Part 1

Circulate Handout 9 to each client.

Ask clients to write their names at the top of the piece of paper and place it on the floor in front of them. The therapists should do the same. Ask the group to get up and move one seat to the right and take the piece of paper and write something nice about the person who is named at the top. Provide some examples: 'friendly', 'nice smile', 'wears smart shoes'. Ask everyone to move to the next seat on their right and again, write something nice about the person who is named at the top. Carry on this activity until people return to their original seat, where each person should have a list of compliments under their name.

Part 2

Give clients a few minutes to read their compliments and reflect on them. Ask if anyone wants to share anything off their list. Therapists should also offer some compliments from their list. Encourage clients to think about how others perceive them. Explain that the way others see you is not always the way that you see yourself. Ask clients if there is anything on their lists that surprised them. Ask how it felt to receive the compliments and what they take away from the fact that they are seen in this way. Therapists should model positive responding and encourage clients to do the same.

Ask clients how it feels to accept compliments and to give them to someone else and discuss different ways in which clients had accept compliments. Explain how giving and receiving compliments can improve social skills, relationships and self-esteem. Finally, therapists should encourage clients to practice giving compliments and also consciously think about how they accept compliments from others.

> Therapists should normalise difficulties in both giving and receiving compliments, especially when people have low self-esteem.

4 BREAK   10 MINUTES

5 RECAP OF GOOD THINGS   5 MINUTES

Therapists should say that there is some time to briefly think about some of the good things that people have put into their boxes or noted on Good Things Cards. Clients should be asked to share some of the things in their Good Things Box. Therapists should model and encourage positive responding.

6 EXERCISE: WHEN I'M AT MY BEST   15 MINUTES

This is an exercise where clients and therapists have the opportunity to think about a time when they have been 'at their best', and to share this with the group. It repeats and practises the exercise in Session 2. Clients should be encouraged to find a new example and not reuse the one they gave in Session 2.

Ask each client to think about a time when they feel they have been 'at their best'. Explain that this may be a time when they have been proud of something they have done, for example, supporting a friend going through a difficult time, completing a course or a time when they have successfully come through a difficult situation. Therapists should provide a short example to model the exercise. Encourage clients to think about what strengths their example shows they have and whether they had realised they had this strength or wanted to develop it further. Therapists should give examples of how strengths have helped them to cope with a particular problem or difficult issue.

Invite feedback of the 'at my best' story to the group. Reflect on how it feels to do this exercise for the second time – is it easier now? Can they identify strengths more easily? Is it easier to feed the example back to the group? Discuss how embracing positive stories about oneself can be beneficial for self-esteem and one's relation to other people.

> Therapists should normalise the experience that for some people it may still be difficult to talk about themselves positively.

7 ONGOING EXERCISE: MAINTENANCE OF GAINS   10 MINUTES

Ask clients to think about what they have learnt from the groups so far and invite them to share their thoughts with the group. Therapists should summarise the main things covered in the sessions so far: savouring, noticing good things, and noticing and using personal strengths, positive responding, embracing and praising positive aspects of oneself. Emphasis should be given to the progress made by the clients in these areas, and that each client should continue to practice each of these activities in order to ensure gains are maintained, both through and after the course. Invite clients to take some time over the coming week to write down in their journals what they have learnt and some ideas for how to continue these lessons.

Discuss ideas for maintenance strategies in the group. Invite everybody to write down strategies that appear suitable and useful to them (even though they may have been somebody else's idea). At the end, encourage clients to feed back what strategies they noted down and explain how and why these will be beneficial in the future and how they will make sure to actually remember to do them.

> If a client has difficulty thinking of something, suggest people reflect on/ repeat what others have suggested and try to think about a way how somebody else's strategy could be adapted to be suitable for their life. Ask the group to help develop suitable strategies for other people using positive responding and compliments.

8 INTRODUCTION TO NEXT SESSIONS   10 MINUTES

Introduce the idea that all strengths and good things become really useful to remember when trying to overcome problems and obstacles. Explain that in the remaining sessions, the group will focus on how we can use the positive things we have learnt (savouring, good things, personal strengths, positive responding, more positive view of oneself) to overcome some things we may find difficult, such as finding positives in negative situations, forgiving people and feeling gratitude.

9 END WITH MINDFUL SAVOURING   5 MINUTES

Case studies

Sally

Sally enthusiastically told the group about the arts and crafts class she had been to. She said she had been anxious beforehand but remembered her strength of perseverance and attended the class. She was pleasantly surprised by her skills and was praised by the facilitator for her painting during the session. She was proud of herself for going and had already signed up to do more of the classes in the following week. The therapists congratulated her on this and reminded her that this was quite a big step she had taken – others in the group also said they had lots of respect for her for going to such a class.

Following the compliments exercise, Sally was quite shy in letting the group know how she felt about the compliments she had been given. After some encouragement from the therapists, she said she was both touched to read them and embarrassed to share them with the group since they were really nice and she wasn't sure whether people had just been kind to her or whether they really meant it. The rest of the group then strongly reassured her they had each meant their comment genuinely. Sally said she was really surprised that people viewed her in these ways, and shared examples such as 'Sally is a warm and friendly person' and 'Sally is a great person to have in a group since she gives really good advice about how to view things in a positive light'. The therapists said this linked very well with Sally's strength of optimism, and Sally should remember she has a further strength – of being a lovely person. The therapists asked if these were things she could look at every day and remind herself of them when her mood went down or things were difficult. Sally agreed it would be lovely thing to cherish and she would put it in her Good Things Box.

Sally's story of when she was at her best was when she had been asked to do a flower arrangement by her sister for someone's funeral, since they knew she was interested in arts and crafts, especially flower arranging. However, Sally explained that her sister had not been very supportive of her over the last few years, and had not treated her well. She decided that since she would enjoy making a flower arrangement, she would offer to do this but would not allow herself to be exploited and would ask to be paid a reasonable amount for doing so. Sally was really happy she had asserted herself, and the therapists praised her and reminded her that wasn't an easy thing to do. They also said given how shy and anxious Sally had been in her first session, she had clearly made a lot of progress already and should be congratulated for that. Sally said she had made the arrangement and had received many compliments about it, including from others who were willing to pay her to do an arrangement for them. A group member reminded Sally that this also showed her strength of perseverance – she wanted to do something but had to assert herself in order to do it in a way in which she wasn't taken for granted, and that she should be proud of herself. Other group members responded in similar positive ways. The therapists asked her how it felt to tell a positive story about herself for a second time in sessions.

Sally said it was easier than last time, and she felt spurred on by the compliments she had received in the earlier sessions.

When the group was asked to think about what progress they had made over the sessions, Sally said she felt she had really made progress with savouring exercises. She said she also used to rush through things and rarely consciously thought about her experiences. She said it was a tool she used in several different ways, which really helped to reduce her anxiety and appreciate the good things in her life. When asked how to maintain the gains she had made, Sally suggested that she make a concerted effort to continue to use her Good Things Box when the sessions had finished, especially to note down things she had savoured. She also said she would continue to try to savour something every day. The therapists also suggested that she write down in her journal her experiences of savouring, and as she thought about different things she could savour, to write a list of these in her journal.

William

When asked about how he had got on with his personal strengths exercise, William said he had booked to go to the gardening club but when it came to it, he didn't have the motivation to go, and was really quite low about it. He said most other people seemed to have been successful, but he hadn't managed his exercise. The therapists reassured him that sometimes these things happened, and asked him what particular barrier he thought had stopped him from going that day. William said it was a feeling that no one would like him when he got there, and that he would feel awkward walking into a group where he didn't know anyone. Another member of the group said William shouldn't worry that people wouldn't like him – he came across as very easy to talk to and amiable in the group, and others nodded in agreement. The therapists also asked him if he had felt awkward about coming to the first session. William said he had done but had managed to go because his doctor said it looked like something that would be very useful for him. He said his anxiety dissipated once he was in the group, and the therapists suggested that he use this previous experience as a reassurance and motivation to attend the next gardening club, and that he wrote these things down in his journal to help him remember the potential benefits of going and what he could do to counter-balance his negative thoughts.

William really enjoyed the compliments exercise, seeming more encouraged after having spoken about his Personal Strengths exercise. His compliments included 'William is always energetic and enthusiastic in the group' and 'William clearly cares a lot for others'. William said that he was really surprised that the group had picked up on these things when he assumed they didn't know him very well. When the therapists asked him if he thought the compliments reflected his strengths, he said they did because he enjoyed working with and helping others.

William's story of a time when he had been at his best recently was when he had been working as a pizza delivery man and had just arrived at a flat to deliver an order. He said when the door opened the person looked over this shoulder, and William saw two guys running off with his bike which he had left parked at the end of the path. William entertained the group in explaining the rest of what had happened, which involved him chasing the two guys with his bike across the park next door, picking up his helmet on the way when they threw it on the ground, and bellowing at them to leave his bike alone otherwise he would 'come to find them'. In the end they apparently left his bike at the entrance of the park and ran away. William said he was very glad he had done this, because the bike belonged to the pizza company and not him, and he did not want to be seen as irresponsible. The therapists asked him what strength he used in that situation. William said his strengths of honesty and bravery, which he realised he had after considering the event. The therapists commended him on these strengths, but also asked the group if they could see how overuse of one of these strengths may have put William in a difficult position. One of the group said perhaps he had been too brave, and that perhaps he had put himself in danger by chasing the two men, when they may have hurt him. William agreed and said he hadn't thought about that, and that it was really useful to hear other people's perspectives on what he had done. The therapists said that nevertheless William should be pleased with himself but should bear in mind that he should think in the future about whether he was potentially overusing his strengths in certain situations. He noted this down in his journal and thanked everyone for their input.

When asked what progress he thought he had made over the course of the sessions, William said that positive responding and recalling good things had really been of benefit to him. He said that he realised that responding positively came quite naturally to him, but it was interesting to see the impact it could have on conversations – both to respond positively yourself but also to have someone respond positively to you. The therapists suggested he write this down in his journal to remind himself of it when the sessions had finished. The therapists asked how remembering good things and looking back at his Good Things Box had made William feel. He said it had really cheered him up and that he also remembered to think about what he had done to make those things happen. He said this made him feel more empowered and confident. Another member of the group suggested that maybe he could introduce a friend of his to the concept of the Good Things Box – something they had done that had been very well received and meant every week they could share something together. William liked this idea and wrote it down, saying he would think about which of his friends would most benefit from having a Good Things Box. The therapists asked him how he planned to maintain his progress so far. William said he would make a concerted effort to continue using his Good Things Box every day. He said he would spend more time thinking about how he could incorporate more savouring experiences into his everyday life, since he felt he really benefited from the context but often did not to remember to think about savouring between sessions.

Session 8: One Door Closes, Another Door Opens

Rationale

It is common for things to happen to people that are very hard to deal with and where it is very hard to see any positives in the situation. However, in most cases, life is not just black and white – especially the smaller things that upset or annoy us every day often have a positive side to them that we find hard to recognise. That contributes to us becoming grumpy, unmotivated and getting into the pattern of not recognising the positives and expecting the negatives. This can be a self-fulfilling prophecy, strengthening the conclusion that things are negative. It can often be beneficial to remember that bigger things that go wrong also often lead to alternative developments that have a different positive outcome. Even traumatic experiences can lead to growth, positive developments and can give life meaning, sometimes in unexpected ways through post-traumatic growth. However, big things, or even traumas, are comparatively rare in comparison to the smaller, more daily annoyances of life. While the exercises discussed and practised in this session can be applied to bigger things and traumas, we will explicitly try to start with practising the concept to reframe smaller things. This is because the reframing of things in a more positive way – seeing the silver lining – can often be challenging if we are used to dwelling on the negatives (which most people are). Once we are used to seeing things not only in black and white but also recognising the positives that come with negative events, it will be easier – or even come naturally – to also find meaning and gain in bigger negative things.

Reframing things to recognise the positive consequences can also be a powerful way to challenge any self-blaming tendencies, which can be a considerable barrier to change and recovery. By helping clients to see how they can benefit from negative situations, they will be helped to see how things are not necessarily their fault. The session should also build on the previous sessions by encouraging clients to remain optimistic in the face of difficult situations.

Aim

The aim of this session is to encourage more positive appraisals of past events in order to decrease self-blame and promote optimism.

Session summary

- Mindful savouring
- Recap of what clients have learnt over the sessions
- Warm-up: Ball challenge
- Ongoing Exercise: One door closes, another door opens
- Mindful savouring

Materials needed

- Music
- Handout 10
- Two balls
- Two other items to throw around the group (e.g. cuddly toys)
- Pens and pencils

Session plan

1 ENTER WITH MINDFUL SAVOURING   **5 MINUTES**

2 WELCOME AND RECAP   **10 MINUTES**

Ask clients to share that they wrote down in their journals regarding what they feel they have learnt from the sessions so far. Also probe for clients to share their ideas about how they might maintain some of these gains and continue the lessons. Ask about one good thing in somebody's box since last week.

3 WARM-UP: BALL CHALLENGE   **15 MINUTES**

This is an exercise where clients begin to see that despite sometimes being difficult, experiences can be enjoyable – and that good things can come out of challenging situations. Perhaps also that you could view a challenge in a fun/humorous way?

Therapists should explain that the group is going to a play a game called the 'ball challenge'. This will involve throwing a ball around the circle, choosing any member of the group, not just the people to either side. Each person should say the name of the person they are throwing it to as they throw it. The therapists should start this off. Once this is going smoothly, the therapists should introduce a second ball and carry on. Therapists can introduce a more playful aspect to the game, but suggesting that when a person calls someone's name and throws the ball to them, they do this looking in the opposite direction! A third object (not a ball, e.g. a cuddly toy) is thrown in, which is harder to throw and catch, and finally a fourth object is thrown in, and people are likely to be starting to drop things.

Therapists should briefly discuss the meaning of the exercise and what lessons the group can take from it. It should be explained that as the exercise became more and more difficult, the group was still able to have lots of fun playing it together. This shows us that we can still see good things in what was otherwise a challenging situation. Clients should be asked to share any reflections they have on the exercise.

Care should be taken to ensure that clients are given the opportunity to roll the ball or pass hand-to-hand if preferred or appropriate. Therapists should ensure the number of objects included in the game is appropriate to the size of the group, for example, using a maximum of three objects for a group of six people. Emphasis should be placed on people enjoying themselves and therapists should try to ensure clients are not left frustrated.

4 BREAK   10 MINUTES

5 ONGOING EXERCISE: ONE DOOR CLOSES, ANOTHER DOOR OPENS   35 MINUTES

This is an exercise in which clients are encouraged to try to find positive aspects of a difficult situation.

Part 1

Therapists should introduce the exercise by acknowledging that when things happen that are very hard to deal with, it is often difficult to see any positives in the situation. However, in most cases, life is not just black and white – the smaller things that upset or annoy us often have a positive side to them that we find hard to recognise. If we do not identify the positive aspects, we can become grumpy and unmotivated, and getting in the pattern of not recognising the positives and expecting the negatives – a self-fulfilling prophecy – strengthens the conclusion that things are negative. Further, research shows that optimists are less likely to blame themselves for negative events and less likely to believe that they are likely to re-occur. So this exercise wants to counter this tendency and to encourage positive appraisals of past events in order to decrease self-blame and promote optimism.

Therapists should provide some examples of finding positive things in negative situations. It should also be emphasised that it is also not necessary to be able to find positives in everything, for example, a bad accident happening to someone close to them.

Therapists may find the following examples useful:

My bus broke down on the way to the library and by the time I got there the library was shut. However, the library had kept a set of second-hand books outside that were free for the public, so I managed to pick up a great book to read and can now lend it to my sister when I've finished with it.

I had made a special effort to cook dinner for my mum, but we got so carried away talking I forgot to take the dinner out of the oven and by the time I remembered the food was too burnt to eat! In the end we grabbed a sandwich and some fruit and sat out in the garden since it was a lovely evening and had a really good catch up.

Part 2

Ask the group if they have ever helped a friend or family member to see the positive in a difficult situation. Discuss one or two examples of these in the group. Explain that it is often much more difficult to apply this principle and compassion to yourself, so that's something the group is going to look at in this exercise.

Circulate Handout 10.

Explain that this is a worksheet where clients can write down times when they have identified positives (sun) out of negative situations (cloud). Ask each client to think of a time where they have managed to find a positive aspect of a negative situation, or when they have come across a difficult situation but have found identifying a positive aspect difficult. Ask clients to share their examples, and ask the group to help find a positive where people are having difficulties. Therapists should ask clients to populate Handout 10 with their examples.

Therapists should conclude by asking that clients try to remember to identify a positive aspect of any difficult situation they encounter over the next week, or try to help someone else identify a positive if they are complaining / finding something is getting them down. Clients should be asked to write down their examples in their journals, and how they were able to see the problem in terms of the opportunities it presents.

Therapists may find the following prompts useful when exploring clients' examples:

- Did you see the positive immediately or did it take a while?
- Did your disappointment or sadness resulting from difficult situation affect your ability to find a positive?
- Are there things you can do in the future to find the positive more readily?

Therapists should be realistic: Normalise negativity in experience; encourage beginning with small examples and focus on recent disappointments (avoid major trauma). Therapists should consider asking for 'lessons learnt' and how to implement them in the future.

---

6 END WITH MINDFUL SAVOURING   5 MINUTES

Case studies

Sally

Sally was enthusiastic at the recap and said she had added a new savouring experience to her list following the last session – she had gone to the park with a picnic, and spent some time lying on her picnic mat with her eyes closed, listening to the sounds of the park: the birds, the wind through the trees, the dogs. She had written about this in her journal. The therapists congratulated her on taking the time to think about another experience and also for writing about it so eloquently. One of the other members said that they would really like to try going to the park and doing the same, and was encouraged to write this down in their journal. When asked if Sally had thought about anything that might help her progress in the future, Sally said she had come up with some more savouring ideas she wanted to try – going for a bike ride down the river and learning how to use the computer, and had noted these in her journal. She was once again praised for her progress.

Sally found the Ball Challenge quite difficult – she managed with one ball but when others were added she seemed uncomfortable in trying to catch them. It was only after one of the therapists emphasised that it wasn't about people being able to complete the task, more about having a try and having fun, that Sally really got stuck into the exercise and was quite animated! In her feedback, she said it had taken her a while to realise the point of the exercise and it showed her that she only really approached things that she thought she could be successful at. She said she now saw she could have a go at difficult things with a sense of humour, and still enjoy it even if it was challenging. The therapists pointed out that this was really impressive and insightful and it was great Sally felt that way.

When the group discussed seeing positives in negative situations, Sally seemed to concentrate on big events, such as her father's death, and found it difficult to think about smaller examples. The therapists helped by giving their own examples, and after hearing these and some from other members of the group, Sally tentatively suggested that perhaps an example would be her making a dinner dish for a friend last week, and finding that she was missing a vital ingredient. Instead of letting this make her annoyed, she looked up a different recipe that she hadn't tried before that would use the ingredients she had. It actually turned out really well. The therapists asked her how this had made her feel. She said she felt proud and also quite empowered that she had solved a problem on her own, without it affecting her mood greatly. She made a note of this example on her handout.

William

During the recap, William shared that he'd had a bad week and hadn't managed to progress with anything. The therapists normalised this and said this was likely to happen from time to time, and other members spoke up and said they had felt like this in other weeks as well. William did recall what he planned to do – share the idea of the Good Things Box with a friend. He said he knew who he wanted to share it with, but had found it difficult to leave the house to put it into action. The therapists asked how he could be supported to help make this happen, but William was quite withdrawn: he looked down and said he didn't know. The therapists said he should be proud of himself for thinking about who he would share the idea with, and that he should be proud that he made it to the session. They suggested that perhaps he wrote down who he planned to share the idea with, and how he might get in touch with them to arrange a time. William said sometimes they were at the community centre together, so he could have a coffee with his friend and explain then. He was encouraged to make a note of this and reassured that it was fine that he hadn't managed it last week, he could just make a plan and do his best to follow it next week.

William joined in the Ball Challenge, but with less enthusiasm than usual. He apologised and said it was difficult for him at the moment to enjoy things. The therapists reassured him that was no problem; it was a great achievement for him to attend and join in so he should remember that. They commented that William had very good coordination and it was impressive how he could catch so many things being thrown so quickly. This brought a little smile to William's face.

When asked to think about a negative experience from which he may be able to find a positive, William said that a few weeks ago, he had locked himself out, but had managed to crawl in through a window he had left open! He was commended for his ingenuity, and asked to identify the negative experience and the positive points of this event. William said it was a horrible experience to have locked himself out, but he was lucky that the window had been left open. The therapists realised that William had missed the point slightly, and picked an example where he felt he had good luck but not necessarily finding a positive in a negative. They explained this to him and asked if he could find a positive thing that had arisen from him solving the problem of how to get into his flat. He said that it had taught him that he must remember to close all windows, since while it was useful for him to get in on such occasions, it was ultimately unsafe to leave the house with windows open. So he said the positive was that he had been reminded about the importance of safety. The therapists said they were impressed with this insight and that William should note this down since it was a very useful illustration.

Session 9: Forgiveness (1)

Rationale

Research shows that forgiveness increases positive emotions about the past and increases self-control, while the bitterness we may feel when someone has let us down causes rumination and resentment. Forgiveness can help us to learn how to change and become more open to our mistakes. Negative responses to being harmed, such as seeking revenge, are likely to have negative physical, mental and relational consequences.[201] However, it has been shown that more positive responses, such as forgiving the person who has caused the harm, often have positive physical,[202] mental[203] and relational[204] consequences. Further, forgiveness may lead to increased optimistic thinking and decreased hopelessness, increased self-efficacy and higher levels of perceived social and emotional support.[205]

Specific forgiveness therapies have been established in recent years, for example, compassion-focussed therapy.[206] And forgiveness is a complex topic that may be dealt with over an extended period of time. The two sessions devoted to forgiveness in Positive Psychotherapy for Psychosis aim to provide a first taste and insight into the potential positive effects of forgiveness, but will most likely not suffice to help people come to terms with major traumatic events or injustices they had to endure. Also, forgiveness may need several attempts before it one is ready to let go. Clients may be prompted to discuss forgiveness also in their individual therapies (if they have such), and it should be offered that the topic of forgiveness is addressed again in the booster sessions (if planned) after the therapy has finished. This will give clients enough time to digest and try forgiveness anew.

This session and the following session is to introduce the idea of forgiving another person who has let us down, thereby transforming feelings of anger and bitterness into feelings of neutrality or positive emotions. The session will also cover difficulties associated with forgiveness, for example, that it does not mean being submissive, 'letting one's guard down' or necessarily liking the other or having to be close to them.

Aims

This session aims to:

a   focus on feeling disappointed or let down by others and forgiveness; and
b   explore the possibility of letting go of a grudge.

Session summary

- Mindful savouring
- Recap of experiences with maintaining a positive outlook in a difficult situation
- Warm-up: Celebrity forgiveness
- Exercise: What is forgiveness?
- Exercise: Feeling disappointed or let down by others
- Ongoing exercise: Sea of forgiveness
- Mindful savouring

Materials needed

- Music
- Handouts 11 and 12
- Flipchart
- Pens and pencils

Session plan

1 ENTER WITH MINDFUL SAVOURING   5 MINUTES

2 WELCOME AND RECAP   5 MINUTES

Ask clients how they found the experience of maintaining a positive attitude when faced with a difficult situation. Clients should be encouraged to share the stories they noted in their journals with the group. Ask a few clients to briefly share with the group one good thing in their Good Things Box and ask for a few volunteers to describe a successful savouring experience over the past week.

3 WARM-UP: CELEBRITY FORGIVENESS   10 MINUTES

This is an exercise where the idea of forgiveness is introduced to the group in an informal way, giving clients the chance to think about for what types of things people are forgiven and whether all forgiveness is the same.

Ask if anyone can think of celebrities who have done something for which they may need to be forgiven? Prompts: Wayne Rooney, Lindsay Lohan, Lance Armstrong, Tiger Woods, politicians. What have they done? What do they need to be forgiven for? Have they asked for forgiveness? Can we identify types of forgiveness? There seem to be both big and small things to forgive. Let's focus on the small things because it is important to first forgive the small things.

> Some clients may relate the examples back to themselves so emphasise that 'We are talking about famous people at the moment'. Acknowledge that not everything can and should be forgiven. Try to avoid discussion about sensitive topics that clients may find difficult emotionally, e.g. celebrities in abuse cases.

4 WHAT IS FORGIVENESS?   15 MINUTES

Therapists should lead a discussion on what forgiveness is and it means to clients. If possible, therapists should use a flipchart or whiteboard and populate it with the thoughts and ideas discussed. Therapists should initiate discussion on the following areas.

What is forgiveness?

For example, a process of reducing negative feelings, letting go of grudges

What is forgiveness not?

For example, excusing a past event, necessarily reconciliation

Why is forgiveness important?

For example, increases self-efficacy, decreases hopelessness

At the end of the discussion, therapists should circulate Handout 11, and explain that much of what has just been discussed is included on the worksheet to aid clients in remembering the key points.

5 BREAK   10 MINUTES

6 EXERCISE: FEELING DISAPPOINTED OR LET DOWN
BY OTHERS   15 MINUTES

This is an exercise that looks at how clients can feel disappointed when they are let down by others.

Part 1

Explain that the group is going to consider occasions when they felt disappointed or let down by someone and how it felt to forgive them. Briefly explain the rationale for the session: thinking about how forgiveness can be beneficial. They should then start the exercise by each giving an example of when they have felt let down by someone and how it felt. Therapists should role-play these examples.

   Invite clients to suggest reasons for why people forgive. These may include 'lifting a burden', 'making peace', 'putting anger/bitterness behind you', 'moving on', becoming a 'better, stronger person'.

Therapists should encourage clients to consider when they felt 'let down by someone' rather than discussing traumatic life experiences. Some clients may automatically choose big examples where it may be difficult, or impossible, to forgive. In this case, guide clients to start with small things that can be forgiven before going onto bigger things. Therapists should also discuss the idea that that forgiveness is personal and a process that takes time. It is also important that therapists acknowledge that forgiveness can be difficult. Discussion should also include the fact that some situations do not need, or are not suitable, to be forgiven.

   Be aware of religious/spiritual connotations of forgiveness and recognise participants' personal ideas about spirituality or religious duties in relation to forgiveness. Forgiveness may indeed be very different depending on religious background.

Part 2

Invite clients to think about when they have felt let down by someone, and how it felt, or may feel, to forgive that person. Ask clients to share their examples and talk about how forgiving a person may feel. Explore the different reasons that there may be to forgive a person in each case.

Therapists may find the following questions helpful:

'Think of a time when someone has let you down and you have forgiven them'

'What did you think when you forgave the person?'

'How did you feel when you forgave the person?'

'What has happened as a result of forgiving?'

7 ONGOING EXERCISE: A SEA OF FORGIVENESS   15 MINUTES

This is an exercise where each member of the group thinks about a grudge they are holding against a person, and encourages members to think about the positive things about the other person as well as the grudge. Circulate Handout 12.

Explain to clients that the exercise involves thinking about a grudge they are holding against a particular person and that the aim of the exercise is to see a difficult situation in its entirety and recall the positive things as well. Tell clients that the grudge is represented by the red circle, and ask clients to write the name of the person and a few words describing the grudge in the bubble. Therapists should then invite clients to think about as many positive things about this person as they can, and to write these down in the circles around the grudge. It should be explained that this exercise aims to loosen the grudge and allow the process of forgiveness to proceed. Clients should be encouraged to start this during the session and complete it during the week before the next session.

Therapists need to anticipate that if you try to find something positive, this will bring up the negatives as well. So say this is normal and will happen as part of the exercise, but we need to focus on finding the positives. Balance this out by saying it's not taking away the hurt, but it's learning to see some positives about the person. Encourage clients to consider that people are often not only 'bad guys'.

Therapists should emphasise that forgiveness is about seeing the benefits for the client, and not the other person.

Depending upon the examples chosen, this may be a good time for therapists to emphasise that sometimes it may not be possible, or people may not want, to forgive someone.

When discussing examples, therapists should probe how it felt for the person to feel let down and to forgive, or at least consider forgiving. Therapists should also be aware of religious views of forgiveness: if a client's religion requires that someone should always forgive, don't question this or try to get them to change.

8 END WITH MINDFUL SAVOURING   5 MINUTES

Case studies

Sally

Sally approached the therapists at the beginning of the session and said that she was hearing voices again and was finding things quite hard, and apologised if she didn't have a lot to contribute this session. She was reassured that it wasn't necessary for her to say anything at all and it was something that may happen from time to time, and she should be proud of the fact that she came to the group that week. Sally didn't offer to share anything she had put in her Good Things Box or a savouring experience and the therapists did not push her for these.

Sally couldn't think of any examples of celebrities who had done something for which they should be forgiven. She did however join in the conversation about celebrities who were suggested by other members of the group, and interestingly started a discussion around whether celebrities, as role models, should be 'assessed' against different ideas for what could be forgiven by members of the public.

Sally suggested that what came to mind for her, about forgiveness, was regaining a relationship with the person being forgiven. The therapists asked what other members thought, and while the majority agreed with Sally, a few said that for them, forgiving someone didn't mean necessarily repairing the relationship. The therapists then led a brief discussion about how it may be possible to forgive someone, but not to continue in the relationship. The therapists emphasised that this was not always the case, but since the focus was on forgiveness being beneficial to the person doing the forgiveness, it may not be necessary to go back to the relationship. This may particularly be the case in an abusive relationship or one where the person being forgiven had taken advantage of the other person. Sally acknowledged this and said it was useful to remember.

Sally's example of when she had been let down was when her mother had offered to bake her a cake to take to a friend's child's christening, since her mother was good at making cakes. The morning of the christening, Sally's mother called to say she hadn't remembered to buy all the ingredients so wouldn't be able to make the cake. Sally was very disappointed and felt she had let down her friend. In the end, Sally went out and bought a lovely cake, and people were very grateful for her bringing a cake to the christening for everyone. The therapists asked Sally how she felt about the situation now. Sally said she still hadn't really forgiven her mother for letting her down, but had tried to forget about it instead. The therapists asked Sally what she thought the benefits to her of forgiving her mother would be. Sally said she would feel less 'eaten up' by the idea her mother had let her down and wouldn't have to play the situation around in her head every few days as she did at the moment.

Sally's example for the Sea of Forgiveness was a teacher at school, who she had hadn't treated her very well at all and had made her quite unhappy. She said she saw the lady again a few months ago, and she was very nice, likeable and interested in what Sally had been up to since she left school. Sally decided that there were these good things about the lady, and that time could change people. She said she could therefore retrospectively forgive the teacher for the unhappiness she caused. Sally was congratulated by the therapists for providing an excellent example for the rest of the group.

William

William arrived early for the session and the therapists congratulated him for making such an effort to be on time. William said he hadn't had any new savouring experiences over the last week but he had added a button to his Good Things Box – he said this represented a new cardigan he had bought which he really liked, and had written a note to accompany the button to remind himself of this. The group agreed this was a lovely thing to add to the box.

William was quick to put forward some celebrities who may be perceived as having done something that could be forgiven, and came up with Tiger Woods and a political figure who had claimed some fraudulent expenses. William suggested that maybe there was a scale of things that could be forgiven and those that can't, and perhaps infidelity was something that couldn't be forgiven and fraudulent expense claims were less 'serious' and could be forgiven. This prompted an interesting discussion within in the group. The therapists brought up the idea of what forgiveness actually means, and what benefit the person forgiving can get from the process. This led into the next discussion about the concept of forgiveness, which William seemed to find quite interesting. He felt strongly that not all things should be forgiven – to which the therapists replied that he could be right, and that the session was not about encouraging people to forgive big things, but to start to think about the concept in relation to smaller things and see the benefits of forgiveness for the person forgiving.

William shared that he had been let down by a friend who he was due to meet for a coffee. While he was waiting for her in a local café, his friend called him to apologise and say she couldn't make it. William said he was quite frustrated about this, but remembered the session and tried to think of a positive. He said he popped next door to buy a paper, and had a nice hour in the café reading the paper and having a hot chocolate. Other members of the group said they thought this was an excellent example and he had done well to think of this at the time. William said he had forgiven his friend because she was usually very reliable, but may not forgive so easily if the same thing happened again. The therapists said this highlighted a very important point – that forgiveness wasn't a blanket rule that should be applied to every situation or to forgive constant wrongs of a person, but that the benefits of forgiveness and the fact that it isn't about excusing the behaviour were important to think about.

William's initial example for the Sea of Forgiveness was an incident where his cousin had been violent towards his mother. The therapists suggested this was quite a big example to use as a way of thinking more about the process of forgiveness, and that perhaps William could start off with a smaller example that might be easier to think about, before moving onto the larger examples. William said another example was when his sister broke a picture while she was very angry at William's house a few months ago. William was encouraged to think about good things about his sister, and managed to come up with quite a few and include them on the worksheet, for example she was a great mother to her children, and a very good support for her father. He did say he found it hard to link these good qualities about her to being able to forgive her but after some discussion, acknowledged that it was beneficial to him to forgive her, since it took away the anger he sometimes felt towards her and the energy it took him to deal with this. He said he felt she was very sorry and would not do it again. The therapists suggested he spend the next week thinking about the situation in light of some of things the group had discussed about what forgiveness was and what it was not, and to see whether he could relate any of this to his example.

Session 10: Forgiveness (2)

Rationale

This is a session that continues with the theme of forgiveness, this time focussing on what letting go of a grudge feels like, as well as giving clients the opportunity to express their forgiveness in the form of a letter. The Tug-of-War exercise is based on the embodied mind thesis, which holds that the nature of the human mind is significantly determined by the form of the human body. It is argued that all aspects of cognition (e.g. higher level mental constructs such as categories, and cognitive task performance such as reasoning) are influenced by aspects of the body (e.g. the motor and perceptual systems). This exercise extends current clinical practice where interventions use the body as a medium for encouraging therapeutic change (e.g. drama therapy, body psychotherapy). The Tug-of-War exercise helps clients to experience the bodily relief of pressure when letting go of a grudge and forgiving. Through this, clients can start to realise their own emotional feelings around forgiveness.

The forgiveness letter helps clients to process difficult feelings, and provides a way to get a release and feel a sense of freedom from them. Such letters are used as part of other therapeutic approaches (e.g. compassion-focussed therapy and cognitive therapy). Clients can use the letter to express their feelings and needs about a situation in which they feel it would be beneficial to forgive. The aim is not for letters to be sent (although clients may decide to do so), but to engender a feeling of empowerment. Moving on from the Tug-of-War exercise, the writing of a forgiveness letter is a further physical way for strong emotions to be externalised and dealt with.

Aims

This session aims to:

a   further explore forgiveness and how it feels to let go of a grudge; and
b   give clients the experience of expressing their forgiveness in a letter.

Session summary

- Mindful savouring
- Recap of experiences with sea of forgiveness exercise and progress with Good Things Box
- Warm-up: Tug-of-war
- Ongoing exercise: Forgiveness letter
- Mindful savouring

Materials needed

- Music
- Rope
- Paper
- Pens and pencils

Session plan

1 ENTER WITH MINDFUL SAVOURING   5 MINUTES

2 WELCOME AND RECAP   10 MINUTES

Therapists should discuss the experience of seeing the grudge in a sea of forgiveness and completing the exercise. This is a difficult exercise and some clients may not have been able to complete it. Prompt clients to look at their worksheets again and feed back what they have written and how they feel about letting go of the grudge, and discuss. If clients have not completed the exercise, normalise this and briefly prompt for some elements that clients can complete in this session or before the next session. If time allows, therapists should ask clients if anyone wants to share anything they added to their Good Things Box over the last week and any successful savouring experiences. Therapists should take the opportunity to remind clients to try to add things to their Good Things Box and to write in their journal any thoughts about the exercises, the topics covered or other positive things that they think may help them.

Therapists should be mindful that this may have been a challenging exercise for some clients and may have brought up difficult emotions. Emphasis should be given to the benefits of forgiveness for the person forgiving, and if relevant, a brief reminder of what forgiveness is, and is not, should be given.

3 WARM-UP: TUG-OF-WAR   35 MINUTES

This is an exercise in which clients have the opportunity to feel how letting go of a grudge and forgiveness feels from a bodily perspective.

Part 1

Therapists should begin by explaining that the exercise is going to encourage the group to think about forgiveness in a different way. Explain the rationale for this exercise by providing a brief explanation of the idea of embodiment: that just as our mind can influence bodily actions, our motor system, for example bodily movements, can have an impact on cognition and the way we think. The exercise will help show clients how thoughts can be experienced physically, as well as in the mind.

> Therapists may find the following example useful when helping clients understand the basics of the embodiment theory. Research has shown that when people hold a pencil in their teeth engaging the muscles of a smile, they comprehend pleasant sentences faster than unpleasant ones, while holding a pencil between their nose and upper lip to engage the muscles of a frown has the reverse effect.

Part 2

Ask clients to think about an incident where they felt let down by someone, and suggest that this is something meaningful and memorable, but nothing too major. Therapists should ask for two volunteers to share their examples and take part in the game. Encourage all clients to give an example and choose the two clients who they think are willing to let go of their grudge and have appropriate examples.

> Therapists should discuss clients' examples to ensure they are appropriate for the exercise, that is, not something too traumatic or likely to be very difficult to forgive. Therapists can suggest that clients' examples may be one from the worksheet if that is most appropriate to them.

Therapists should bring out the rope and explain that there is now going to be a game of tug-of-war. One volunteer should be asked to hold one end of the rope, and to let it represent the occasion when they have felt let down, and how it feels. One of the therapists should then take the other end of the rope, and explain that they are going to represent the person that let the client down. The volunteer should be asked to pull the rope gently, feeling the tension in the rope as it gets tauter. Ask the client to continue to think about the grudge, and envisage how it felt to be let down, imaging that the rope represents the anguish of feeling let down. Let the client do this for about 30 seconds, and prompt to ask how the client is feeling. The client should then be asked to drop the rope and take a step back. Therapists should ask the client how it felt to drop the rope, and therefore, in some ways, to let go of the grudge. Ask if the client still feels annoyed, or if they still feel the other person has power over them. Explain to the rest of the group that the exercise shows how people can take control over forgiveness and also the relief of tension that forgiveness may bring.

This should be repeated with another volunteer. Therapists should ask for reflections on the exercise from the group.

4 BREAK   10 MINUTES

5 ONGOING EXERCISE: FORGIVENESS LETTER   15 MINUTES

This is an exercise in which clients think about a person they would like to forgive, and write a letter to them, expressing their forgiveness. This letter does not need to be sent to the addressee.

Therapists should explain that in this exercise, the group is going to look further at forgiveness and also at its beneficial consequences, which were touched on briefly last session. It should be explained that the remainder of the session will be spent writing a forgiveness letter to someone who has let you down, where you explain that you have forgiven them. Clients should be asked to think about an example they have used before, or they can pick a new one if they want to. Therapists should go around the group and briefly ask clients who they picked, why they picked that person and why it may be beneficial to forgive that person.

Therapists should give clients the opportunity to write a greeting card or draw a picture to express their forgiveness if they don't want to write a letter. Other alternatives that therapists may suggest are painting, making something, or writing a poem or song. **Therapists should make it clear that the letter is just for the client – it is not intended that they send their letters.** This is because the focus in this session is on how forgiveness feels for the client, not for the person being forgiven. Ask clients to start the letter (or equivalent) in the session and try to finish over the next week. Remind clients that they can reflect on writing their letter in their journals.

Emphasise that not everyone needs to be forgiven, and that just because they may choose to forgive someone, does not mean they need to stay friends with that person.

Therapists should steer clients towards appropriate examples – that is, a person and a situation that the client genuinely wants to try to forgive. Therapists should acknowledge that it may be quite a difficult exercise for some clients, and that's why starting it in the group is important, so clients can ask questions and seek support from the therapists. As clients start the exercise, ask them to share if they are finding it difficult and how they can be helped to write the letter.

---

6 END WITH MINDFUL SAVOURING   5 MINUTES

Case studies

Sally

Sally did not attend this session. In her subsequent between-session call, she said she had started some new medication and had just not managed to get up early enough. The therapist said this was fine and that the group had been thinking of her. The therapist asked if she wanted to talk about the Sea of Forgiveness from the last session she had been to, and also what she had missed. Sally was quite quiet and reluctant to do so – so the therapist suggested maybe she came 10 minutes early to the next session and they could sit down and go through what she had missed, and that she shouldn't be worried about it at all. Sally was really grateful for this and said she would see the therapists a little earlier the next week.

William

William shared that he had completed the Sea of Forgiveness with some more positive attributes about his sister, which made forgiving her a lot easier. He said it had been a useful exercise and that he would remember it in the future.

William offered to take part in the Tug-of-War exercise. He said he had wanted to meet his friend David to play tennis, but David didn't turn up and hadn't given any warning. This was apparently not the first time David had let William down in this way. William said he was initially quite angry, especially as he had expected that this might happen anyway. The therapists asked William what options he felt he had. William said he could end his friendship with David (but he didn't want to since there were lots of good things about their friendship). He said he could tell David how angry he was, but that this may make David upset and may not change his behaviour in the future. The therapists suggested that perhaps William could concentrate on letting go of his anger about the situation, which may encourage forgiveness. William took part in the exercise, and shutting his eyes really gave some thought to tugging the rope and letting go. His body visibly relaxed after letting go of the rope. When asked how the exercise had affected him, William said he was surprised at how much physical energy the grudge had been taking up, and that by symbolising the rope as letting go of the grudge, William felt a great release and a lot less angry about the situation. He said that this didn't mean he would forgive David if he did it again, but could see the benefits to himself from forgiving David for this incident. Other members commented that they had learnt a lot from seeing William taking part in the exercise and hearing how it had affected him.

William decided to write the forgiveness letter to his sister in relation to the incident where she broke the picture. He started writing it in the session and planned to finish it over the next week.

Session 11: Gratitude

Rationale

Gratitude has a very strong correlation with mental health and life satisfaction, even more so than optimism, hope or compassion. It has been shown that people who feel grateful experience higher levels of positive emotions, such as joy, enthusiasm, love, happiness and optimism.[200] Further, it has been suggested that gratitude can also have a protective function – protecting us from negative feelings of envy, resentment and greed. People who experience gratitude are better able to deal with stress, recover more quickly from illness and show increased resilience when faced with traumatic situations.[207] This research suggests that gratitude is therefore incompatible with negative emotions and that it may even offer protection against psychiatric disorders.

Research has shown that gratitude is linked with positive emotions including contentment, happiness, pride and hope.[208] The same study found that clients who were randomly assigned to keep gratitude journals on a weekly basis exercised more regularly, reported fewer physical symptoms, felt better about their lives as a whole and were more optimistic about the upcoming week compared with those who recorded hassles or neutral life events.

Aims

This session aims to:

a   focus on the feeling of gratitude;
b   discuss the benefits of feeling grateful and expressing gratitude; and
c   introduce the gratitude letter.

Session summary

- Mindful savouring
- Recap of experiences with forgiveness letters
- Warm-up: Desert island ball
- Exercise: Feeling grateful
- Exercise: Gratitude timeline
- Ongoing exercise: Gratitude letter

Materials needed

- Music
- Handout 13
- Ball
- Pens and pencils

Session plan

1 ENTER WITH MINDFUL SAVOURING   5 MINUTES

2 WELCOME AND RECAP   5 MINUTES

Ask clients to share their experiences about writing their forgiveness letters. Therapists should probe how clients felt in writing the letter and any difficulties that may have arisen. Ask a few clients to share an item they have added to their Good Things Box and a successful savouring experience.

3 WARM-UP: DESERT ISLAND BALL   15 MINUTES

This is a game that gives clients the opportunity to think about those things in their life that they find valuable and for which they are grateful.

Therapists should introduce the exercise by explaining that it is designed to help clients identify and focus on those things in their lives that are particularly valuable to them. Encourage clients to form a circle, and explain the game is about throwing a ball around the circle, and when someone passes the ball, they should say something that they would like to take with them if they went to a desert island. Therapists should start the first round by saying that people should name physical objects they would want to take with them (examples might be: favourite music, chocolate, comfortable shoes, sunscreen). The second round should move onto choosing other people or qualities or characteristics that people really value and don't want to miss that you would like to take with you (examples might be: my sister, my neighbour's kindness, my mum's cooking, my friend's sense of humour).

> Therapists should ensure that it is emphasised that examples of objects can be as valuable as people, and that things do not need to be the 'necessities' of life, but more things that each client values as important to them.

Therapists should conclude by asking everyone to take a seat and briefly reflect on the task and what they had chosen to take with them.

4 EXERCISE: FEELING GRATEFUL   15 MINUTES

This is an exercise where clients learn to appreciate the benefits of feeling grateful and to discuss how feeling grateful feels.

Therapists remind clients that in the last session the group looked at forgiveness and thinking about how forgiving someone can sometimes be beneficial for the person doing the forgiving. They should explain that this session will continue by looking at our gratitude for positive outcomes and events. Therapists should inform the group that research has shown that gratitude is linked with positive emotions including contentment, happiness, pride and hope. The rationale for the session should be explained: to express gratitude towards another person, thus shifting attention away from bitter aspects of relationships towards embracing positive aspects.

Therapists should each provide a small, accessible, personal example of an occasion when they felt grateful and how being grateful felt. The therapists should then encourage discussion by the group of other examples where people have felt grateful for people, being careful to probe how being grateful felt for each client. Therapists may also want to ask clients if they expressed their gratitude to the person concerned, and if so, how this was received.

Explain that you don't have to be thankful for every miniscule thing others do for you – and that doing so may even elicit a feeling of powerlessness ('I am always the one who is helped'). Touch upon the fact that gratefulness can sometimes be a bittersweet feeling – but it's still beneficial to remember what we are thankful for.

Examples of occasions where people may feel grateful that may be useful:

- I forgot my purse when I went to the post office to a buy a stamp, and luckily I bumped into a friend there who generously lent me the money for a stamp. Her kindness really made me fortunate and cared for, and feeling grateful was a really warm feeling. I told my friend I really appreciated her kindness and she smiled and said I was welcome.

- I was running down the road in the rain to catch the bus, which had pulled into my stop a few hundred metres in front of me. A very nice lady asked the bus driver to hold the bus for me and kept the doors open until I reached it. I really appreciated her thoughtfulness – there are only two buses an hour and it really made a difference to catch this bus and not wait in the rain for the next one. I thanked the lady for being so kind and she accepted my thanks warmly.

---

5 BREAK   10 MINUTES

6 EXERCISE: GRATITUDE TIMELINE   15 MINUTES

This is an exercise where clients get to think about people in their lives to whom they are grateful.

Therapists should explain that in this exercise, the group is going to think about people in their lives that deserve recognition, and identify which of their actions in particular deserve recognition. Explain that the group is also going to think about how being grateful feels. Circulate Handout 13.

Therapists should briefly discuss the timeline and how it should be used, that is, going through each time period and writing down people in our lives to whom we're grateful, including a short note of what they have done that the client is grateful for. Therapists should each provide an example from their own timeline. When clients have completed the handout with some examples, ask for volunteers to briefly share their gratitude experiences.

Therapists should be aware that this may be a difficult exercise for some clients – who may have had traumatic experiences and so may find the need to recall their lives, challenging. Normalise these difficulties, and reassure clients that it's not necessary to give more than one example if they don't come to mind. It may also be the case that one person was especially important throughout a client's life (e.g. my mother did many things for which I am grateful).

7 ONGOING EXERCISE: GRATITUDE LETTER   10 MINUTES

This is an exercise where clients have the opportunity to think about a person to whom they are grateful, and experience and express their feelings of gratitude in a letter.

Therapists should explain that the ongoing exercise is writing a letter to someone to whom you are grateful. Like the forgiveness letter, this can be in the form of a painting, picture, poem or whatever a client chooses as most practical for them. What is the rationale about why this should help? Ask each client to think about a person to whom they feel especially grateful – this may be someone they mentioned on their gratitude timeline or a different person (potentially from a more recent single event for which they are grateful). Ask each client to briefly share with the group the person they are going to write to. Therapists should ensure the example is appropriate (i.e. realistic, suggesting of a situation where the client may feel genuinely thankful etc.). Where examples are not appropriate, therapists should gently try to get the client to suggest alternatives.

When clients are happy with their examples, ask everyone to start writing a letter to the person, describing their gratitude, and suggest that clients finish the letter over the next week. Therapists should discuss the boundaries of the exercise: the feelings of the letter recipients, if the letter is to be sent, if and when to send the letter, etc.

Therapists should remember that this may be a very difficult exercise for some clients, and this should be acknowledged and support provided accordingly. Therapists should empower clients to consider appropriate levels of gratitude. The reciprocal ('give and take') nature of many interactions should be emphasised to contextualise the concept of gratitude.

Therapists should remind clients to bring their Good Things Box to the next session.

8 END WITH MINDFUL SAVOURING   5 MINUTES

147

Case studies

Sally

As arranged, Sally arrived 10 minutes early for the session and ran through what she had missed with one of the therapists. While Sally couldn't practice the Tug-of-War exercise at home, she said she understood the concept of the exercise and would give it some thought in relation to people she felt had let her down. The therapists said they would go over some of the exercises again in the between-session call if that would help Sally, and Sally agreed and thanked the therapists for this.

Sally said she would take her cat and her favourite CDs with her to a desert island. When they moved onto the second part of the exercise, Sally said she would take her best friend's wit and her mother's kindness, since these were so important to her and she would miss them if she didn't take them with her. She said that it was interesting for her to think about what she was grateful for her in her life, and that she thought she would continue to make a note of these and add it to her Good Things Box. Other group members said this was a great idea and they would try to do it too.

Sally's example of feeling grateful was when the librarian gave her a lift home from the library when it was pouring with rain. Sally had waited half an hour until she hoped the rain had stopped, but at closing time it was still very heavy. One of the librarians offered to give Sally a lift home, for which Sally was very grateful, especially as she didn't know the librarian well. When asked how this made her feel, she said it made her feel like there were some really caring people in the world who did do lovely things, and that she was fortunate to meet one of them. She also said that the person offering the lift must also have gained some benefit in terms of caring for another and providing a favour, to which the therapists agreed this was another view of the situation and one that showed there are benefits to both feeling and grateful and doing something for which someone else is grateful.

Sally really enjoyed completing the Gratitude Timeline, and said it was really useful for her to think about how grateful she had been to people throughout her life. She said she had never really taken the time to remember this, but may use the timeline alongside the Good Things Box to remember good things in her life.

For her gratitude letter, Sally decided she would write it to her mother, who had looked after her so well after the death of her father when she was a child. She said her mother had sacrificed so much to give her a good life, and that she was still her best friend. She said while she said thank you to her for individual things, she didn't feel she had really got across to her mother how grateful she was for everything she had done. She said she understood she didn't need to give the letter to her, but said she would consider it once it was written.

William

William said he found it quite difficult to write a forgiveness letter to his sister. It took him some time to think through the reasons he was going to forgive her, but looked through the notes from the last session and reminded himself what forgiveness was, and what it wasn't, and he found it a lot easier. He did not plan to send the letter, but was glad he did it because it really made him think about the topic. The therapists congratulated him for his insight into forgiveness – they said it was very mature and he had clearly taken the time to try to understand it.

William started suggesting a lot of things he would take to a desert island, including his favourite foods, friends, clothes, music, etc. The therapists suggested maybe he thought about those things that he would miss the most, rather than everything he liked in his life. William then said he would probably take his favourite CDs and a pair of shoes he always felt comfortable in. When it came to thinking about people or feelings he would take with him – he said he would take his best friend, who was always supportive to him and made him laugh when he was feeling low. He said it was useful to think about the things in his life that were really important to him, and wrote these things down in his journal.

William's example of feeling grateful was when he had forgotten his keys, and had called his neighbour who had a spare pair. Despite his neighbour being in the local supermarket, he quickly came back and gave William his keys so he didn't have to wait long. William said he was so thankful to his neighbour and said he was really grateful. He said that feeling grateful was a nice feeling, and that he realised his example was something quite big, but that he would continue to think about things for which he was grateful, and would note them down.

William found the gratitude timeline quite difficult to complete, since he could think of people from his childhood (his parents) and currently (his friends), but that his life had been difficult in the middle and he was struggling to think of someone to whom he was grateful. The therapists said this didn't need to be anything big, just someone who may have done or said something small that William may have recalled. William said that when he had first attended his local day centre, his mentor had been really helpful in terms of training him to use a computer, and spending time teaching him, giving him skills that he still used today. The group agreed this was an excellent example and William noted this down.

William said he was going to write his gratitude letter to one of his primary school teachers, who had believed in him and helped him get some qualifications despite the fact that sometimes he was badly behaved and not that popular with the other children. He said it will always be something that he remembered, and that the teacher's support had really helped shape his character and given him the determination and belief that he could overcome difficult times. He said he would consider giving it to this teacher, who still lived locally, but would think about it over the coming week.

Session 12: Looking Back, Moving Forward

Rationale

This session encourages clients to think about the progress they have made over the sessions and to think about ways in which they can maintain gains that they have made – a session with a similar aim to Session 7. It also provides therapists with a chance to explain the importance of continuing work carried out in the sessions, after the therapy has finished. Research has shown that often gains made during a course of therapy are not maintained after the end of the therapy, and it has been suggested that this is in part down to the belief of clients that work carried out in the sessions is not something to be continued when the group ends. Further, literature shows that continuing exercises that have been carried out in therapy can help to maintain such gains, and therefore the emphasis on such maintenance is introduced in this session.

Aims

This session aims to:

a   give clients the opportunity to share with the group what they have put in their Good Things Box;
b   help clients think about positive experiences in their lives when they have been at their best; and
c   encourage discussion about how to maintain progress and continue using what has been learnt across the sessions.

Session summary

- Mindful savouring
- Recap of experiences with writing gratitude letters
- Exercise: Good Things Box
- Exercise: When I'm at my best
- Ongoing exercise: Maintenance – how to continue using what we have learnt
- Mindful savouring

Materials needed

- Music
- Handout 14
- Pens and pencils

Session plan

1 ENTER WITH MINDFUL SAVOURING   **5 MINUTES**

2 WELCOME AND RECAP   **10 MINUTES**

Therapists should explore with clients their experiences of writing their gratitude letters. Clients should be invited to share their letters with the group if they want to. Therapists should take this opportunity to remind the group about positive responding and model this in relation to people's stories and experiences of gratitude. Ask for volunteers to share one successful savouring experience they have had over the last week.

3 EXERCISE: GOOD THINGS BOX   **15 MINUTES**

This is an exercise in which the group gets to share some of the good things that they have put into their Good Things Box.

Therapists should explain that this is a good opportunity to remind themselves of some of the good things they have put into their Good Things Box, and to share some of these with the group. Therapists should share some of the things in their own Good Things Box first, and ensure that they emphasise what they had to do to make those good things happen.

> Therapists should ensure they use accessible examples of good things, and share a mixture of examples, such as objects and Good Things Cards, reminders of small things that meant a lot and bigger events, etc. Positive responding should be modelled and encouraged by the therapists.

Each client should then be asked to share a few items in their Good Things Box, and explain what those items or notes on Good Things Cards mean to them. Therapists should probe to ensure clients have made a note of the dates on which these good things happened. Once this has been completed, therapists should encourage a short discussion on the meaning of these good things, and how their Good Things Box can be used going forward. For example, clients can continue to collect things and add them to the boxes, can get copies, or make their own copies of, additional good things cards, and should go back to the Good Things Box when they are finding things difficult, to remind themselves of good things that have happened.

4 EXERCISE: WHEN I'M AT MY BEST   **15 MINUTES**

This is a repeat of the 'When I'm at my best' exercise in Sessions 2 and 7, and gives the clients an opportunity to think of another occasion when they have been 'at their best' and reflect on it with the group.

Therapists should remind clients about the same exercise that they did in Sessions 2 and 7 and explain that the group is going to consider this exercise again, and share another story of when people were at their best.

Therapists should emphasise that clients may well look at situations in different ways following some of the sessions, and should be encouraged to come up with a different, and more recent example. More recent examples should be provided by the therapists, together with a brief explanation of what they thought they learnt from such an experience. Clients should then be encouraged to share their own stories, together with that they have learnt from them.

Positive responding should again be modelled and encouraged by the therapists. Some clients may find this difficult – it may be useful for therapists to have considered their post-session notes on clients' progress through the sessions, in order to be able to provide some relevant prompts from examples clients have given in previous sessions.

---

5 BREAK   10 MINUTES

6 EXERCISE: WHEN I'M AT MY BEST (CONTINUED)   10 MINUTES

The exercise should be continued to allow all clients the opportunity to provide a story of when they have been at their best. Reflect on how thinking about and telling these stories now feels different to how it felt like the first time around. Elicit and reinforce feedback on gains in self-esteem and positive self-images.

7 ONGOING EXERCISE: MAINTENANCE – USING WHAT
WE HAVE LEARNT   15 MINUTES

This is an exercise where therapists discuss with clients how they can continue using what they have learnt and how to maintain the progress and gains they have made.

Therapists should explain to clients that it is important not only to recognise what each of them has learnt over the sessions, but also to think about how they can continue to use what they have learnt, and maintain the progress and gains they have made.

Therapists should remind clients about the key learning topics from Positive Psychotherapy for Psychosis – Savouring, Good Things, Personal Strengths, Gratitude, Forgiveness, and One Door Closes, Another Door Opens, Positive Responding and Positive Self-Image. Circulate Handout 14.

Ask clients to remember the work they have done, and look over their handouts (especially Handout 9). If clients have not brought handouts with them, encourage them to think about what they had included on it. Discuss whether clients have practised the skills they developed in sessions in the rest of their life. If they have practised these, encourage clients to think about ways to improve their strategy. If clients have not managed to practise, reflect on why they didn't manage to do this and what clients could do differently that may be more helpful. Following this, ask clients to note these strategies down on Handout 12. Clients can start noting methods they think about during the session in their journals, and continue to do this over the next week.

> Therapists should then ask clients to suggest ways in which they can keep each of these things going after the sessions. Approaches might include practising the exercises again, continuing to use the journal to note down experiences, using their Good Things Box, remembering the benefits of forgiveness and gratitude, trying to savour something different each week, etc. Be specific. Encourage clients to think about when and how they are going to practise each of these things (e.g. think about a positive thing that happened every evening when brushing their teeth or remembering to savour one bite of breakfast every morning).

8 END WITH MINDFUL SAVOURING   5 MINUTES

Case studies

Sally

Sally's mood seemed to have improved a little over the last week. She said she had finished her gratitude letter to her mother, and it had been quite an emotional process for her and had made her remember everything she had done for her and how it had made her feel. She said she planned to give it to her but only after giving herself some time to fully appreciate the emotions that had been generated. The therapists reminded her that the intention was not for the letter to be sent, and that it was optional, but if she wished to send it then of course she could.

Sally shared some of the things in her Good Things Box. She had put in a few pictures of her and her best friend having a picnic, and had written the date on the back, and the steps involved in her making the picnic happen. She was congratulated for remembering to do this. She also had a Good Things Card on which she had written about a trip to the cinema she had made with her brother to see a film she had really enjoyed, and again she had remembered to put down the date and what she had done (booking the tickets and checking the bus times). She said she would continue to use the Good Things Box as she really identified with the purpose and it was good to boost her mood.

Sally's example of when she had been at her best was when she had confronted her anxiety and attended a church event where she had offered to run a stall making fun balloon figures for children all day. It had been a long day (and her fingers had hurt from the balloon modelling by the end!), but she was really pleased she had achieved the goal, interacted with people and received a lot of praise for her efforts. She said this taught her to challenge her fears and that once she got there, she felt a lot better. Sally hadn't written this down yet, so the therapist suggested she made a note of this in her journal and came back to it later to remind herself of her achievements.

When asked how she had got on with her plans for maintaining her progress which she completed in Session 7, Sally said she felt she had done quite well. She had planned to continue to make good use of her Good Things Box, and felt she had done this, with which the rest of the group agreed. She wanted to make a note of more savouring experiences, which she had done, and tried putting these into action. Sally showed the group a list of savouring experiences she had compiled in her journal. Next to each one she had completed, she had written briefly about the experience and how it made her feel. Several members of the group said they would try this too since it sounded like a useful method. Among Sally's favourite savouring activities was baking bread. She had started making different breads and experimenting with different recipes. She said on the weekend she really enjoyed listening to classical music and baking bread, and enjoying the smell as it baked, and the taste when she had some of the bread for lunch. One client said she had really described the experience very well, and it was interesting that Sally used all five senses in this experience. This client was commended for such an insight, and there was a brief discussion after this about using different senses in savouring experiences.

Sally said she wanted to extend her savouring experiences to include activities with others, since she acknowledged her activities did not involve anyone else. The therapists praised her for challenging herself even more, and asked her to write this down in her journal.

William

William brought his gratitude letter written to his teacher to the session, and read part of it out. He said he had written it over a few days to give himself sufficient time to remember everything his teacher had done for him. The group responded positively to him, especially with regard to how well he had written down his feelings of gratitude. He said he was not going to send it but would keep it in his journal and look back at it.

William shared a few things from his Good Things Box, including a pen. He said this was the pen he had used when he passed a test in basic electrics at his day centre, and reminded him of how proud he was of this achievement. The group congratulated him on this achievement and liked the way in which he had chosen to remember this. William hadn't written any notes about this event, so was encouraged to also complete a Good Things Card noting down the event, the date and what he had done to make it happen.

William's story about when he had been at his best over the past few weeks was how he had refused to let an acquaintance sleep on his sofa.

He said the man always wanted to stay, and he ended up taking advantage, eating all William's food and taking some of his things. William was proud he had stood up to him, because he had been scared about the man's response. He said this had actually just been accepted and he hadn't heard anything about it since. William said he thought about the work he had done on forgiveness and thinking about overusing strengths. He said his strength was kindness but he had been overusing that and had been taken advantage of. He said he had forgiven the man, but this didn't mean he excused his behaviour or would be maintaining the relationship. The therapists were really pleased – William had used many of the things he had learnt and really showed a mature way of thinking. The rest of the group were really impressed with William's account, and said it was a good example for them.

William said he felt he had really continued making progress, and that he had also succeeded in his goal from Session 7 – to think more about savouring experiences. He said he tried to savour a few new things every week and make a note of these. One example he gave was enjoying watching the Saturday afternoon football games at his friend's house – they would have a good catch up about the week and he would enjoy the match. He hadn't written a note about this but said he would. He said he had also shared some of the things in his Good Things Box with one of his friends, as he had planned to do. He was worried his friend wouldn't understand, but actually his friend thought it was a great idea and went and got a box for himself! To continue maintaining his progress, William thought he needed to move his Good Things Box to the side of his bed, so he remembered it before going to bed every night. He also said he wanted to write more about each savouring experience, as Sally had been doing, since he thought this would be very useful for him. The therapists praised him for taking such responsibility for his progress and for his determination.

Session 13: Celebration

Rationale

This celebration session provides an opportunity for clients to think about what they have learned and enjoyed throughout the sessions, and to cement key learning by reviewing and discussing main learning points. This will build clients' confidence in how far they have come. Clients are also given Positive Psychotherapy for Psychosis certificates to congratulate them on their completion. This will reinforce positive self-image, self-esteem and belief in their abilities. In advance of the session, therapists write letters to each client, highlighting their progress across the sessions. The session notes taken on each client following each session can serve as a basis for writing these letters. These letters provide lasting mementoes of each client's contribution to, and learning from, the sessions.

Aims

The aims of this session are to:

a   revisit positive experiences throughout the sessions; and
b   celebrate achievements with a certificate ceremony.

Session summary

- Mindful savouring
- Recap of maintaining gains
- Learning experiences
- Certificate and letter ceremony
- Mindful savouring

Materials needed

- Music
- Completed and signed certificates (shown in Appendix 3)
- Personalised end-of-session letters
- Celebratory food and drink
- Pen and pencils

Therapist preparation

Therapists should prepare two documents for each client before the session:

Certificates

An example certificate is included in Appendix 3. This should be completed for each client and signed by both therapists.

End of session letters

Therapists should try to write these letters together, referring to the post-session notes they made for each client. These letters should be a couple of short paragraphs, mentioning specific, personalised examples of all the praised aspects referred to in the letters. Language should be kept simple and easy to understand.

Session plan

1 ENTER WITH MINDFUL SAVOURING   **5 MINUTES**

2 WELCOME AND RECAP   **10 MINUTES**

Discuss clients' experiences of noting ways to maintain gains and progress that they should have noted in their journals over the last week. Also ask for volunteers for one good thing they noted in their Good Things Box and one new successful savouring exercise they undertook.

3 EXERCISE: LEARNING EXPERIENCES   **15 MINUTES**

Go around the group and ask clients what they feel they have learned across the sessions and exercises, and what they have particularly enjoyed. Specifically encourage discussion on target areas of Positive Psychotherapy for Psychosis and how clients feel these areas have benefited them throughout the sessions. Prompt clients with key session topics where necessary. Suggest clients make a brief note of these things in their journals, and continue this after the session.

4 BREAK   **10 MINUTES**

If possible, a special selection of cakes (or similar) should be provided. Clients should be invited to think about savouring their cakes or drinks and reflecting on how this feels for them, especially in the context of the celebratory nature of the food.

5 CERTIFICATE AND LETTER CEREMONY   **40 MINUTES**

Music should be playing in the background throughout the second half of the session, and refreshments can continue to be served. The room can be decorated too if the therapists wish! Explain that the last half of the session will be spent recognising and celebrating the achievements of everyone in the group across the sessions. Further explain that each client will be receiving a certificate, as a record of their achievements over the course, and also a personal letter to the client setting out their achievements and strengths. Clients should also be given the choice as to whether to read out their letter to the group, have one of the therapists read the letter to the group, or for the client to read to himself.

For each client in turn, therapists should present them with a certificate and letter. Give clients some time to read the letter silently for themselves. Then give them the option to have either the clients themselves or therapist, if wanted, read out the letter to the group. Therapists should encourage positive responding from other members of the group. Ask each client what they think about the letter, how they feel about it and what they would add. Ask the group for more feedback and for things they would add to the letter.

For some clients, reading out their letters may be very challenging and/or daunting. Therapists should therefore try to gauge the group before the exercise to see what process may be more appropriate.

6 END WITH MINDFUL SAVOURING   5 MINUTES

Since it is the last session, therapists should ask if any of the group wants to lead the last mindful savouring exercise. Emphasise that it doesn't need to be perfect; it would just be a nice opportunity for someone to have a go if they want to. If more than one person volunteers, let them take responsibility for savouring different parts (i.e. first half) of the music.

If booster sessions are being offered, remind clients of the invitation to optional booster sessions and briefly explain again what these would consist of. Invite clients to note down their contact details to receive a booster session reminder in the future.

Case studies

Sally

Sally seemed to really enjoy this session. She said she had written down her new plans for maintaining the progress she had made. When discussing the things that each of the group had learnt, Sally felt she had really benefited from thinking about her strengths – she said it was difficult to start with, since she had never really thought there was anything she was good at. However, through the sessions, she began to see she had a number of strengths and realised that by using these, she could increase her confidence and discover new areas of interest. She said the other main things she had learnt were savouring, which helped her to relax and appreciate small things in her life, and gratitude – for her this was a really strong emotion and she felt it was useful to think about all she had to be thankful for.

Sally was proud to receive her certificate and seemed really pleasantly surprised when she read out her letter. She said she had no idea that she had been perceived in so many positive ways, and that the therapists thought her progress had been excellent. She said she was more inclined to believe this following her recounting her stories of when she had been at her best. She planned to keep the letter and put it in her Good Things Box. She thanked the therapists for such a lovely letter, and the rest of the members said it had been great to have Sally in the group, and she had taught them a lot.

Sally joined in the last mindful savouring session with enthusiasm, and said she planned to attend the booster sessions since it would be useful to see how she had continued her progress and get some more support.

William

William felt he had noted down his key progress points over the week, and intended to go to the booster session to try to ensure his progress continued. He felt his key learning experiences from the sessions were learning how to savour activities, using the Good Things Box and learning about the concept of forgiveness, especially the benefits to the person forgiving and also what forgiveness means and doesn't mean. He said he had been holding a lot of negative emotions about people who had let him down, and that by using what he had learnt in the sessions, he had let go of many of these things, sometimes choosing to maintain the friendship and other times deciding he would be better off not continuing the relationship. The therapists said they were really impressed by his progress over the sessions and how much he had learnt. This was reflected in William's end-of-session letter – which he managed to read out despite not finding reading easy and getting quite emotional when going through it. The letter included many references to William's progress and William was amazed that the therapists had remembered these things. The group congratulated William and said his sense of humour and caring nature had made him a real asset to the group. William seemed touched by all of this, and sat down smiling.

William offered to lead the mindful savouring of music – and did a very good job! He had clearly progressed from the first session where he found it quite difficult to concentrate. He had listened intently to the therapists in the previous sessions and guided the exercise impressively. The rest of the group and the therapists thanked him afterwards for doing this so well.

Appendix 1

Positive Psychotherapy for Psychosis

JOURNAL

This is your journal.

Please remember to bring it to every session.

WELCOME TO POSITIVE PSYCHOTHERAPY FOR PSYCHOSIS

Session 1

WHAT IS THIS SESSION ABOUT?

You will be introduced to Positive Psychotherapy for Psychosis and you will also be given your journal.

What will we be doing in this session?

- Pass the ball warm-up exercise
- Introduction to Positive Psychotherapy for Psychosis
- Expectations
- Introduction to the journal
- Ongoing exercises – what are they?
- Exercise: Pass the ball

POSITIVE EXPERIENCES

Session 2

WHAT IS THIS SESSION ABOUT?

You will be introduced to positive responding and also have the opportunity to share with the group a time when you feel you have been 'at your best'.

What will we be doing in this session?

- One thing about you warm-up exercise
- Introducing positive responding
- Exercise: At my best
- Ongoing exercises – continued
- Exercise: Pass the ball

Ongoing exercise

Note down your positive story 'at my best' in your journal.

SAVOURING

Session 3

WHAT IS THIS SESSION ABOUT?

We practise slowing down and consciously enjoying experiences.

What will we be doing in this session?

- Learning about the process of savouring
- Exercise: Mindful eating – enjoying the taste, texture
- Exercise: Mindful listening – enjoying the sounds we can hear

Ongoing exercise

Think of some experiences to savour in your own time. Record some of these experiences in your journal.

GOOD THINGS

Session 4

WHAT IS THIS SESSION ABOUT?

We concentrate on good things that happen and how recording this experiences can be good for your wellbeing.

What will we be doing in this session?

- Stand up who . . . warm-up

- Good Things: Think of good things that have happened today

- Consider what you did to make this good thing happen

Ongoing exercise

Add mementoes of good things that have happened to you every day or write about them on a Good Things Card and put them in your Good Things Box.

165

IDENTIFYING A PERSONAL STRENGTH

Session 5

WHAT IS THIS SESSION ABOUT?

We focus on our personal strengths and how recognising these can be helpful in maintaining mood and mental health.

What will we be doing in this session?

- The Last Roll – warm-up
- Exercise: Personal Strengths
- Exercise: Identifying a personal character strength

Ongoing exercise

Reflect on your personal character strength and write about it in your journal.

USING PERSONAL STRENGTHS

Session 6

WHAT IS THIS SESSION ABOUT?

We consider how we can put our strengths into practice by planning a personal strength activity.

What will we be doing in this session?

- Recap of identifying personal strengths
- Playing to your strengths – warm-up
- Exercise: Identify and plan a personal strength activity

Ongoing exercise

Carry out your personal strength activity and record your experiences in your journal.

167

AT MY BEST

Session 7

WHAT IS THIS SESSION ABOUT?

We focus on the strengths you share with other people.

What will we be doing in this session?

- Compliments – warm-up
- Recap of Good Things
- Exercise: When I'm at my best
- Introduction to next sessions

Ongoing exercise

Exploring ways to maintain gains in progress, noting these down and plans of how to put these into action.

ONE DOOR CLOSES, ANOTHER DOOR OPENS

Session 8

WHAT IS THIS SESSION ABOUT?

We look at difficult experiences from which we can see a positive outcome.

What will we be doing in this session?

- Ball Challenge warm-up

- Exercise: Think about times when negative events in your past had positive outcomes

Ongoing exercise

Try and identify more situations where you can see positive aspects of negative experiences and record these experiences in your Good Things Box or journal.

FORGIVENESS (1)

Session 9

WHAT IS THIS SESSION ABOUT?

We focus on forgiveness as a way of changing bitter feelings into neutral or positive ones.

What will we be doing in this session?

- Celebrity Forgiveness warm-up

- Exercise: What is forgiveness?

- Exercise: Feeling disappointed or let down by others

- Exercise: Grudge Surrounded by a Sea of Forgiveness – identify a grudge you hold against someone and consider their positive characteristics

Ongoing exercise

Continue with and complete the Sea of Forgiveness exercise.

170

FORGIVENESS (2)

Session 10

WHAT IS THIS SESSION ABOUT?

We continue to think about the importance of forgiveness.

What will we be doing in this session?

- Tug of War – warm-up

- Exercise: Forgiveness Letter – write to someone who has let you down and express your forgiveness

Ongoing exercise

Complete your forgiveness letter and reflect on it in your journal.

GRATITUDE

Session 11

WHAT IS THIS SESSION ABOUT?

We focus on gratitude and its link with positive emotions.

What will we be doing in this session?

- Desert Island Ball – warm-up
- Exercise: Feeling grateful
- Exercise: Gratitude timeline

Ongoing exercise

Write a gratitude letter to someone to whom you are grateful and reflect on it in your journal.

LOOKING BACK, MOVING FORWARD

Session 12

WHAT IS THIS SESSION ABOUT?

Sharing with the group some of the things in the Good Things Boxes, a further time recently where people have been 'at their best' and discussion about maintaining progress.

What will we be doing in this session?

- Gratitude Letter – Reflect on your gratitude letter and share your experiences

- Good Things Box – Have a look and see what you have collected over the past weeks

- Exercise: When I'm at my best

Ongoing exercise

Thinking about maintenance – how to continue using what you have learnt.

173

CELEBRATION

Session 13

WHAT IS THIS SESSION ABOUT?

We look back at what we have achieved!

What will we be doing in this session?

- Exercise: learning experiences
- Certificate and letter ceremony

Ongoing exercise

Keep up the good work. Remember, you can use the exercises and your journal at any time!

Appendix 2

Handouts

Handout	1	Positive Psychotherapy for Psychosis overview
Handout	2	Positive responding
Handout	3	Savouring
Handout	4	Things I plan to savour this week
Handout	5	Good Things Cards
Handout	6	Good Things Cards (blank)
Handout	7	Identifying Personal Strengths
Handout	8	Personal Strength Activity
Handout	9	Compliments
Handout	10	One Door Closes, Another Door Opens
Handout	11	Forgiveness
Handout	12	Sea of Forgiveness
Handout	13	Gratitude Timeline
Handout	14	How can I maintain my progress?

POSITIVE PSYCHOTHERAPY FOR PSYCHOSIS OVERVIEW

Handout 1

WHAT IS POSITIVE PSYCHOTHERAPY FOR PSYCHOSIS?

Positive Psychotherapy for Psychosis aims to increase wellbeing. This is done by helping you to identify and use your strengths, meaning and positive relationships.

WHAT DO WE DO IN EACH SESSION?

Each session lasts for 90 minutes including a 10-minute break. You will be given a journal to record your personal experiences.

SESSIONS:

Session 1: Welcome to Positive Psychotherapy for Psychosis
Session 2: Positive Experiences
Session 3: Savouring
Session 4: Good Things
Session 5: Personal Strengths
Session 6: Personal Strength Activity
Session 7: At My Best
Session 8: One Door Closes, Another Door Opens
Session 9: Forgiveness (1)
Session 10: Forgiveness (2)
Session 11: Gratitude
Session 12: Looking Back, Moving Forward
Session 13: Celebration

GROUP GUIDELINES:

- Try to arrive on time

- Switch off mobile phones

- Stories, personal details and experiences shared in this group stay in the room

- Listen to others when they are speaking

- Be considerate towards other group members

POSITIVE RESPONDING

Handout 2

A friend tells you he/she has managed to get a part-time voluntary job. How do you respond?

'That is wonderful! I am so happy for you. You will be an excellent volunteer! What will the work involve?'

Responding enthusiastically; maintaining eye contact, smiling, displaying positive emotions; showing interest

'But if you start volunteering, I won't be able to see you as much.'

Pointing out the downside; displaying negative feelings

'That's nice, that you are volunteering.'

Happy but lacking enthusiasm; little to no active emotional expression

'Oh. Remind me again when we are going to the cinema next week.'

Lacking interest; displaying little to no eye contact; turning away or leaving the room

177

SAVOURING

Handout 3

SAVOURING GUIDANCE

Give yourself breaks for savouring every day. In order to savour, you need to set aside some time. Try to slow things down. Even a few seconds can bring about a positive feeling. Here are some guidelines you can follow:

1   Savouring needs time

2   Let yourself savour

3   Everyone is different – know what you like and what you want to savour!

4   Savouring is something you can do every day

5   Take time to find out which of your senses (sight, hearing, taste, smell and touch) you want to use to savour

SAVOURING SUGGESTIONS

Here are some examples of everyday experiences that you could savour:

- Eating a meal you've cooked yourself
- Having a bubble bath
- Talking to friends
- Going for a walk in the park
- Listening to music

178

THINGS I PLAN TO SAVOUR THIS WEEK

Handout 4

Date: _____

Date: _____

GOOD THINGS CARDS

Handout 5

It is common for people to worry about things that went wrong that day and what might go wrong in the future. The aim of this session is to counteract this natural tendency to focus on negatives. This exercise wants to encourage you to look at the positives.

Think of at least one good thing that has happened to you and fill out some **Good Things Cards** (see example below)

- Place the cards in your personal Good Things Box

- Instead of filling out a card, you may consider putting a small object into your box (e.g. newspaper clippings if you enjoyed reading an article, a sachet of sugar from a café where you enjoyed having a drink)

- By the end of the group, you should have collected a number of things, which remind you of positive experiences. You may even find it useful to refer back to your Good Things Box when you are feeling low.

Example of a completed **Good Things Card**

GOOD THINGS CARD
Date: *day/month/year*   Place: *Café*
Good thing that happened today: *I met my friend and we went to a cafe for a cup of coffee. We had a really good time catching up ...*
How I helped this happen: ✓ *called my friend and arranged the meeting* ✓ *got myself ready to leave the house* ✓ *got on a bus in order to get to a cafe*

180

GOOD THINGS CARDS

Handout 6

GOOD THINGS CARD

Date: _____   Place: _____

Good thing that happened today:

How I helped this happen:

GOOD THINGS CARD

Date: _____   Place: _____

Good thing that happened today:

How I helped this happen:

IDENTIFYING PERSONAL STRENGTHS

Handout 7

Do you identify with any of the strengths below?

Appreciation
of beauty

Enthusiasm

Bravery

Fairness

Capacity to love
and be loved

Forgiveness

Caution

Gratitude

Creativity

Honesty

Curiosity

Humour

IDENTIFYING PERSONAL STRENGTHS

Handout 7 *continued*

Kindness

Leadership

Love of learning

Modesty

Perseverance

Open-mindedness

Optimism

Self-control

Spirituality

Social skills

Teamwork

Wisdom

183

PERSONAL STRENGTH ACTIVITY

Handout 8

My chosen activity for next week is:

_____

_____

Where? _____

When? (Day, time)_____

What will I will in order to do this?
(This could be money, transport, information, materials, help from other people, etc.)

- _____

_____

- _____

_____

- _____

_____

What personal strengths can I use to achieve this?

- _____

- _____

- _____

- _____

- _____

184

COMPLIMENTS

Handout 9

Name _____

Here are your compliments:

ONE DOOR CLOSES, ANOTHER DOOR OPENS

Handout 10

Write about a time in your life when you lost out on something important or when a big plan collapsed. Then consider what doors opened after other doors closed.

Here is an example:

 ### When something bad happened

My bus broke down on the way to the library and by the time I got there the library was shut.

 ### What good thing(s) came out of it

However, the library had kept a set of second-hand books outside that were free for the public, so I managed to pick up a great book to read and can now lend it to my sister when I've finished with it.

 ### When something bad happened

 ### What good thing(s) came out of it

 ### When something bad happened

 ### What good thing(s) came out of it

186

FORGIVENESS

Handout 11

WHAT IS FORGIVENESS?

Forgiveness increases positive emotions about the past and self-control while bitterness causes rumination and resentment. Forgiving another person can help to transform feelings of anger and bitterness into feelings of neutrality or positive emotions.

Forgiveness is . . .

- ✓ a process of change
- ✓ being understanding and generous to someone who has let you down
- ✓ a process of reducing negative feelings
- ✓ letting go of grudges
- ✓ about releasing the hold that the person has over you
- ✓ _____
- ✓ _____

Forgiveness is NOT . . .

- ✗ an event
- ✗ mindlessly replacing feelings
- ✗ overlooking or ignoring a wrongdoing
- ✗ giving permission for hurtful behaviour to continue
- ✗ excusing a past event
- ✗ necessarily reconciliation
- ✗ _____
- ✗ _____

187

SEA OF FORGIVENESS

Handout 12

The tinted circle represents a grudge that you are holding. While you are holding this grudge in mind, write something positive about the person in each circle.

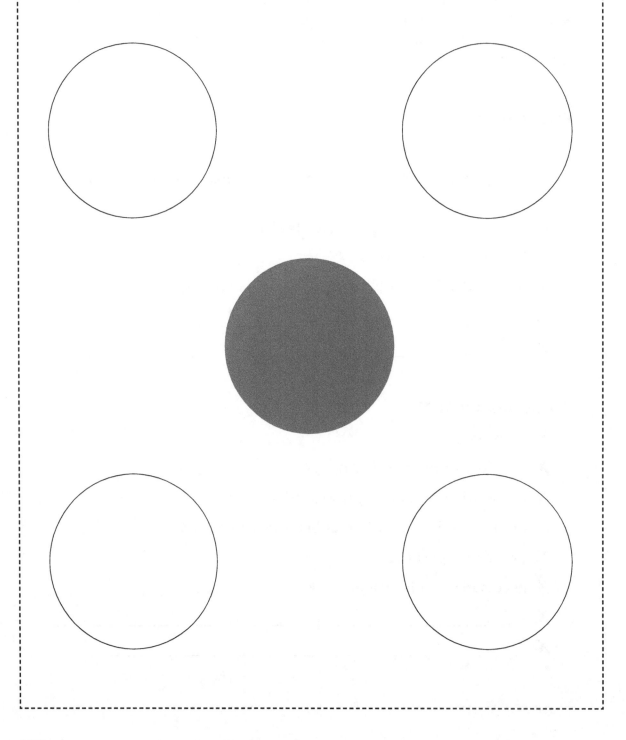

SEA OF FORGIVENESS

Handout 12 *continued*

As you look at the sea of forgiveness, how are you able to see the situation differently? In what way do you feel differently about the person?

Do you feel more ready or willing to work towards forgiveness (remember, forgiveness is for you, not the person who wronged you)? What will you do?

Do you feel as though you would like to restore your relationship with that person?

GRATITUDE TIMELINE

Handout 13

Think of one or more important people that played a positive role in your life.

To help you remember, use the timeline below.

Adulthood

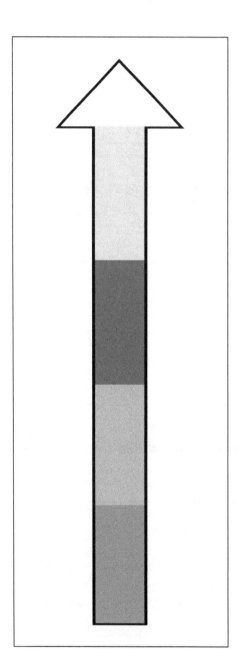

Early years

HOW CAN I MAINTAIN MY PROGRESS?

Handout 14

What have I found useful in these sessions?

- Positive responding

- Savouring

- Good Things Box

- Good Things Cards

- Personal strengths

- Gratitude

- Forgiveness

- One door closes, another door opens

What will I do to keep these going in the future?

For example, practising the exercises, using the journal, using the Good Things Box, remembering the benefits of forgiveness and gratitude, trying to savour something different every day, etc.

_____

_____

_____

How will I remember?

For example, think about a positive thing that happened every evening when brushing my teeth, savour one bite of breakfast every morning

_____

_____

_____

191

Appendix 3

Additional resources

Positive Psychotherapy for Psychosis equipment checklist

Example Music List

Personal Strengths Cards

Certificate

POSITIVE PSYCHOTHERAPY FOR PSYCHOSIS
EQUIPMENT CHECKLIST

All sessions

- Music
- Pencils
- Felt-tip pens
- Refill pad
- Refreshments
- Plastic cups
- Napkins

Session 1   Welcome to Positive Psychotherapy for Psychosis

- Journals containing all pages in Appendix 1
- Ball
- Handout 1

Session 2   Positive experiences

- Flipchart
- Scissors
- Blu-tack
- Handout 2

Session 3   Savouring

- Food (chocolate, grapes, popcorn)
- Music for savouring
- Handouts 3 and 4

Session 4 Good Things

- Good Things Boxes
- Handouts 5 (x1) and 6 (x2)

Session 5 Identifying a Personal Strength

- Toilet paper rolls
- Strengths pictures (shown in Appendix 3)
- Handout 7

Session 6 Personal Strengths

- Flipchart
- Handout 8

Session 7 At My Best

- Handout 9

Session 8 One Door Closes, Another Door Opens

- Two balls
- Two other items that can be thrown
- Handout 10

Session 9 Forgiveness (1)

- Flipchart
- Handouts 11 and 12

Session 10 Forgiveness (2)

- Rope

Session 11   Gratitude

- Ball
- Handout 13

Session 12   Looking Back, Moving Forward

- Handout 14

Session 13   Celebration

- Personalised end-of-session letters
- Ball
- Completed and signed certificates (see p. 202)
- Celebratory food and drink

Example Music List

- Joseph Haydn, Opus 20 ("the Sun Quartets"), String Quartet No.1 in C Major, Moderato

- Blank & Jones, Desire (Ambient Mix)

- Georg Friedrich Händel, Concerti grossi in B-flat Major, Allegro ma non troppo

- Nacho Sotomayor, *Café del Mar*

- Single Cell Orchestra, *Transmit Liberation*

- D'Note, *D'Votion*

- Joseph Haydn, Opus 20 ("the Sun Quartets"), String Quartet No.6 in A Major, Adagio

- Nova Nova, *Tones*

- dZihan & Kamien, *Homebase*

- Wolfgang Amadeus Mozart, Piano Concerto No. 9, 1st movement

- Ludwig van Beethoven, Opus 68, Symphony No.6 in F Major ("Pastoral Symphony"), 1st movement, Allegro ma non troppo

Appreciation of beauty

Bravery

Capacity to love/ be loved

Caution

Creativity

Curiosity

Kindness

Leadership

Love of learning

Modesty

Perseverance

Open-mindedness

Enthusiasm/energy

Fairness

Forgiveness

Gratitude

Honesty

Humour

Optimism

Self-control

201

Spirituality

Social skills

Teamwork

Wisdom

POSITIVE PSYCHOTHERAPY FOR PSYCHOSIS CERTIFICATE

Positive Psychotherapy for Psychosis

This certificate is awarded to

_____

for

_____

your achievements in the Positive Psychotherapy for Psychosis group

Signature _____

Date _____

References

1   The Schizophrenia Commission. *The Abandoned Illness: A Report from the Schizophrenia Commission*. London: Rethink Mental Illness; 2012.

2   Andrews A., Knapp M., McCrone P., Parsonage M., Trachtenberg M. *Effective Interventions in Schizophrenia the Economic Case: A Report Prepared for the Schizophrenia Commission*. London: Rethink Mental Illness; 2012.

3   Slade M. Mental illness and well-being: The central importance of positive psychology and recovery approaches. *BMC Health Services Research* 2010; **10**: 26.

4   Mankiewicz P., Gresswell D., Turner C. Happiness in severe mental illness: Exploring subjective wellbeing of individuals with psychosis and encouraging socially inclusive multidisciplinary practice. *Mental Health and Social Inclusion* 2013; **17**: 27–34.

5   Werner S. Subjective well-being, hope, and needs of individuals with serious mental illness. *Psychiatry Research* 2012; **30**(196): 214–9.

6   Hanlon P., Carlisle S. What can the science of well-being tell the discipline of psychiatry – and why might psychiatry listen? *Advances in Psychiatric Treatment* 2008; **14**: 312–219.

7   Riches S., Schrank B., Rashid T., Slade M. Wellfocus PPT: Modifying Positive Psychotherapy for Psychosis. *Psychotherapy* 2016; **53**(1): 68–77. doi.org/10.1037/pst0000013.

8   Schrank B., Brownell T., Jakaite Z., Larkin C., Pesola F., Riches S., Tylee A., Slade M. Evaluation of a positive psychotherapy group intervention for people with psychosis: Pilot randomized controlled trial. *Epidemiology and Psychiatric Sciences* 2015; **25**(3): 235–246. doi:10.1017/S2045796015000141.

9   Brownell T., Schrank B., Jakaite Z., Larkin C., Slade M. Mental health service user experience of positive psychotherapy. *Journal of Clinical Psychology* 2015; **71**: 85–92.

10 Schrank B., Brownell T., Riches S., Chevalier A., Jakaite Z., Larkin C., Lawrence V., Slade M. Staff views on wellbeing for themselves and for service users. *Journal of Mental Health* 2015; **24**: 48–53.

11 Schrank B., Riches S., Bird V., Murray J., Tylee A., Slade M. A conceptual framework for improving well-being in people with a diagnosis of psychosis. *Epidemiology and Psychiatric Sciences* 2014; **23**: 377–87.

12 Schrank B., Riches S., Coggins T., Rashid T., Tylee A., Slade M. WELLFOCUS PPT – modified positive psychotherapy to improve well-being in psychosis: Study protocol for pilot randomised controlled trial. *Trials* 2014; **15**: 202.

13 Schrank B., Brownell T., Tylee A., Slade M. Positive psychology: An approach to supporting recovery in mental illness. *East Asian Archives of Psychiatry* 2014; **24**: 95–103.

14 Schrank B., Bird V., Tylee A., Coggins T., Rashid T., Slade M. Conceptualising and measuring the well-being of people with psychosis: Systematic review and narrative synthesis. *Social Science and Medicine* 2013; **92**: 9–21.

15 Schrank B., Riches S., Coggins T., Tylee A., Slade M. From objectivity to subjectivity: Conceptualisation and measurement of well-being in mental health. *Neuropsychiatry* 2013; **3**: 525–34.

16 Wissing M., van Eeden C. Empirical clarification of the nature of psychological well-being. *South African Journal of Psychology* 2002; **32**: 32.

17 Cummins R.A., Eckersley R., Pallant J., van Vugt J., Misajon R. Developing a national index of subjective wellbeing: The Australian unity wellbeing index. *Social Indicators Research* 2003; **64**(2): 159–90.

18 Hicks N., Streeten P. Indicators of development: The search for a basic needs yardstick. *World Development* 1979; **7**(6): 567–80.

19 Glock C. The sense of well-being: Developing measures. *Science* 1976; **194**: 52–4.

20 Beaumont J. *Measuring National Well-Being – Discussion Paper on Domains and Measures*. Newport: Office for National Statistics; 2011.

21 Gill T.M., Feinstein A.R. A critical appraisal of the quality of quality-of-life measurements. *JAMA: The Journal of the American Medical Association* 1994; **272**(8): 619–26.

22 Kaplan R., Bush J., Berry C. Health status: Types of validity for an index of well-being. *Health Services Research* 1976; **11**: 478–507.

23 Bech P., Olsen R.L., Kjoller M., Rasmussen N.K. Measuring well-being rather than the absence of distress symptoms: A comparison of the SF-36 mental health subscale and the WHO-Five well-being Scale. *International Journal of Methods in Psychiatric Research* 2003; **12**(2): 85–91.

24 Skevington S., McCrate F. Expecting a good quality of life in health: Assessing people with diverse diseases and conditions using the WHOQOL-BREF. *Health Expectations* 2011; **15**: 49–62.

25 EuroQol Group. EuroQol – a new facility for the measurement of health-related quality of life. The EuroQol Group. *Health Policy* 1990; **16**(3): 199–208.

26 Hays R.D., Morales L.S. The RAND-36 measure of health-related quality of life. *Annals of Medicine* 2001; **33**(5): 350–7.

27 van Nieuwenhuizen C., Schene A.H., Koeter M.W., Huxley P.J. The lancashire quality of life profile: Modification and psychometric evaluation. *Soc Social Psychiatry and Psychiatric Epidemiology* 2001; **36**(1): 36–44.

28 Priebe S., Huxley P., Knight S., Evans S. Application and results of the manchester short assessment of quality of life. *International Journal of Social Psychiatry* 1999; **45**: 7–12.

29 Katschnig H. How useful is the concept of quality of life in psychiatry? In: Katschnig H.F., H., Sartorius N., eds *Quality of Life in Mental Disorders*. Chichester: John Wiley & Sons, Ltd; 2005: 3–17.

30 Hunt S.M., McKenna S.P. The QLDS: A scale for the measurement of quality of life in depression. *Health Policy* 1992; **22**(3): 307–19.

31 Mechanic D., McAlpine D., Rosenfield S., Davis D. Effects of illness attribution and depression on the quality of life among persons with serious mental illness. *Social Science & Medicine* 1994; **39**(2): 155–64.

32 Katschnig H. How useful is the concept of quality of life in psychiatry? *Current Opinion in Psychiatry* 1997; **10**: 337–45.

33 Vothknecht S., Schoevers R., De Haan L. Subjective well-being in schizophrenia as measured with the subjective well-being under neuroleptic treatment scale: A review. *Australian and New Zealand Journal of Psychiatry* 2011; **45**: 182–92.

34 Wright B.A., Lopez S.J. Widening the diagnostic focus. A case for including human strengths and environmental resources. In: Snyder C.R., Lopez S.J., eds *Handbook of Positive Psychology*. New York, NY: Oxford University Press; 2002: 26–44.

35   Kiefer R.A. An integrative review of the concept of well-being. *Holistic Nursing Practice* 2008; **22**(5): 253–4

36   McDowell I. Measures of self-perceived well-being. *Journal of psychosomatic research* 2010; **69**(1): 69–79.

37   Böckerman P., Johansson E., Saarni S. Do established health-related quality-of-life measures adequately capture the impact of chronic conditions on subjective well-being? *Health Policy* 2011; **100**(1): 91–5.

38   Bettazzoni M., Zipursky R.B., Friedland J., Devins G.M. Illness intrusiveness and subjective well-being in schizophrenia. *The Journal of Nervous and Mental Disease* 2008; **196**(11): 798–805. doi: 10.1097/NMD.0b013e31818b6457.

39   Magyar-Moe J.L. *Therapist's Guide to Positive Psychological Interventions*. New York, NY: Elsevier Science & Technology; 2009.

40   Spiro A.I., Bosse R. Relations between health-related quality of life and well-being: The gerontologist's new clothes? *International Journal of Ageing and Human Develoment* 2000; **50**: 297–318.

41   Ryan R.M., Deci E.L. On happiness and human potentials: A review of research on hedonic and eudaimonic well-being. *Annual Review of Psychology* 2001; **52**(1): 141–66.

42   Veit C.T., Ware J.E. The structure of psychological distress and well-being in general populations. *Journal of Consulting and Clinical Psychology* 1983; **51**: 730–42.

43   Bruffaerts R., Vilagut G., Demyttenaere K., Alonso J., Alhamzawi A., Andrade L.H., Benjet C., Bromet E., Bunting B., de Girolamo G., Florescu S., Gureje O., Haro J.M., He Y., Hinkov H., Hu C., Karam E.G., Lepine J.P., Levinson D., Matschinger H., Nakane Y., Ormel J., Posada-Villa J., Scott K.M., Varghese M., Williams D.R., Xavier M., Kessler R.C. Role of common mental and physical disorders in partial disability around the world. *British Journal of Psychiatry* 2012; **200**(6): 454–61.

44   Joseph S., McCollam P. A bipolar happiness and depression scale. *Journal of Genetic Psychology* 1993; **154**: 127–9.

45   Lewis C., McCollam P., Joseph S. Convergent validity of the depression-happiness scale with the bradburn affect balance scale. *Social Behavior and Personality* 2000; **28**: 579–84.

46   Sisask M., Varnik A., Kolves K., Konstabel K., Wasserman D. Subjective psychological well-being (WHO-5) in assessment of the severity of suicide attempt. *Nordic Journal of Psychiatry* 2008; **62**(6): 431–25.

47   Ware J.E., Sherbourne C.D. The MOS 36-item short-form health survey (SF-36). I. conceptual framework and item selection. *Medical Care* 1992; **30**: 473–83.

48   McDowell I., Praught E. On the measurement of happiness. An examination of the bradburn scale in the Canada health survey. *American Journal of Epidemiology* 1982 **116**(6): 949–58.

49   Watson D., Clark L.A., Tellegen A. Development and validation of brief measures of positive and negative affect: The PANAS scales. *Journal of Personality and Social Psychology* 1988; **54**(6): 1063–70.

50   Tennant R., Joseph S., Stewart-Brown S. The Affectometer 2: A measure of positive mental health in UK populations. *Quality of Life Research* 2007; **16**: 687–95.

51   Uher R., Goodman R. The everyday feeling questionnaire: The structure and validation of a measure of general psychological well-being and distress. *Social Psychiatry and Psychiatric Epidemiology* 2010; **45**(3): 413–23.

52   Diener E., Robert E., Randy L., Griffin S. The satisfaction with life scale. *Journal of Personality Assessment* 1985; **49**: 71–5.

53   Hills P., Argyle M. The Oxford happiness questionnaire: A compact scale for the measurement of psychological well-being. *Personality and Individual Differences* 2002; **33**(7): 1073–82.

54 Cummins R. The second approximation to an international standard for Life satisfaction. *Social Indicators Research* 1998; **43**: 307–34.

55 Schwarz N., Clore G.L. Mood, misattribution, and judgments of well-being: Informative and directive functions of affective states. *Journal of Personality and Social Psychology* 1983; **45**(3): 513–23.

56 Diener E., Suh E.M., Lucas R.E., Smith H.L. Subjective well-being: Three decades of progress. *Psychological Bulletin* 1999; **125**(2): 276–302.

57 Ryff C.D., Keyes C.L.M. The structure of psychological well-being revisited. *Journal of Personality and Social Psychology* 1995; **69**: 719–27.

58 Cummins R.A. Normative life satisfaction: Measurement issues and a homeostatic model. *Social Indicators Research* 2003; **64**(2): 225–56.

59 Brickman P., Coates D., Janoff-Bulman R. Lottery winners and accident victims: Is happiness relative? *Journal of Personality and Social Psychology* 1978; **36**(8): 917–27.

60 Oswald A., Wu S. Objective confirmation of subjective measures of human well-being: Evidence from the U.S.A. *Science* 2010; **327**: 576–9.

61 Ryff C.D. Happiness is everything, or is it? Explorations on the meaning of psychological well-being. *Journal of Personality and Social Psychology* 1989; **57**(6): 1069–81.

62 Stewart-Brown S., Tennant A., Tennant R., Platt S., Parkinson J., Weich S. Internal construct validity of the Warwick-Edinburgh Mental Well-being Scale (WEMWBS): A Rasch analysis using data from the Scottish Health Education Population Survey. *Health Qual Life Outcomes* 2009; **7**: 15.

63 Tennant R., Hiller L., Fishwick R., Platt S., Joseph S., Weich S., Parkinson J., Secker J., Stewart-Brown S. The Warwick–Edinburgh Mental Well-being Scale (WEMWBS): Development and UK validation. *Health and Quality of Life Outcomes* 2007; **5**: 63.

64 Badoux A., Mendelsohn G.A. Subjective well-being in French and American samples: Scale development and comparative data. *Quality of Life Research* 1994; **3**(6): 395–401.

65 World Health Organization. *Promoting Mental Health. Concepts, Emerging Evidence, Practice.* Geneva: World Health Organization; 2004.

66 King L., Napa C. What makes a life good? *Journal of Personality and Social Psychology* 1998; **75**: 156–65.

67 Vaillant G.E. Mental health. *American Journal of Psychiatry* 2003; **160**(8): 1373–84.

68 Keyes C.L.M. Mental illness and/or mental health? Investigating axioms of the complete state model of health. *Journal of Consulting and Clinical Psychology* 2005; **73**: 539–48.

69 Ryff C.D., Keyes C.L.M. The structure of psychological well-being revisited. *Journal of Personality and Social Psychology* 1995; **69**(4): 719–27.

70 Keyes C., Dhingra S., Simoes E. Change in level of positive mental health as a predictor of future risk of mental illness. *American Journal of Public Health* 2010; **100**: 2366–71.

71 Department of Health and Ageing. *Fourth National Mental Health Plan: An Agenda for Collaborative Government Action in Mental Health 2009–2014.* Canberra: Commonwealth of Australia; 2009.

72 Mental Health Commission of Canada. *Changing Directions, Changing Lives: The Mental Health Strategy for Canada.* Calgary: Mental Health Commission of Canada; 2012.

73 Department of Health Social Services and Public Safety (Northern Ireland). *Service Framework for Mental Health and Wellbeing.* Belfast: DHSSPS (NI); 2010.

74 New Freedom Commission on Mental Health. *Achieving the Promise: Transforming Mental Health Care in America. Final report.* Rockville, M.D.: U.S. Department of Health and Human Services; 2003.

75 HM Government. *No Health without Mental Health. Delivering Better Mental Health Outcomes for People of all Ages.* London: Department of Health; 2011.

76 Slade M., Adams N., O'Hagan M. Recovery: Past progress and future challenges. *International Review of Psychiatry* 2012; **24**: 1–4.

77 Olij L., de Haan E. *Naar herstel en gelijkwaardig burgerschap* [Restoring dignity and equal citizenship]. Amsterdam: GGZ Nederland; 2009.

78 Oades L.G., Anderson J. Recovery in Australia: Marshalling strengths and living values. *International Review of Psychiatry* 2012; **24**(1): 5–10.

79 Amering M., Mikus M., Steffen S. Recovery in Austria: Mental health trialogue. *International Review of Psychiatry* 2012; **24**: 11–8.

80 Tse S., Cheung E., Kan A., Ng R., Yau S. Recovery in Hong Kong: Service user participation in mental health services. *International Review of Psychiatry* 2012; **24**(1): 40–7.

81 Mental Health Commission. *Blueprint II: How Things Need to Be*. Wellington: Mental Health Commission; 2012.

82 Anthony W.A. Recovery from mental illness: The guiding vision of the mental health system in the 1990s. *Psychosocial Rehabilitation Journal* 1993; **16**: 11–23.

83 Cooke A., Basset T., Bentall R., Boyle M., Cupitt C., Dillon J., Freeman D., Garety P., Harper D., Johnstone L., Kinderman P., Kuipers E., Lavender T., Lea L., Longden E., May R., Morrison T., Meddings S., Onyett S., Peters E., Pilgrim D., Read J., Slade M., Weaver Y., Wykes T. *Understanding Psychosis and Schizophrenia*. London: British Psychological Society; 2014.

84 Department of Health. *From Values to Action: The Chief Nursing Officer's Review of Mental Health Nursing*. London: HMSO; 2006.

85 College of Occupational Therapists. *Recovering Ordinary Lives: The Strategy for Occupational Therapy in Mental Health Services 2007–2017*. London College of Occupational Therapists; 2006.

86 Care Services. Improvement Partnership RCoP, Social Care Institute for Excellence. *A Common Purpose: Recovery in Future Mental Health Services*. Leeds: CSIP; 2007.

87 Allen R. *The Role of the Social Worker in Adult Mental Health Services*. London: College of Social Work; 2014.

88 American Psychiatric Association. *Position Statement on the Use of the Concept of Recovery*. Washington, D.C.: American Psychiatric Association; 2005.

89 Slade M., Amering M., Farkas M., Hamilton B., O'Hagan M., Panther G., Perkins R., Shepherd G., Tse S., Whitley R. Uses and abuses of recovery: Implementing recovery-oriented practices in mental health systems. *World Psychiatry* 2014; **13**: 12–20.

90 Leamy M., Bird V., Le Boutillier C., Williams J., Slade M. A conceptual framework for personal recovery in mental health: Systematic review and narrative synthesis. *British Journal of Psychiatry* 2011; **199**: 445–52.

91 Slade M. Everyday solutions for everyday problems: How mental health systems can support recovery. *Psychiatric Services* 2012; **63**: 702–4.

92 Le Boutillier C., Leamy M., Bird V.J., Davidson L., Williams J., Slade M. What does recovery mean in practice? A qualitative analysis of international recovery-oriented practice guidance. *Psychiatric Services* 2011; **62**: 1470–6.

93 Anthony W. The principle of personhood: The field's transcendent principle. *Psychiatric Rehabilitation Journal* 2004; **27**: 205.

94 Foresight Mental Capital Wellbeing Project. *Mental Capital and Wellbeing: Making the Most of Ourselves in the 21st Century. Final Project Report*. London: Government Office for Science; 2008.

95 Keyes C.L.M. Promoting and protecting mental health as flourishing. A complementary strategy for improving national mental health. *American Psychologist* 2007; **62**: 95–108.

96 Slade M., Amering M., Oades L. Recovery: An international perspective. *Epidemiologia e Psichiatria Sociale* 2008; **17**(2): 128–37.

97 Fredrickson B., Joiner T. Positive emotions trigger upward spirals toward emotional well-being. *Psychological Science* 2002; **13**: 172–5.

98 Schueller S.M., Parks A.C. Disseminating self-help: Positive psychology exercises in an online trial. *Journal of medical Internet research* 2012; **14**(3): e63.

99 Schrank B., Bird V., Rudnick A., Slade M. Determinants, self-management strategies and interventions for hope in people with mental disorders: Systematic search and narrative review. *Social Science and Medicine* 2012; **74**: 554–64.

100 Henry J. Positive psychology and the development of well-being. In: Haworth J., Hart G., eds *Well-being: Individual, Community and Societal Perspectives*. Basingstoke: Palgrave Macmillan; 2007: 25–40.

101 Seligman M., Csikszentmihalyi M. Positive psychology: An introduction. *American Psychologist* 2000; **55**: 5–14.

102 Craig P., Dieppe P., Macintyre S., Michie S., Nazareth I., Petticrew M. Developing and evaluating complex interventions: The new Medical Research Council guidance. *British Medical Journal* 2008; **337**(7676): a1655.

103 Seligman M., Ernst R., Gillham J., Reivich K., Linkins M. Positive education: Positive psychology and classroom interventions. *Oxford Review of Education* 2009; **35**: 293–311.

104 Gould D. Sport psychology in the New Millenium: The psychology of Athletic Excellence and Beyond. *Journal of Applied Sports Psychology* 2002; **14**: 137–9.

105 Hershberger P. Prescribing happiness – positive psychology and family medicine. *Family Medicine* 2005; **37**: 630–4.

106 Coyne J., Tennen H., Ranchor A. Positive psychology in cancer care: A story line resistant to evidence. *Annals of Behavioral Medicine* 2010; **39**: 35–42.

107 Evans J. Positive psychology and brain injury rehabilitation. *Brain Impairment* 2011; **12**(02): 117–27.

108 Wood A., Tarrier N. Positive clinical psychology: A new vision and strategy for integrated research and practice. *Clinical Psychology Review* 2010; **30**: 819–29.

109 Cloninger R. The science of well-being: An integrated approach to mental health and its disorders. *World Psychiatry* 2006; **5**: 71–6.

110 Siegler V. *Measuring National Well-being – An Analysis of Social Capital in the UK*. London: Office for National Statistics; 2015.

111 Randall C., Corp A. *Measuring National Well-being: European Comparisons, 2014*. London: Office for National Statistics; 2014.

112 Curtis S. Socio-economic status and geographies of psychiatric inpatient service use. Places, provision, power and well-being. *Epidemiologia e psichiatria sociale* 2007; **16**: 10–5.

113 Resnick S.G., Rosenheck R.A. Recovery and positive psychology: Parallel themes and potential synergies. *Psychiatric Services* 2006; **57**(1): 120–2.

114 Slade M., Hayward M. Recovery, psychosis and psychiatry: Research is better than rhetoric. *Acta Psychiatrica Scandinavica* 2007; **116**(2): 81–3.

115 Sin N.L., Lyubomirsky S. Enhancing well-being and alleviating depressive symptoms with positive psychology interventions: A practice-friendly meta-analysis. *Journal of Clinical Psychology* 2009; **65**(5): 467–87.

116 Bolier L., Haverman M., Westerhof G.J., Riper H., Smit F., Bohlmeijer E. Positive psychology interventions: A meta-analysis of randomized controlled studies. *BMC Public Health* 2013; **13**: 119.

117 Hatch S., Harvey S., Maughan B. A developmental-contextual approach to understanding mental health and well-being in early adulthood. *Social Science and Medicine* 2010; **70**: 261–8.

118 Schwarzer R., Luszczynska A., Boehmer S., Taubert S., Knoll N. Changes in finding benefit after cancer surgery and the prediction of well-being one year later. *Social Science and Medicine* 2006; **63**: 1614–24.

119 Mak W., Cheung R., Law R., Woo J., Li P., Chung R. Examining attribution model of self-stigma on social support and psychological well-being among people with HIV+/AIDS. *Social Science and Medicine* 2007; **64**: 1549–59.

120 Seligman M.E., Steen T.A., Park N., Peterson C. Positive psychology progress: Empirical validation of interventions. *American Psychologist* 2005; **60**(5): 410–21.

121 Rashid T., Seligman M.E. *Positive Psychotherapy: A Manual*. Oxford University Press; in press.

122 Rashid T., Seligman M.E. Positive psychotherapy. In: Wedding D., Corsini R.J., eds *Current Psychotherapies*. Belmont, C.A.: Cengage. 98.; 2013: 461–98.

123 Rashid T., Anjum A., Lennex C., Quinlin D., Niemiec R., Mayerson D., Kazemi F. Assessment of positive traits in children and adolescents. In: Proctor C., Linley P., eds *Research, Applications, and Interventions for Children and Adolescents: A Positive Psychology Perspective*. Netherlands: Springer; 2013: 81–114.

124 Kashdan T., Rottenberg J. Psychological flexibility as a fundamental aspect of health. *Clinical Psychology Review* 2010; **30**: 865–78.

125 Rosenberg T., Pace M. Burnout among mental health professionals: Special considerations for the marriage and family therapist. *Journal of Marital and Family Therapy* 2006; **32**: 87–99.

126 McKenzie D., Gurris N., Traue H. Factors affecting burnout and compassion fatigue in psychotherapists treating torture survivors: Is the therapists' attitude to working through trauma relevant? *Journal of Traumatic Stress* 2007; **20**: 63–75.

127 Harrison R., Westwood M. Preventing vicarious traumatization of mental health therapists: Identifying protective practices. *Psychotherapy* 2009; **46**: 203–19.

128 Lyubomirsky S., Layous K. How do simple positive activities increase well-being? *Current Directions in Psychological Science* 2013; **22**: 57–62.

129 Pedrotti J.T. Broadening perspectives: Strategies to infuse multiculturalism into a positive psychology course. *Journal of Positive Psychology* 2011; **6**(6): 506–13.

130 Duckworth L.A., Steen T.A., Seligman M.E. Positive psychology in clinical practice. *Annual Review of Clinical Psychology* 2005; **1**: 629–51.

131 Olfson M., Marcus S. National trends in outpatient psychotherapy. *American Journal of Psychiatry* 2010; **167**: 1456–63.

132 Smith E., Aaker J. Millennial Searchers. New York Times. 2013 November 30.

133 Seligman M., Rashid T., Parks A.C. Positive psychotherapy. *American Psychologist* 2006; **61**(8): 774–88.

134 Asgharipoor N., Farid A.A., Arshadi H., Sahebi A. A comparative study on the effectiveness of positive psychotherapy and group cognitive-behavioral therapy for the patients suffering from major depressive disorder. *Iranian Journal of Psychiatry and Behavioral Sciences* 2010; **6**(2): 33–41.

135 Cuadra-Peralta A., Veloso-Besio C., Pérez M., Zúñiga M. Resultados de la psicoterapia positiva en pacientes con depression. *Terapia Psicológica* 2010; **28**(1): 127–34.

136 Bay M., Csillic A. *Comparing Positive Psychotherapy with Cognitive Behavioral Therapy in Treating Depression*. Unpublished manuscript: Paris West University Nanterre La Défense (Université Paris Ouest Nanterre La Défense); 2012.

137 Rashid T., Anjum A. *Positive Psychotherapy for Young Adults and Children. Handbook of Depression in Children and Adolescents*. New York, NY: Guilford Press; US; 2008: 250–87.

138 Seligman M.E., Rashid T., Parks A.C. Positive psychotherapy. *The American Psychologist* 2006; **61**(8): 774–88.

139 Parks-Sheiner A.C. Positive psychotherapy: Building a model of empirically supported self-help. *Dissertation Abstracts International: Section B: The Sciences and Engineering* 2009; **70**(6-B): 3792.

140 Lü W., Wang Z., Liu Y. A pilot study on changes of cardiac vagal tone in individuals with low trait positive affect: The effect of positive psychotherapy. *International Journal of Psychophysiology* 2013; **88**(2): 213–7.

141 Schueller S.M., Parks A.C. Disseminating self-help: Positive psychology exercises in an online trial. *Journal of Medical Internet Research* 2012; **14**(3): e63.

142 Cromer T.D. Integrative techniques related to positive processes in psychotherapy. *Psychotherapy* 2013; **50**(3): 307–11.

143 Kahler C.W., Spillane N.S., Day A., Clerkin E., Parks A., Leventhal A.M., Brown R.A. Positive psychotherapy for smoking cessation: Treatment development, feasibility, and preliminary results. *The Journal of Positive Psychology* 2013: 1–11.

144 Bertisch H., Rath J., Long C., Ashman T., Rashid T. Positive psychology in rehabilitation medicine: A brief report. *NeuroRehabilitation* 2014; **34**(3): 573–85.

145 Huffman J.C., DuBois C.M., Healy B.C., Boehm J.K., Kashdan T.B., Celano C.M., Denninger J.W., Lyubomirsky S. Feasibility and utility of positive psychology exercises for suicidal inpatients. *General Hospital Psychiatry* 2014; **36**(1): 88–94.

146 Celano C.M., Beale E.E., Moore S.V., Wexler D.J., Huffman J.C. Positive psychological characteristics in diabetes: A review. *Current Diabetes Reports* 2013; **13**(6): 917–29.

147 DuBois C.M., Beach S.R., Kashdan T.B., Nyer M.B., Park E.R., Celano C.M., Huffman J.C. Positive psychological attributes and cardiac outcomes: Associations, mechanisms, and interventions. *Psychosomatics* 2012; **53**(4): 303–18.

148 Huffman J.C., Mastromauro C.A., Boehm J.K., Seabrook R., Fricchione G.L., Denninger J.W., Lyubomirsky S. Development of a positive psychology intervention for patients with acute cardiovascular disease. *Heart International* 2011; **6**(2): 47–54.

149 Feldman M.A., Condillac R.A., Tough S., Hunt S.L., Griffiths D. Effectiveness of community positive behavioral intervention for persons with developmental disabilities and severe behavior disorders. *Behavior Therapy* 2002; **33**(3): 377–98.

150 Rashid T[N.1]. Positive psychotherapy: A strength-based approach. *The Journal of Positive Psychology* 2014; (ahead-of-print): 1–16.

151 Meyer P.S., Johnson D.P., Parks A., Iwanski C., Penn D.L. Positive living: A pilot study of group positive psychotherapy for people with schizophrenia. *The Journal of Positive Psychology* 2012; **7**(3): 239–48.

152 Schrank B., Stanghellini G., Slade M. Hope in psychiatry: A review of the literature. *Acta Psychiatrica Scandinavica* 2008; **118**(6): 421–33.

153 Popay J., Roberts H., Sowden A., Petticrew M., Arai L., Rodgers M., Britten N., Roen K., Duffy S. *Guidance on the Conduct of Narrative Synthesis in Systematic Reviews. Results of an ESRC Funded Research Project*. Lancaster: University of Lancaster; 2006.

154 Office for National Statistics. *Measuring National Well-being: Summary of Proposed Domains and Measures*. London: Office for National Statistics; 2012.

155 Willig C. *Introducing Qualitative Research in Psychology*. Second Edition. Maidenhead: Open University Press; 2008.

156 Braun V., Clarke V. Using thematic analysis in psychology. *Qualitative Research in Psychology* 2006; **3**: 77–101.

157 Seligman M. *Flourish*. London: Nicholas Brealy Publishing; 2011.

158 Ludwig J., Duncan G., Gennetian L., Katz L., Kessler R., Kling J., Sanbonmatsu L. Neighborhood effects on the long-term well-being of low-income adults. *Science* 2012; **337**: 1505–10.

159 Gademan M., Deutekom M., Hosper K., Stronks K. The effect of exercise on prescription on physical activity and wellbeing in a multi-ethnic female population: A controlled trial. *BMC Public Health* 2012; **12**: 758.

160 Clare L., Hindle J., Jones I., Thom J., Nelis S., Hounsome B., Whitaker C. The age well study of behavior change to promote health and wellbeing in later life: Study protocol for a randomized controlled trial. *Trials* 2012; **13**: 115.

161 Luthans F., Avolio B., Avey J., Norman S. Positive psychological capital: Measurement and relationship with performance and satisfaction. *Personnel Psychology* 2007; **60**: 541–72.

162 Priebe S., Omer S., Giacco D., Slade M. Resource-oriented therapeutic models in psychiatry – a conceptual review. *British Journal of Psychiatry* 2014; **204**: 256–61.

163 Amering M. Recovery, science and human rights. *Epidemiology and Psychiatric Sciences* 2012; **21**: 367–9.

164 Longmore R.J., Worrell M. Do we need to challenge thoughts in cognitive behavior therapy? *Clinical psychology review* 2007; **27**(2): 173–87.

165 Rashid T. *Positive Psychotherapy. Positive Psychology: Exploring the best in people, Vol 4: Pursuing Human Flourishing*. Westport, CT: Praeger Publishers/Greenwood Publishing Group; US; 2008: 188–217.

166 Kilcommons A.M., Morrison A.P. Relationships between trauma and psychosis: An exploration of cognitive and dissociative factors. *Acta Psychiatrica Scandinavica* 2005; **112**(5): 351–9.

167 Beards S., Gayer-Anderson C., Borges S., Dewey M.E., Fisher H.L., Morgan C. Life events and psychosis: A review and meta-analysis. *Schizophrenia Bulletin* 2013; **39**(4): 740–7.

168 Varese F., Smeets F., Drukker M., Lieverse R., Lataster T., Viechtbauer W., Read J., van Os J., Bentall R.P. Childhood adversities increase the risk of psychosis: A meta-analysis of patient-control, prospective- and cross-sectional cohort studies. *Schizophrenia Bulletin* 2012; **38**(4): 661–71.

169 Lancaster G.A., Dodd S., Williamson P.R. Design and analysis of pilot studies: Recommendations for good practice. *Journal of Evaluation in Clinical Practice* 2004; **10**: 307–12.

170 Guney S. The Positive Psychotherapy Inventory (PPTI): Reliability and validity study in Turkish population. *Social and Behavioral Science* 2011; **29**: 81–6.

171 Bryant F. Savoring Beliefs Inventory (SBI): A scale for measuring beliefs about savouring. *Journal of Mental Health* 2003; **12**: 175–96.

172 Schrank B., Woppmann A., Grant Hay A., Sibitz I., Zehetmayer S., Lauber C. Validation of the integrative hope scale in people with psychosis. *Psychiatry Research* 2012; **198**: 395–9.

173 Schmitt D., Allik J. Simultaneous administration of the Rosenberg self-esteem scale in 53 nations: Exploring the universal and culture-specific features of global self-esteem. *Journal of Personality and Social Psychology* 2005; **89**: 623–42.

174 Rogers E., Ralph R., Salzer M. Validating the empowerment scale with a multisite sample of consumers of mental health services. *Psychiatric Services* 2010; **61**: 933–6.

175 Eriksson M., Lindstrom B. Antonovsky's sense of coherence scale and the relation with health: A systematic review. *Journal of Epidemiology and Community Health* 2006; **60**: 376–81.

176 Wing J.K., Beevor A.S., Curtis R.H., Park S.B., Hadden S., Burns A. Health of the Nation Outcome Scales (HoNOS). Research and development. *British Journal of Psychiatry* 1998; **172**: 11–8.

177 Overall J.E., Gorham D.R. The Brief Psychiatric Rating Scale (BPRS): Recent developments in ascertainment and scaling. *Psychopharmacology Bulletin* 1988; **24**: 97–9.

178 Jauhar S., McKenna P., Radua J., Fung E., Salvador R., Laws K. Cognitive-behavioural therapy for the symptoms of schizophrenia: Systematic review and meta-analysis with examination of potential bias. *British Journal of Psychiatry* 2014; **204**: 20–9.

179 Fusar-Poli P., Nelson B., Valmaggia L., Yung A., McGuire P. Comorbid depressive and anxiety disorders in 509 individuals with an at-risk mental state: Impact on psycho-pathology and transition to psychosis. *Schizophrenia Bulletin* 2014; **40**: 120–31.

180 Buckley P., Miller B., Lehrer D., Castle D. Psychiatric comorbidities and schizophrenia. *Schizophrenia Bulletin* 2009; **35**: 383–402.

181 Waller H., Craig T., Landau S., Fornells-Ambrojo M., Hassanali N., Iredale C., Jolley S., McCrone P., Garety P. The effects of a brief CBT intervention, delivered by front-line mental health staff, to promote recovery in people with psychosis and comorbid anxiety or depression (the GOALS study): Study protocol for a randomized controlled trial. *Trials* 2014; **15**: 255.

182 Worthington E., Kurusu T., Collins W., Berry J., Ripley S., Baier S. Forgiving usually takes time: A lesson learned by studying interventions to promote forgiveness. *Journal of Psychology and Theology* 2000; **28**: 3–20.

183 Seligman M.E.P., Rashid T., Parks A.C. Positive psychotherapy. *American Psychologist* 2006; **61**(8): 774–88.

184 Topor A., Borg M., Mezzina R., Sells D., Marin I., Davidson L. Others: The role of family, friends, and professionals in the recovery process. *American Journal of Psychiatric Rehabilitation* 2006; **9**: 17–37.

185 Slade M. *Personal Recovery and Mental Illness.* Cambridge: Cambridge University Press; 2009.

186 Fredrickson B. The value of positive emotions: The emerging science of positive psychology is coming to understand why it's good to feel good. ***American Scientist*** 2003; **91**: 330–5.

187 Gable S., Reis H., Impett E., Asher E. What do you do when things go right? The intrap-ersonal and interpersonal benefits of sharing positive events. *Journal of Personality and Social Psychology* 2004; **87**: 228–45.

188 Grossman P., Niemann L., Schmidt S., Walach H. Mindfulness-based stress reduction and health benefits: A meta-analysis. *Journal of Psychosomatic Research* 2004; **57**: 35–43.

189 Flor R., Monir K., Bita A., Shahnaz N. Effect of relaxation training on working memory capacity and academic achievement in adolescents. *Procedia – Social and Behavioral Sciences* 2013; **82**: 608–13.

190 Isen A., Daubman K., Nowicki G. Positive affect facilitates creative problem solving. *Journal of Personality and Social Psychology* 1987; **52**: 1122–31.

191 Fredrickson B. What good are positive emotions? *Review of General Psychology* 1998; **2**: 300–19.

192 Fredrickson B., Losada M. Positive affect and the complex dynamics of human flour-ishing. *American Psychologist* 2005; **60**: 678–86.

193 Beck A.T., Rush A.J., Shaw B.F., Emery G. *Cognitive Therapy of Depression.* New York, NY: Guilford Press; 1979.

194 Gander F., Proyer R., Ruch W., Wyss T. Strength-based positive interventions: Further evidence for their potential in enhancing wellbeing and alleviating depression. *Journal of Happiness Studies* 2012; **14**: 1241–59.

195   White M. Deconstruction and therapy. In: Epston D., White M., eds *Experience, Contradiction, Narrative and Imagination: Selected Papers of David Epston & Michael White, 1989–1991*. Adelaide, Australia: Dulwich Centre; 1992.

196   Snyder C. Hope theory: Rainbows in the mind. *Psychological Inquiry* 2002; **13**: 249–75.

197   Garland E., Fredrickson B., Kring A., Johnson D., Meyer P., Penn D. Upward spirals of positive emotions counter downward spirals of negativity: Insights from the broaden-and-build theory and affective neuroscience on The treatment of emotion dysfunctions and deficits in psychopathology. *Clinical Psychology Review* 2010; **30**: 849–64.

198   Burns A., Brown J., Sachs-Ericsson N., Plant E., Curtis J., Fredrickson B., Joinera T. Upward spirals of positive emotion and coping: Replication, extension, and initial exploration of neurochemical substrates. *Clinical Psychology Review* 2008; **44**: 360–70.

199   Mitchell J., Stanimirovic R., Klein B., Vella-Brodrick D. A randomised controlled trial of a self-guided internet intervention promoting well-being. *Computers in Human Behaviour* 2009; **25**: 749–60.

200   Emmons R., Stern R. Gratitude as a psychotherapeutic intervention. *Journal of Clinical Psychology* 2013; **69**: 846–55.

201   Witvliet C., Ludwig T., Vander Laan K. Granting forgiveness or harbouring grudges: Implications for emotion, physiology, and health. *Psychological Science* 2001; **121**: 117–23.

202   Worthington E., Scherer M. Forgiveness is an emotion-focused coping strategy that can reduce health risks and promote health resilience: Theory, review, and hypotheses. *Psychology and Health* 2004; **19**: 385–405.

203   Karremans J., Van Lange P., Ouwerkerk J., Kluwer E. When forgiving enhances psychological well- being: The role of interpersonal commitment. *Journal of Personality and Social Psychology* 2003; **84**: 1011–26.

204   Fincham F., Paleari G., Regalia C. Forgiveness in marriage: The role of relationship quality, attributions and empathy. *Personal Relationships* 2002; **9**: 27–37.

205   Thoresen C., Harris A., Luskin F. Forgiveness and health: An unanswered question. In: McCullough M., Pargament K., Thoresen C., eds *Forgiveness: Theory, Research, and Practice*. New York, NY: Guilford Press; 2000: 254–80.

206   Gilbert P., Procter S. Compassionate mind training for people with high shame and self_criticism: Overview and pilot study of a group therapy approach. *Clinical Psychology & Psychotherapy* 2006; **13**: 353–79.

207   Emmons R. *THANKS! How the New Science of Gratitude Can Make You Happier*. Boston, MA: Houghton-Mifflin; 2007.

208   Emmons R., McCullough M. Counting blessings versus burdens: An experimental investigation of gratitude and subjective wellbeing in daily life. *Journal of Personality and Social Psychology* 2003; **84**: 377–89.

Index